7.50

IRISH NEUTRALITY AND THE U.S.A.
1939-47

T. Ryle Dwyer

IRISH NEUTRALITY
AND THE USA
1939-47

GILL AND MACMILLAN
ROWMAN AND LITTLEFIELD

First published in Ireland in 1977

Gill and Macmillan Limited
15/17 Eden Quay
Dublin 1
and internationally through association with the
Macmillan Publishers Group

© T. Ryle Dwyer 1977

Gill and Macmillan SBN: 7171 0823 6

First published in the United States in 1977
Rowman and Littlefield
81 Adams Drive, Totowa, N.J.

ISBN 0–87471–994–1

Printed (and bound in Great Britain) by
Bristol Typesetting Co. Ltd, Barton Manor, St Philips, Bristol

To My Mother

Contents

PREFACE   ix

1. NEUTRAL BY NECESSITY
   De Valera and the coming of World War II   1

2. FROM NON-INTERVENTION TO WAR
   Roosevelt, the Irish-Americans and the World Crisis
   September 1939–December 1941   24

3. DAVID GRAY, THE USA AND PARTITION
   De Valera refuses to bargain with Irish Neutrality
   March–July 1940   47

4. THREATENING THE BELLIGERENTS
   The small neutral and the Great Powers
   April–November 1940   66

5. THE SCREWS ARE TIGHTENED
   Irish ports and the Battle of the Atlantic
   November 1940–March 1941   85

6. THE AIKEN MISSION TO USA
   The seeds of future discord
   March–June 1941   107

7. NEUTRALS AT ODDS
   US-Irish relations in the months before Pearl Harbour
   May–December 1941   122

contents continued

8. THE UNITED STATES ENTERS THE WAR
American troops in Northern Ireland
December 1941–October 1942   139

9. TO SEEK OR NOT TO SEEK THE
IRISH PORTS?
Irish threats to the Anglo-American alliance
October 1942–December 1943   160

10. AXIS REPRESENTATIVES IN DUBLIN
The 'American Note' and de Valera's refusal to expel them
December 1943–June 1944   179

11. THE BITTER END
June 1944–June 1947   201

12. CONCLUSION
Upstaging the Playboy of the Western World   211

NOTES   222

GLOSSARY   231

INDEX   237

Preface

THOUGH a neutral country of barely three million people, Ireland nevertheless figured prominently in the diplomacy of the Second World War. Initially this was because the British thought that Irish bases were important to the Allied war effort. On 20 September 1939, for example, shortly before he took up his post as Britain's wartime representative to Ireland, Sir John Maffey candidly told Éamon de Valera, the Irish leader, that if Irish ports became vital, then Britain would seize them. 'But,' he admitted, 'we must think twice and count the gain and the loss.'

During the early years of the war, therefore, de Valera's policy was to convince Britain that seizing Irish facilities would cause more trouble than they were worth. He did this by making subtle appeals to the United States in such a way as to convince the London government that Irish-Americans might undermine American aid for Britain, if Britain violated Irish neutrality. Winston Churchill countered by appealing to the administration of Franklin D. Roosevelt to use its influence to get the Irish-Americans to put pressure on Dublin to allow Britain to use Irish ports.

When British efforts began to meet with some success and the American news media called on de Valera to facilitate the British, the Dublin government resorted to less subtle methods and began involving itself directly in American politics by associating with prominent American isolationists and appealing openly for Irish-American help. The diplomatic manoeuvring thus led to a situation in which Dublin was trying to get Americans to support Irish neutrality while the American leadership was seeking to get Ireland to abandon neutrality. Under these conditions relations between the two governments inevitably became strained.

One of the central characters in those relations was the United States Minister, David Gray, who was probably the most influential diplomat ever to serve in Ireland. Connected with the Roosevelt family by marriage, he had access to the highest Allied counsels and had private wartime discussions on Ireland with such people as Roosevelt, Hull, Churchill, Attlee, Eden, and even de Gaulle.

Believing that the United States should provide Britain with all the help necessary to defeat Hitler, Gray worked diligently to secure facilities for the British in Ireland. He begged, bribed, and flattered de Valera, but to no avail. Then turning sour, he warned, threatened, and schemed against Irish neutrality, going so far as to suggest to the White House contingency plans to starve, bomb, and even invade Ireland. Eventually the American Minister used his influence to mastermind a plan to discredit de Valera because he thought the Irish leader posed a threat to postwar peace and stability.

A detailed study of Gray's actions, based mainly on his voluminous wartime correspondence with Roosevelt, reveals the enormity of the task facing de Valera as he successfully sought to keep Ireland out of the Second World War. It also reveals that even before entering the conflict, the United States played a vital—if somewhat reluctant—role in helping de Valera to preserve neutrality. For, in the last analysis, it was not the Irish Army but American public opinion which afforded Ireland the most effective protection against the British and to a lesser extent against the Germans. As a result Irish neutrality cannot be properly understood unless seen within the context of American politics and against the background of the role played by Irish-Americans in those politics, because Irish-Americans not only helped to mollify the German threat to Ireland, but also played a vital part in convincing the British government that it had more to lose than gain by violating Irish neutrality.

My interest in United States relations with Ireland developed quite by chance on coming across documentary material while partaking in a seminar on American diplomatic history. Being an American citizen who had lived in Ireland for fifteen years and being the son of a United States Army officer who was killed in Europe during the war, I developed a natural curiosity in the wartime relations between the United States and Ireland.

Previously my only exposure to recent Irish history had been in connection with my master's thesis, which concerned events surrounding the Anglo-Irish Treaty of 1921. In it I was critical of the role played by de Valera, so in this study of Irish neutrality I have not been attracted to that particular dynamism of his personality that has enchanted so many people in both Ireland and the United States, nor have I been impressed by his neutral policies on account of any misgivings about American involvement in the Second World War. For, even though I believe that the United States of America has engaged in some misguided wars, she was never more right than in the fight against Hitler.

I would like to thank all those who have helped me, especially those mentioned in the notes who answered my letters, with particular thanks going to Mr Paul O'Dwyer of New York and Mr Kevin Boland of Dublin for enclosing some very useful material. I would also like to thank the members of my family, my brother, Dr Sean Dwyer in Racine, Wisconsin, who secured research material for me; my aunt and uncle, Dr and Mrs J. N. Hassett in Medicine Hat, Canada; and Dr and Mrs Aidan Kennedy who were kind hosts on my frequent visits to Dublin. In addition, I would like to thank Ronnie H. King in Dallas, Texas, for forwarding research material to me and for checking on sources.

TRD
Tralee
October, 1976

1. Neutral by Necessity

DE VALERA AND THE COMING OF WORLD WAR II

On 7 May 1945 while much of Europe was rejoicing at the news that Germany was about to formally surrender, there were some ugly anti-American scenes in Ireland as an angry crowd stoned the offices of the United States Consul-General in Dublin. The incident was indicative of a deterioration in the wartime relations between the United States and neutral Ireland.

Friction between the two countries had actually been so acute at one point during the war that many Irish people feared an American invasion was imminent. At the centre of the strained relations was Ireland's American-born Taoiseach (Prime Minister), Éamon de Valera.

It was nothing new for de Valera to be involved in controversy. He had been a figure of contention throughout most of his political career.[1] Indeed, if the Irish people had been asked for their opinion of him on the eve of the Second World War, they would undoubtedly have had conflicting views, because he was an enigmatic figure.

Opponents saw him as a malignant ogre who promoted discord and division wherever he went. To the Fine Gael opposition, de Valera was a narrow, vain, dictatorial reprobate who divided the Irish-Americans when Ireland needed their help, who divided the Irish people in their hour of triumph, who plunged Ireland into a bloody civil war over a mere quibble, and who accentuated the divisiveness in Irish society for his own selfish political ends. On the other side of the political spectrum, the Irish Republican Army (IRA) and kindred organisations tended to see the Taoiseach as a renegade who prostituted his ideals for the power and prestige of political office.

To his own supporters, however, de Valera was the personification of Irish independence, a military genius who had distinguished himself during the Easter Rising, a brilliant organiser who had founded the Fianna Fáil Party, a superlative leader who had led his party to power, and a tremendous diplomatic tactician who had revised most of the obnoxious portions of the Anglo-Irish Treaty of 1921. To admirers, in short, he was the greatest statesman ever to represent Ireland.

Since coming to power seven years earlier de Valera had distinguished himself in the international arena. On making his initial appearance before the League of Nations in 1932, for instance, he had been particularly fortunate in that it fell to the Irish delegation to provide the President of the Council of the organisation. So he filled the position himself, and did so with distinction.

In succeeding years he secured world recognition both by having the temerity to criticise the major powers for the drift towards war and by his willingness to ignore public opinion at home in Ireland on some issues on which the country's predominantly Roman Catholic population held strong views. Not only did he push for the admittance of the atheistic government of the Soviet Union into the League of Nations, but he supported the League's sanctions against Roman Catholic Italy during the Ethiopian crisis and also endorsed the international body's non-intervention policy during the Spanish Civil War, in spite of the almost frenzied sympathy that the Irish people had for the forces of General Franco. The Taoiseach gained such a reputation for statesmanship that even his old enemy, Britain, voted for him in 1938 when he was elected President of the Assembly of the League of Nations.

By the outbreak of the Second World War de Valera's international prestige was at its zenith. Ironically, the neutrality he subsequently pursued, which most Irish people—including many of his most ardent critics—considered his finest accomplishment, greatly damaged his international reputation. By the end of the war he was discredited in the eyes of many people throughout the world as a Nazi sympathiser. What made the irony even greater was the fact that he had actually pursued a neutrality that was benevolently disposed towards the Allies.

Why then did so many people come to believe that de Valera sympathised with the Nazis, or that at best he was indifferent to the plight of the Allies?

The answer to that question is to be found in a detailed examination of the wartime relations between the United States and Ireland, because it was the Americans who tarnished de Valera's reputation and thus distorted the truth about Irish neutrality. They did so in order to ensure that he would not be able to cause trouble in the postwar period by injecting the Ulster question into international politics.

It was not that partition *per se* was of major international importance. Rather, it was because of the significance that Irish affairs had for millions of Irish-Americans who exerted a tremendous influence on politics in the United States.

American authorities were afraid that de Valera would induce Irish-Americans to oppose any general postwar settlement that did not end partition. And this, in turn, raised the spectre of a repetition of the debacle surrounding the American rejection of the Versailles Treaty following the First World War. Hence the Americans discredited de Valera in order to minimise the possible support that he might receive in the United States, if he were to launch an anti-partition campaign following the war.

On numerous occasions during his political career de Valera had tried to use American public opinion to serve Irish political ends. In fact, he demonstrated that he was even prepared to involve himself directly in United States politics in order to enlist American support.

Of course, de Valera, who was born in New York in 1882, had more reason than most people to appreciate the influence of the United States public. After all it was indirectly due to American opinion that his own life had been spared in 1916 following the Easter Rising. The British had planned to execute him then, but commuted the sentence because they were afraid that executing an American citizen would antagonise people in the United States at a crucial stage of the First Word War. The following year the British even granted an amnesty to de Valera and others involved in the rising in order to win public favour in the United States. Consequently in the autumn of 1917 when the Irish independence movement united under the banner of the Sinn Féin Party, de Valera, as the only surviving commandant of the rising, became a natural choice for the leadership of the movement.

Following a resounding success in the general election of 1918 Sinn Féin representatives refused to take their seats at Westminster. Instead they set up a government in Dublin, Dáil Éireann, which reaffirmed the establishment of the Irish Republic proclaimed during the Easter Rising. De Valera was elected *Príomhaire* (Prime Minister), but he assumed the title of President, apparently because it afforded him a more impressive platform from which to appeal to Americans.

When the Dáil's efforts to secure international recognition were ignored by the Paris Peace Conference, de Valera went to the United States to appeal for American support over the head of President Woodrow Wilson.[2] He later explained that he had three basic aims in going to the United States—to defeat the League of Nations, to raise funds, and to obtain official recognition for the Irish Republic.[3]

Touring the United States the Irish leader campaigned against the Covenant of the League of Nations on the grounds that its controversial Article X was so vague that it could be interpreted to mean that the league would help Britain to suppress the independence movement in Ireland.[4] He thereby helped to rouse Irish-American opposition to the Versailles Treaty and thus contributed not only to the rejection of the agreement in the United States but also to the various ramifications of the resulting American decision not to enter the League of Nations.

Paradoxically, however, de Valera was not nearly so opposed to the League of Nations as were some of the Irish-American leaders. He was prepared to accept the covenant with the exception of Article X. On the other hand, Irish-American leaders like Daniel Cohalan of the Friends of Irish Freedom and John Devoy, editor of the *Gaelic-American*, were opposed to the League in any form that would allow for co-operation between the United States and Britain. Staunch anglophobes, they were anxious to destroy Britain's position as a major power. They actually hoped that once Ireland had secured her independence, she could be used as a base for disrupting British trade and thus wrecking the British Empire.

But de Valera realised that this very threat was enough to make the British reluctant to ever grant independence to Ireland. He therefore suggested that the British government should issue a proclamation against foreign involvement in the British Isles, just as the United States had used the Monroe Doctrine to prevent outside interference in the western hemisphere.

During an interview with a correspondent of the *Westminster Gazette* in February 1920, de Valera proposed that Britain should agree to a treaty with Ireland similar to a 1901 treaty between the United States and Cuba which stipulated that the latter would not enter an agreement with any foreign power that would tend to impair the island's independence.

'Why doesn't Britain make a stipulation like this to safeguard herself against foreign attack as the United States did with Cuba?' the Irish leader asked. 'Why doesn't Britain declare a Monroe Doctrine for the two neighbouring islands?' He then went on to explain that the Irish people would co-operate in such an arrangement 'with their whole soul'.

Cohalan and Devoy were outraged at the interview. The latter was highly critical in the columns of the *Gaelic-American*, while Cohalan wrote a personal letter to the president denouncing the *Westminster Gazette* article:

A British Monroe Doctrine that would make Ireland an ally of England, and thus buttress the failing British Empire so as to further oppress India and Egypt and other subject lands would be so immoral and so utterly at variance with the ideals and traditions of the Irish people as to make it indefensible to them as it would be intolerable to the liberty-loving people of the world.

After the interview a split that had been developing for some time between de Valera and Cohalan became public. The basic difference between them was that Cohalan felt that the Irish leader was interfering in American affairs, while de Valera was annoyed that the Irish-Americans, who considered themselves as Americans first, were trying to speak for Ireland.

There was really a certain amount of truth to both positions. By attacking the Irish leader over the *Westminster Gazette* interview, the Irish-Americans were taking it upon themselves to speak on what was essentially a matter for the Irish, but Cohalan had justification for criticising de Valera for interfering in American affairs, especially when the latter went to the conventions of the major political parties in 1920. De Valera even disrupted efforts to include an expression of support for the Irish Republic in the Republican Party's election platform.

With some difficulty Cohalan had persuaded the platform committee to agree to a plank recognising Irish independence, but the plank was couched in the vague terms usually associated with American election documents. De Valera therefore denounced it as too vague, and the resolutions committee—annoyed at the foreign interference—reversed itself and killed the whole idea. As a result Irish independence was not even mentioned in the party's final platform.

When de Valera returned to Ireland in December 1920 he had collected several million dollars for the Irish cause, but he had not secured United States recognition. In addition, he left the Irish-Americans bitterly split in his wake. One year later the Irish Independence movement would itself be seriously divided with de Valera leading one faction in opposition to the Anglo-Irish Treaty of 1921.[5]

Much has already been written about that split, so there is no need to go into detail here. Whether or not de Valera was right about the treaty need not concern us. Yet it is important to note that many people thought that he was wrong. They believed that there was little real difference between what he was seeking and what the Treaty actually secured. They therefore blamed him for splitting Sinn Féin over a mere quibble, and they held him primarily responsible for the resulting civil war.

The controversy centred around Ireland's status as defined in the Anglo-Irish Treaty. De Valera indicated that he would accept the *de facto* status of the dominions such as Canada and South Africa. In practice, these countries were independent because, even though the British Crown had a *de jure* right to intervene in their affairs, Britain was too far away to enforce that right. In Ireland's case, however, Britain was close enough to intervene, so de Valera insisted that the *de facto* status of the dominions should be made *de jure* for Ireland. To achieve that end he put forward a plan that became known as External Association. In accordance with it, Ireland would be associated with—though not actually a member of—the British Commonwealth.

External Association was modelled on Woodrow Wilson's ideas for the League of Nations, but de Valera decided not to make the same mistake that the American President had made by attending the Paris Peace Conference. Instead the Irish leader stayed in the background and declined to be a member of the delegation which went to London to negotiate the settlement.

The Irish representatives pressed for External Association, but the British, with their extraordinary attachment to the symbols of the Crown and Empire, refused to accept such an arrangement. They offered, instead, to write into the Treaty any phrase that the Irish delegation desired to ensure that as a dominion Ireland would have the same *de facto* status as Canada.

Insisting that the Irish would have to accept membership of the British Commonwealth and subscribe to an oath of allegiance to the Crown, Lloyd George, the British Prime Minister, issued an ultimatum on 5 December 1921, warning that unless the British terms were accepted and an agreement signed, Britain would 'wage an immediate and terrible war' on Ireland. The Irish delegation duly concluded the agreement in the early hours of the following mornng.

Although de Valera repudiated the Treaty, the Dáil accepted it by a narrow margin. He then resigned as President.

The more radical members of the IRA refused to accept the Dáil's decision. They seized some prominent buildings in Dublin and refused to withdraw, even after an election in June 1922 indicated that a majority of the electorate supported the Treaty. When the government ejected them the following week, it sparked off a civil war.

Although the government won a decisive victory in less than a year, the fighting was extremely bitter. Each side resorted to brutal murder and blatant intimidation with the resulting bitterness leaving an indelible imprint on Irish political life for the next half century.

De Valera and his colleagues blamed the pro-Treaty people for the Civil War on the grounds that the latter had exceeded their mandate by abandoning the republican ideal. On the other hand, supporters of the Treaty reviled de Valera. They held that his condemnation of the Treaty and his failure to control militant elements among his supporters had been primarily responsible for the conflict. As a result there would henceforth be little trust or co-operation between de Valera and his opponents. Even though he and W. T. Cosgrave were to lead the strongest wings of the nationalist movement for most of the next twenty-five years, they were never again on speaking terms.

Probably the greatest paradox of the whole Treaty controversy was the paucity of opposition in the Dáil to the agreement's provisions concerning Northern Ireland. This was undoubtedly because most people concluded that the Treaty incorporated a real chance of ending partition by providing for the setting up of a Boundary Commission to redraw the border of Northern Ireland, in accordance with the wishes of inhabitants of the border areas.

People in Ireland were convinced that the Boundary Commission would transfer contiguous areas of the Six Counties in which nationalists were a majority. These areas included the bulk of two counties, Fermanagh and Tyrone, and parts of Derry, Armagh, and Down. Once deprived of so much territory, it seemed likely that Northern Ireland would be economically unable to survive.

Coming to that conclusion in 1925 the Boundary Commission caused a surprise by ruling that the rendering of Northern Ireland into an uneconomical unit would be repugnant to a phrase in the Treaty stipulating that the transfer of territory should 'be compatible with economic and geographic conditions'. The Commission was actually prepared to award some areas to Northern Ireland, but the report was suppressed and, in return for some financial considerations from the British, the Dublin government dropped its demand for territory.

Irish people could hardly have been blamed for thinking that the Boundary Commission robbed them of extensive territory and committed many of their nationalist brethren to live under the discriminating rule of the Stormont parliament in Belfast. Lloyd George had already explained publicly that the phrase concerning 'economic and geographic conditions' had been included in the Treaty simply to ensure that the Commission would not attempt to transfer isolated areas such as Roman Catholic parts of Belfast or Protestant pockets in Dublin. Henceforth the Ulster question was to become a central issue in Irish politics, and the Treaty, which first afforded nationalist recognition to partition, became the focal point for further controversy. Inevitably the government of W. T. Cosgrave suffered from the resulting public discontent.

The government actually compounded its political problems in 1925 by concluding the so-called 'Ultimate Financial Agreement' with Britain by which the Free State agreed to pay the British government land annuities arising out of legislation of the late nineteenth and early twentieth centuries that had helped Irish tenants to purchase land. Although the Cosgrave government felt obliged to pay these debts, some opponents argued that the financial agreement drawn up at the time of the Boundary Commission fiasco absolved them from the payments.

In spite of the growing public discontent, however, the government had essentially a free hand in the Dáil, because members of the republican opposition refused to take their seats. They were adopting the same abstentionist policy towards the Dáil as had earlier been applied to Westminster. Claiming the Sinn Féin banner for themselves, they argued that they were the legitimate government of the whole island and that the IRA was the legitimate army. As President of Sinn Féin, de Valera sought to modify the abstentionist policy at the party's convention in 1926, but he was defeated in a narrow vote. He then resigned, formed his own party, Fianna Fáil, and began preparations for his return to power.

Although Fianna Fáil quickly established itself as a formidable force in Irish politics by promising to revise the 1921 Treaty, de Valera felt that the party was being seriously handicapped by a lack of newspaper support. He therefore turned to the United States for financial help in an effort to found his own daily newspaper. He made two fund-raising visits there and stayed about eight months in all. Eventually on 5 September 1931 the first issue of the *Irish Press* was published. De Valera finally had a newspaper in which to put forward his own ideas.

At the time there was no shortage of popular issues on which the *Irish Press* could berate the government, which had been pursuing unpopular policies with an almost masochistic zeal. On the economic front, for example, the government—like so many other governments of the day—adopted austere financial policies in an attempt to rescue the country from the Great Depression. Fianna Fáil, on the other hand, advocated welfare policies coupled with a programme of economic nationalism. Yet issues surrounding the 1921 Treaty still took centre stage in the political life of Ireland.

Having fought against anti-Treaty forces during the Civil War, members of the government appeared to become inflexible in their support of the Treaty. Thus they did nothing to rob de Valera of one of his most potent issues. They could easily have abolished the controversial oath of allegiance in 1931 following the enactment of the Statute of Westminster, which acknowledged that the dominions were 'autonomous communities'. But instead of trying to placate opponents of the Treaty with revisionist legislation, the government sought to suppress the more radical elements by taking a strict law and order stance. In 1931 it passed a stringent public safety bill proscribing twelve organisations, among them the IRA. Wide powers of arrest and detention were conferred upon the police, and military tribunals were established.

De Valera vigorously opposed the government, so that in the general election of 1932 the IRA and kindred elements strongly supported him, with the result that Fianna Fáil won seventy-two seats. Supported by seven Labour Party deputies, de Valera was thus able to form a government with himself as the dominant figure.

According to his authorised biographers, Lord Longford and Thomas O'Neill, de Valera permitted his cabinet the fullest range of discussion and normally sought to have unanimous consent for his decisions. If every cabinet member did not agree with him, then he would usually postpone decision until such time as he would either win over the sceptic or else wear him down by a process of attrition. He was, in the words of one of his first biographers, a *'Unique Dictator'*.[6]

Believing that the most important matters confronting the government were in the area of foreign policy, de Valera retained the portfolio of External Affairs for himself and began undoing what he believed were the obnoxious portions of the 1921 Treaty. The oath of allegiance was immediately abolished and the land annuity payments suspended.

The British responded by placing heavy duties on Irish imports as a means of collecting substitute revenue, and this gave rise to what became known as the 'economic war' that was to last until 1938. Since Fianna Fáil had been anxious to pursue a policy of economic nationalism in order to build up Irish industries, de Valera was not too perturbed by the 'economic war', as it allowed him to appeal to the strong nationalistic instincts of the Irish people. Indeed some would say that his government deliberately exploited the anglophobia of the people by calling upon them to 'burn everything British but their coal'.

The next step towards dismantling the 1921 Treaty was taken during the British abdication crisis of 1936 when de Valera had the Dáil pass the External Relations Act, which was quickly followed by a new constitution that was ratified in a popular referendum. Together these two pieces of legislation excluded the British monarchy from the internal affairs of Ireland, but retained the links for international matters as an inducement for the majority in Northern Ireland to accept Irish unity. In effect this was the External Association idea first put forward in 1921.

From the domestic standpoint Ireland had become, in essence, a republic. The office of Governor-General, the link with the British Crown, was abolished and an elected President became Head of State. With the use of native terms very much in vogue on the continent, the Prime Minister, who was Head of Government, assumed the title of Taoiseach, the Gaelic for leader or chief. One of the more controversial aspects of the constitution was an article claiming sovereignty over the whole island, though another article then qualified this by recognising the existence of a separate regime in Northern Ireland. In other words the existence of Northern Ireland was accepted, but its right to exist was not.

Meanwhile the 'economic war' continued, but in time the British began to make overtures to de Valera to settle the controversy. The first man to move to end the conflict was Malcolm MacDonald, the Dominions Secretary. He had a number of secret meetings with de Valera over a period of more than a year and these eventually culminated in the convening of a conference in London in January 1938.

De Valera explained that his principal grievances were partition and Britain's retention of three Irish ports—Queenstown (now Cobh), Berehaven, and Lough Swilly—in accordance with the terms of the 1921 Treaty. He concentrated on the partition issue, arguing that there was no intention of coercing Ulster. He was perfectly content to let Northern Ireland retain its parliament in Belfast, on condition the latter agreed to be represented in a general parliament in Dublin. If the British would settle the question, he indicated that he would then be willing to conclude a naval agreement to Britain's satisfaction.

When the British retorted that they could do nothing, de Valera appealed to President Franklin D. Roosevelt of the United States to use his 'influence to get the British government to realise' that the ending of partition would open the way for closer co-operation between the democracies by removing the opposition of Irish exiles to ties with Britain.[7] This was particularly important in the United States, where Irish-Americans imbued with a deep anglophobia were bitterly opposed to Anglo-American co-operation.

Roosevelt was 'very much interested' in an Ulster settlement, but he was loath to intervene 'officially or through diplomatic channels'. Yet he did intervene discreetly by personally instructing Joseph P. Kennedy, who had recently been appointed Ambassador to Britain, to tell Neville Chamberlain, the British Prime Minister, that the White House hoped that the Ulster question could be settled.[8]

Writing to Roosevelt the following April, de Valera explained that 'the knowledge of the fact that you were interested came most opportunely at a critical moment in the progress of the negotiations. Were it not for Mr Chamberlain personally the negotiations would have broken down at the time, and I am sure that the knowledge of your interest in the success of the negotiations had its due weight in determining his attitude.'[9]

Even though the Ulster problem proved insoluble, the British delegation did make a goodwill gesture in handing over the three bases and also coming to a financial agreement ending the 'economic war' on terms favourable to Dublin. The agreement not only provided de Valera with a major diplomatic success but also made it possible for Ireland to remain neutral during the coming war.

Although in the political wilderness at the time, Winston Churchill, who had been instrumental in securing the provision granting Britain the ports in 1921, put up a spirited opposition to the new agreement. He denounced it as a surrender, warning that the day might come when the ports would be vital to Britain's survival and if the Irish refused to hand them over, Britain might be placed in the unenviable position of having to seize them and thereby suffer great damage in the eyes of public opinion throughout the world. 'To violate Irish neutrality should it be declared at the moment of a great war', Churchill told the House of Commons, 'may put you out of court in the opinion of the world, and may vitiate the cause by which you may be involved in the war.'[10]

According to MacDonald, however, most of Chamberlain's cabinet believed that the 'very importance of those ports in the event of war threw the balance of argument, paradoxically, on the side of our voluntarily resigning our Treaty right to occupy them'. This view was unanimously supported by the Chiefs of Staff who contended that they could count on French and Northern Irish bases to provide sufficient protection for the North Atlantic trade route. As a result, in spite of Churchill's opposition, the agreement was ratified by Westminster without much difficulty.[11]

Nevertheless the agreement did little to defuse the partition issue, which had been exerting an inordinate influence on Irish politics. Over the years the IRA had become estranged from de Valera and more militant in its attitude towards Britain.[12]

In January 1939 the IRA issued an ultimatum to the British government to leave Northern Ireland within four days. And when London failed to comply, the organisation—encouraged by Germany and financed mainly by money from the United States—initiated a bombing campaign in a number of British cities, placing explosives in mail boxes, railroad stations, bridges, and other public places. The most serious of the more than one hundred outrages occurred on 25 August 1939, when a bomb exploded in a Coventry thoroughfare, killing five people, including an eighty-one-year-old man and a fifteen-year-old boy. The bombings outraged public opinion, not only in Britain, but also in Ireland, where the public image of the IRA suffered great damage and the comparative freedom of action that the organisation had previously enjoyed was seriously restricted.

In June 1939 the IRA was proscribed after the Dáil passed the Offences against the State Act. It established military tribunals to deal with political offences and empowered the government to intern people without trial—actions that de Valera had condemned when introduced by his predecessor some years earlier.

The Taoiseach later charged that the IRA bombings had destroyed the climate for a campaign that he was planning to wage in order to enlist the support of world opinion to get Britain to end partition. Circumstances had seemed propitious for such a campaign following the Munich agreement of 1938. After all Chamberlain had been involved in handing over the Sudetenland to Adolf Hitler on the grounds that the area had been cut off from Germany by the treaty imposed at Versailles. Seeing that the Six Counties had been severed from the rest of Ireland by legislation imposed by the British, Dublin could point to a precedent in its quest for the return of the lost territory.

If the majority in the Six Counties were unwilling to accept an arrangement whereby Stormont would retain its existing powers while the authority vested in Westminster would be transferred to an all-Ireland parliament, then de Valera intended to call for the adoption of a transfer of populations formula similar to a provision in the Treaty of Lausanne (1923) in accordance with which Greece and Turkey exchanged certain populations. Although admitting that it would be a costly solution, the Taoiseach seemed to believe that the Ulster question could be settled by transferring Scottish-Irish Protestants from Northern Ireland to Britain and replacing them with Roman Catholics of Irish extraction from Britain. He not only had established precedents to which he could allude, but also a formidable platform from which to speak, because in the midst of the Sudeten crisis he had been elected President of the nineteenth Assembly of the League of Nations. Thus armed with the imposing title of President of the international assembly he was guaranteed a great opportunity to expound upon his views on the Northern Irish situation, especially in the United States, where he planned to visit in May 1939.

By the spring of 1939, however, the conditions once favourable for an anti-partition campaign were rapidly disintegrating following Hitler's seizure of all of Czechoslovakia in violation of the Munich agreement. Another major European war seemed inevitable, and since the great majority of Americans sympathised with the Allies, the opportunity for securing United States support on the partition issue was seriously damaged. Indeed John Cudahy, the United States Minister to Ireland, believed that any effort to enlist American support for a cause that might be considered anti-British would be counter-productive.

In April Cudahy reported that he warned de Valera 'not to talk too much about partition' during his coming visit to the United States. 'I told him very emphatically', the American Minister wrote, 'that if he were to dwell in his speeches upon any movement which would be considered an attack upon England, this would be resented by the people in our country and would react to the detriment of the Irish cause.'

De Valera replied that he understood the situation, and he promised that anything he had to say would be said with tact. But Cudahy obviously remained uneasy because he advised President Roosevelt to 'hammer home' to the Irish leader 'the necessity of treading very lightly on any controversial issue directed against England'.[13]

The President did not have to act on Cudahy's advice because international developments forced de Valera to cancel the visit. First, during late April 1939 there was a political crisis when the British government announced its intention of introducing compulsory military service. The Roman Catholic minority in the Six Counties were bitterly opposed to the idea, and de Valera demanded that the measure should not be applied to Northern Ireland. When the affair was resolved with Chamberlain's decision to exclude Northern Ireland from the conscription bill, the Taoiseach's American visit was rearranged for September 1939, but it too had to be cancelled with the outbreak of war in Europe.

In an address to the American people the following Christmas de Valera left little doubt that he would have ignored Cudahy's counsel had the visit not been cancelled. The Taoiseach explained that the 'chief aim' of his tour would have been to get the people of the United States to support his government's efforts to end partition. Subsequently, American authorities were understandably afraid that the Irish leader would renew his postponed efforts to involve Americans in the partition question and this, in turn, was to have a profound influence on relations between the United States and Ireland during the final months of the war. But when the war began, the primary importance of the partition question was that its very existence virtually compelled the Irish government to remain neutral.

De Valera personally favoured the British but, confronted with the anglophobia of the IRA, it would have been impossible for him to conclude an alliance with Britain without provoking civil strife in Ireland. Tired of the internal bitterness of almost two decades of recrimination, intimidation, and murder, the Irish people could not be expected to court another civil conflict, and since the approval of the Dáil was necessary for a declaration of war, de Valera had little choice but to pursue a neutral policy.

Even if the IRA menace had not existed, however, it was unlikely that de Valera would have pursued any other course, seeing that he thought that small countries like Ireland were better off neutral. In 1936, for instance, he warned the League of Nations that world peace depended upon the will of the major powers. 'All the small states can do, if the statesmen of greater states fail in their duty,' he said, 'is resolutely to determine that they will not become the tools of any Great Power, and that they will resist with whatever strength they may possess, every attempt to force them into a war against their will.'[14]

Believing that Ireland should remain neutral, the Taoiseach made no real preparations for war, with the result that the country was totally unprepared for the conflict. The Irish army only numbered 12,500 men, a few anti-aircraft guns, and a handful of obsolete planes, while two small patrol boats was the extent of the country's naval protection. For a country so poorly defended to go to war would have been sheer madness.

There was also one other consideration that undoubtedly entered the picture. By remaining neutral while Britain was at war, the Irish government demonstrated once and for all that Ireland was indeed an independent country, in spite of her ties with the British Commonwealth. A similar consideration actually prompted the Canadian government to adopt what amounted to a token neutrality at the outbreak of hostilities. The Canadians accomplished this by waiting for almost a week after Britain entered the conflict before adopting a separate declaration of war themselves.

Neutrality 'visibly strengthened Irish national self-consciousness', according to Edouard Hempel, the German Minister in Dublin. But he was under no illusions about the attitude of the people of Ireland. There was, he reported, 'widespread aversion to present-day Germany, especially for religious reasons', as a result of the German attack on Poland, a predominantly Roman Catholic country.*

While the Germans therefore welcomed the news that Ireland was remaining neutral, the British were disappointed, especially when they learned that naval vessels, submarines, and military aircraft would be prohibited from using Irish waters and airspace. They wanted to voice their disapproval to de Valera personally but they were hampered because they had no representative in Ireland to explain their case. Consequently Sir John Maffey, who had had a long and distinguished career in the colonial service, was asked to come out of retirement and become Britain's representative in Ireland. It was, however, first necessary to settle a diplomatic impasse between Dublin and London over the acceptance of a British representative.

The problem revolved around whether or not Ireland was actually a member of the British Commonwealth. Contending that she was only externally associated with it—and not actually a member—de Valera was unwilling to accept a representative with the rank of High Commissioner. The British, on the other hand, were not prepared to recognise Ireland's withdrawal from the Commonwealth by appointing an Ambassador, or a Minister. During two meetings which Maffey had with de Valera in September 1939 a compromise formula was agreed upon in accordance with which Maffey simply assumed the title of British Representative to Ireland.[15]

In the course of his initial meeting with de Valera on 14 September Maffey complained about Ireland's rigid neutrality. He said that the stringent rule affecting British ships and aircraft had been viewed with profound disappointment in London. In reply, de Valera explained that on the whole the measures helped Britain, because German U-boats would be denied access to Irish harbours for either supplies or repairs. He added that it had been necessary to include aircraft and ships in the exclusion order because, if the policy were directed against U-boats alone, critics would charge that it was entirely anti-German.

De Valera made it clear that he sympathised with Britain in her plight. Chamberlain had 'done everything that a man could

*Except where otherwise noted, the source of material on German-Irish relations is *Documents on German Foreign Policy, 1918–1945, Series D,* Washington, D.C., 1949–1964.

do to prevent this tragedy', he said. 'There was a time when I would have done anything in my power to help destroy the British Empire. But now my position has changed.' Nevertheless he noted that the difficulties created by partition prevented him from giving open expression to his sympathies.

Why did Chamberlain not put his foot down and stop the follies and oppressions of Northern Ireland? the Taoiseach asked. 'Look at what a picture we might have—a united, independent Ireland! Think of the effect in America where the Irish element had ruined and would ruin any possibility of Anglo-American understanding.' He simply could not understand why the British could not see this weakness.

Notwithstanding his desire to keep up the appearance of strict neutrality, de Valera noted that Irish authorities had already shown their goodwill towards Britain by allowing a British plane that had come down in Ireland to escape, but he warned that the affair had been the subject of such widespread comment that under similar circumstances in future offending crews would have to be interned.

Suddenly by a strange coincidence the telephone rang. The Taoiseach answered it and then turned to Maffey: 'There you are!' he said. 'One of your planes is down in Ventry Bay. What am I to do?'

According to Maffey, both of them 'were much relieved when the telephone rang again an hour later to report that the plane had managed to get away—or rather had been allowed to get away'.

At their second meeting on 20 September 1939 when Maffey suggested joint Anglo-Irish patrols, de Valera rejected the idea but did come up with an ingenious plan to help Britain while at the same time preserving the appearance of strict neutrality. He said that once Irish authorities located any submarine, the information of its whereabouts would be radioed. 'Not to you especially', he added. 'Your Admiralty must pick it up. We shall wireless it to the world. I will tell the German Minister of our intention to do this.' Not that this was going to be of much assistance to the Germans. They were too far from Ireland to use such information, but the British were near enough to take action.

In subsequent weeks Dublin further demonstrated the benevolence of its neutrality by allowing the British not only to fly in an air corridor over County Donegal but also to station a tug boat at Cobh for air-sea rescue purposes. In addition, Irish authorities turned over seven modern oil tankers to British registry and complied with a British request that Ireland would not charter neutral ships except through Britain. In this way Anglo-Irish competition for neutral shipping could be eliminated in order to keep chartering rates down. Of course, the latter agreement was mutually advantageous to both countries. So also was the Irish government's initial policy towards emigration. In the early years of the war no efforts were made to prevent Irish people from going to Britain to volunteer for British forces or to work in factories. In fact, the de Valera government, which was confronted with chronic unemployment at home, actually encouraged this emigration by ordering that the British Ministry of Labour's *National Clearing House Gazette* should be displayed at employment exchanges throughout Ireland.[16] Later, restrictions were placed on emigration, especially from the agricultural sector, but by then Dublin had shown further benevolence towards Britain by agreeing to secret Anglo-Irish co-operation on military and intelligence matters.

The co-operation that the British wanted most, however, was not forthcoming. The Irish were unwilling to give back to Britain the ports that were handed over in the previous year. Churchill, who became First Lord of the Admiralty immediately after the outbreak of hostilities, was particularly annoyed at this. Ever a man to rely on his own intuition, he was not prepared to defer to the judgement of the Chiefs of Staff—rendered shortly before the ports were handed over—that naval facilities in the Twenty-Six Counties were not important to Britain.

In a memorandum for the First Sea Lord, the Deputy Chief of Naval Staff, and the Director of Naval Intelligence, Churchill noted that 'three-quarters of the people of Southern Ireland are with us, but the implacable, malignant minority can make so much trouble that de Valera dare not do anything to offend them.' The First Lord went on to reject the possibility of promoting co-operation with Dublin by ending partition, because, he explained, Britain 'cannot in any circumstances' betray the loyalists of Northern Ireland. He therefore asked that the naval leaders should consider the Irish situation with his 'observations as the basis upon which Admiralty dealings with Southern Ireland should proceed'.

Churchill was not really looking for guidance. He had already made up his mind. In the same memorandum he went on to contend that if the German submarine menace were to increase in the Atlantic, then Britain 'should coerce' the Twenty-Six Counties for the use of ports and for coast watching facilities. Explaining that the denial of such concessions was likely to continue for some time, Churchill ordered that 'the Admiralty should never cease to formulate through every channel its complaints about it, and I will from time to time bring our grievances before the cabinet. On no account must we appear to acquiesce in, still less be contented with, the odious treatment we are receiving.'

In mid-October Churchill brought his supposed grievance before the cabinet. He contended that the ports were indispensable to Britain's security, and he produced a report by the Chief of Naval Staff concluding that it was 'of vital importance' that the control of Ireland's 'waters shall be available for the use of the Navy which protects Irish as well as British trade and soil'. As a result Chamberlain instructed that Maffey should make an informal approach to de Valera concerning the ports.

Maffey found de Valera immovable on the subject on 21 October 1939. The Taoiseach contended that if the British had paved the way towards Irish unity as he had asked the previous year, then Ireland 'might' have been able to help, but as things stood his hands were tied because the Irish people would not stand for handing over the ports. Although there was a 'vague majority sentiment' in Ireland favouring an Allied victory, de Valera explained that there were still many people who were willing to welcome Britain's defeat at any price. He admitted that the latter sentiment was based on ignorance but pointed out that it had its roots in the years of hostility between the two islands. Emphasising his determination to remain neutral, the Irish leader said that he would neither reconsider his decision, nor would he meet with Chamberlain to discuss the situation. He concluded the interview by expressing 'full agreement' with the course followed by Chamberlain in the events leading up to the war. 'England has a moral position today', the Taoiseach said; Hitler might have his early successes, but the moral position would tell.

The British were anything but gratified at what Anthony Eden, then Dominions Secretary, described as 'the rigid and unsatisfactory attitude adopted by Mr de Valera'. Churchill talked about seizing the ports but Eden pointed out that the Taoiseach would appeal to world opinion on moral grounds and would alienate not only the Irish people from Britain, but also many in the dominions and the United States.

Appreciating the logic of Eden's argument, Churchill was particularly worried about the possible American reaction. He therefore suggested that Britain should not move against Ireland until the United States Congress repealed its neutrality law prohibiting the sale of munitions to belligerents. After much discussion the Chamberlain cabinet decided not to attempt to seize Irish ports unless the matter became a question of life or death.

Meanwhile de Valera had to concentrate on domestic affairs as the IRA made no secret of its intention of doing everything in its power to help bring about the defeat of Britain. The Emergency Powers Act was passed giving virtual dictatorial powers to the government, which then introduced a strict press censorship under the direction of Frank Aiken, Minister for Co-ordination of Defensive Measures. De Valera explained to the Dáil that the purpose of censorship was to prevent pro-German or pro-British elements from trying to drag Ireland into the war on one side or the other.[17]

But this did not stop the IRA, which declined to submit copies of its clandestine *War News* to the censor. On 28 October 1939, for instance, in the first of a sporadic run of *War News*, the Republican Publicity Bureau appealed to the Irish people :

England's Difficulty—Ireland's Opportunity has ever been the watchword of the Gael. British Cities and Ports are now beleaguered by Germany's Aeroplanes and Submarines. Now is the time for Irishmen to take up arms and strike a blow for our Ulster people. By destroying the Orange Ascendancy, by expelling the British Army, by abolishing the Border, *we shall cut away the cancer that is gnawing at the heart of Ireland*.

A number of prominent IRA members were arrested, but they resorted to hunger strikes, demanding their unconditional release. The Taoiseach was placed in a thorny position. The prisoners

B

were employing essentially the same tactics against his government as had been used during the Civil War when he and
most of his cabinet colleagues were themselves members of the
IRA. One of the hunger-strikers, Patrick McGrath, had been a
comrade during the Easter Rising, Black and Tan War, and
Civil War. Now McGrath was dying because he was unwilling
to abandon the same cause for which he had previously fought
alongside members of the government.

Ever since Terence MacSwiney, the Lord Mayor of Cork,
died in a British jail after a protracted hunger strike in October
1920, the hunger strike had become a very effective weapon for
securing public sympathy in Ireland. Thus, in 1939 the government was faced with the danger of alienating people, if men like
McGrath were allowed to die. But, on the other hand, de Valera
told the Dáil that 'If we let these men out we are going immediately afterwards to have every single man we have tried to detain
and restrain going on hunger strike.'[18]

In the midst of the growing crisis Seán MacBride, the eminent
lawyer, argued successfully before the courts that the law under
which some of the men were being held had been unconstitution-
ally applied, with the result that the cabinet decided to release
all the internees in early December 1939.[19] This was a decision
that the Taoiseach was soon to regret because some months
later McGrath was again arrested and subsequently executed for
his part in a shooting incident in which two police detectives
were killed.

On 23 December 1939 the government was confronted with
a serious challenge when the IRA raided the Magazine Fort in
the Phoenix Park, Dublin, and seized more than a million rounds
of ammunition. Although an embarrassing setback for the
authorities, the raid soon proved to be a pyrrhic victory for the
IRA, because the police and army acted quickly and recovered
most of the stolen material. In addition, the government secured
legislation closing the legal loopholes exploited by MacBride.

In view of the challenges posed by the IRA, coupled with
the lull in the European fighting that became known as the
'phoney war', foreign affairs faded into the background in
Ireland during the last months of 1939 and early 1940. So much
so that de Valera refused to preside over the opening of the
twentieth Assembly of the League of Nations.

Ignoring encouragement that he take advantage of his position as President of the Assembly to make a genuine peace effort, the Taoiseach declined to have any further dealings with the moribund institution. According to the American Minister, Cudahy, de Valera 'spoke very bitterly and cynically of the League, describing it as "debris". He said that the only country which could possibly speak with any effectiveness now was the United States, and it would do no good for us if we did not follow words with actions.' The Taoiseach added that the only language that had persuasion at the time was, 'Tanks, Bombs and Machine Guns.'[20]

Cudahy, who had earlier served as Ambassador to Poland, was becoming very restless in Ireland because he believed that the country would remain aloof from the European conflict and he feared that he would thus be unable to play any part in the great developing drama. He therefore bombarded the White House, State Department, and friends of the President with requests that he be sent to the continent.

Eventually Cudahy had his way. In January 1940 he was appointed Ambassador to Belgium, and he hurriedly left Ireland to assume his new position.

It was not until early April that David Gray filled the vacancy in Dublin. He was to have a profound influence on the course of relations between the United States and Ireland for the remainder of the war and for some time thereafter.

2. From Non-Intervention to War

ROOSEVELT, THE IRISH-AMERICANS AND THE WORLD CRISIS
September 1939—December 1941

DURING the Second World War the Irish-American influence on United States politics played a very important role in shaping both British and American policy towards Ireland. Before proceeding further, therefore, it is necessary to examine in some depth the attitudes of Irish-Americans towards the war and also towards President Roosevelt and his pro-Allied policies.

Although Irish-Americans comprised only about fifteen per cent of the population of the United States, their political importance far outweighed their numerical strength. For one thing their concentration in the most populous states and their tendency to support Democratic candidates made them a very potent force within the Democratic Party. Indeed they controlled the party's political machines in some of the larger cities like New York, Philadelphia, Boston, Chicago and St Louis. In addition, Irish-Americans filled many of the influential positions within the Roman Catholic Church in the United States. For most of the war both the country's cardinals and a majority of the archbishops and bishops were Irish-Americans. Consequently the Irish-American influence also extended to millions of Americans of other than Irish ancestry.

Only in the presidential election of 1920 did Irish-Americans bolt the Democratic Party in really significant numbers, and that was apparently in reaction to President Wilson's lack of sympathy for the Irish cause. Although this defection was only one of a number of reasons why the Democrats lost the White House in that election, it did provide a warning that the Irish-American vote could not be taken for granted. One man who undoubtedly learned that lesson was the party's vice-presidential nominee, Franklin D. Roosevelt.

By 1932 when Roosevelt ran for President himself, the Irish-

Americans were solidly back in the Democratic fold. Only four years earlier the party had nominated one of their own for President, Governor Alfred E. Smith of New York. He was not only partly of Irish ancestry, but was the first Roman Catholic to be nominated by a major party. Although heavily defeated by Herbert Hoover in the ensuing election, his candidacy nevertheless helped to entrench Irish-Americans with the Democratic Party, with the result that they voted almost en masse for Roosevelt in both 1932 and 1936, even though Smith himself campaigned for the Republican Party's candidate in the latter election.

In 1936 the break with Smith concerned domestic issues, as foreign policy was only of secondary concern to the American people who were still struggling to extricate themselves from the Great Depression. Isolationism thrived during those years, especially after Congressional hearings held under the chairmanship of Senator Gerald Nye concluded that the First World War had resulted from the imperial ambitions of the European antagonists. The United States had supposedly become involved due to the machinations of American munitions manufacturers who, having extended enormous credits to the Allies, pushed for American involvement in order to salvage their investments when it appeared that the Allies were going to lose the war. With the aid of a great deal of insidious Allied propaganda, the businessmen supposedly managed to convince the American people that the Allies were fighting a war to end all wars and that the preservation of democracy and the rights of small nations depended on an Allied victory.

Although the Nye committee findings were much too simplistic, most Americans accepted them at the time. Consequently when the spectre of another war began to hang over Europe, there were wide-spread calls for legislation that would ensure that the United States could remain neutral, thereby preventing a repetition of the previous disaster. Congress passed neutrality laws establishing rigid government controls over the export of munitions, with their shipment to belligerent nations being strictly prohibited. In addition, credit or loans to countries at war were banned and the President was authorised to forbid Americans to travel on ships of belligerents.

While this legislation undoubtedly reflected the public mood of the United States at that time, it did not mean that either Congress or the American people were indifferent about the outbreak of hostilities in Europe a few years later. In fact, the vast majority of them sympathised strongly with the Allies. As a result there was little surprise when President Roosevelt asked Congress to repeal the provision of the neutrality laws that prohibited the sale of armaments to belligerents, seeing that this actually favoured the Germans because they did not have the capability of transporting any equipment from the United States. The Allies, on the other hand, did have the ability, but the munitions embargo prevented them from making proper use of their naval superiority.

Initially the White House did not expect any difficulty in securing legislation that would permit belligerents to purchase munitions on a 'cash and carry' basis, but the repeal proposal ran into a shower of isolationist criticism, much of which emanated from Irish-American circles.

The ethnic Irish-American press was unanimously critical of the repeal move. The *Irish World* (New York), one of the more moderate of the Irish-American newspapers, carried a simple admonition that Americans should avoid any involvement in the war because it was 'neither the war to end war, nor is it a struggle to uphold democracy. It does not concern us in any way, and the sooner it is over, the better.' The more radical *Gaelic-American* warned that repeal amounted to the same kind of mistake that the United States had made during the First World War when it sympathised with the Allies, with disastrous consequences. Americans were therefore advised to avoid any assistance to Britain and France—the countries which the *Gaelic-American* held responsible for the Versailles Treaty and thus for the Second World War itself. 'It is to aid the empires that framed the Versailles crime', the editor asserted, 'that President Roosevelt has asked [for] the elimination of the Arms and Ammunition provision of the Neutrality Act.' The San Francisco *Leader* went somewhat further when it called on its readers to reject Roosevelt's request. 'Let us resolve', the *Leader* declared, 'to save our country from entanglement in this mess, and to take advantage of every opportunity offered by the difficulties of England to secure the freedom of Ireland.'

Irish-American newspapers failed to give even a semblance of balanced coverage of the issues surrounding repeal. People who supported the measure were generally ignored, while prominence was given to reports concerning the speeches and actions of those opposing the President, such as Senator Patrick A. McCarran's denunciation of repeal during an address to the Keep America Out of War Committee in New York, or Senator David I. Walsh's letter to every priest in the United States asking for suggestions on ways of opposing repeal. The ethnic press also gave full coverage to Father Charles E. Coughlin, the radical founder of the National Union for Social Justice, when he called for the defeat of the repeal measures on his weekly radio broadcast carried over forty-eight radio stations. He warned that repeal was 'a step which definitely means farewell to democracy and hail to dictatorship; a step which means the end of free institutions in this world for years to come.' He called on his listeners to urge their Congressional representatives to oppose repeal. Father Edward Lodge Curran, president of the International Truth Society and national director of its 'anti-war crusade', did likewise in a radio address in which he criticised Alfred E. Smith for supporting the repeal proposal.

Smith was actually only one of many Irish-Americans supporting repeal. In fact, a Gallup poll indicated that sixty-one per cent of Americans whose fathers were born in Ireland favoured the measure.[1] Somewhat incredulous, the *Gaelic-American* denounced the poll, and noted that the United Irish Societies of New York could not find one of its members supporting the provisions. Certainly anyone reading only the ethnic press and the various resolutions of the different Irish-American organisations could hardly have avoided the conclusion that the vast majority of Irish-Americans was opposed to furnishing any kind of assistance to the Allies.

One is immediately confronted with the problem of determining just who were the Irish-Americans. Generally speaking they were all Americans of Roman Catholic Irish descent, but not all were imbued with Irish-American nationalism nor had all retained their Roman Catholic heritage. Many of those whose forebears had moved to states with few Roman Catholic priests, had adopted Protestant religions, while many more had simply assimilated into American society, especially in the 1920s and 1930s. During those years American interest in Irish affairs was at a low ebb and Irish-Americans were preoccupied with their own problems. They had begun their flight to suburban America where they formed loyalties and attachments to their new neighbourhoods, to their various economic groups, and to their professions. Irish-American nationalism had therefore been seriously weakened even before the Second World War.

Such nationalism was found mainly in areas where Irish-Americans congregated in closely knit communities, especially in the large urban centres of such north-eastern states as Massachusetts, Connecticut, Rhode Island, New York, New Jersey, and Pennsylvania, or in mid-western states like Illinois and Michigan, or further west in California. Irish-American nationalists—or professional Irish-Americans, as they were often called—controlled the ethnic newspapers that circulated within these communities, and since the daily press of larger cities devoted little attention to ethnic affairs, the nationalists had a virtual monopoly on such news coverage. Hence the strength of isolationist sentiment of Irish-Americans tended to be rather distorted. Indeed, the repeal legislation was actually backed by over sixty per cent of Congressmen with Irish surnames.

Yet the fact that so many of them favoured repeal of the embargo in 1939 should not be taken as indicative of interventionist sentiment. Many people actually viewed repeal as the best way to keep America out of the conflict, seeing that the President had astutely included a provision in his bill forbidding American ships to travel in waters in a zone extending around belligerent countries and including such neutrals as Belgium, Holland and Ireland. Thus, it was argued, the bill reduced the danger that American opinion might be inflamed either by a deliberate or accidental sinking of an American ship.

John Cudahy, who later became one of the most outspoken critics of Roosevelt's foreign policy, wrote an encouraging letter to the President in September 1939. 'Those of us who believed in the arms embargo realise in experience that we were wrong,' he wrote, 'and I am sure you will convince the country that your recommendations are the soundest course to keep us out of war, by avoiding the proximate courses which drew us into the last war.'[2] From London, Ambassador Joseph P. Kennedy warned that 'It would be sheer disaster for England and France if such a bill refused to pass.'

The embargo was lifted in early November 1939 and this gave rise to widespread confidence in the United States that the Allies had sufficient strength to overcome the Nazis, but that confidence was soon undermined by the German successes of May 1940. Winston Churchill, who took over as Prime Minister in Britain, began sending frantic requests for the loan of forty or fifty destroyers, several hundred aircraft, anti-aircraft guns, and other material. Clearly the American assistance that had previously amounted to only what could be purchased in the private sector, was not going to be enough if the Allies were to survive.

Roosevelt had to move cautiously, however, because public opinion in the United States was strongly opposed to war. One opinion poll published in late May, for instance, showed that less than eight per cent of the people would support immediate intervention and only nineteen per cent were in favour of such a move if it appeared that the Allies would otherwise be defeated. Consequently the White House had to be careful not to give any impression that there was some kind of secret commitment to join the Allies.

The President therefore temporarily rejected the request for destroyers, but he did promise to supply other equipment, including some twenty torpedo boats that were under construction at the time. He used the occasion of Italy's entry into the war on 10 June 1940 to inform the American people of his plans to aid the Allies more directly. In spite of strong representations from the State Department that he modify the tone of his address, the President delivered a forceful speech in Charlottesville, Virginia, making it clear that he detested the fascists. 'The whole of our sympathies', he declared, 'lies with those nations that are giving their life blood in combat against these forces.' The United States, he said, was therefore going to 'extend to the opponents of force the material resources of this nation'. This was a tremendous commitment—the extent of which few could have envisioned at the time.

The following week Roosevelt moved to strengthen his power base by including two Republicans in his cabinet, Henry L. Stimson as Secretary of War, and Frank Knox as Secretary of the Navy. Both men were outspoken interventionists as well as very influential members of the Republican Party. Stimson already had a long distinguished career in public service, having served in the cabinets of two different Presidents, while Knox had been the vice-presidential nominee on the unsuccessful Republican ticket that had opposed Roosevelt in the 1936 Presidential election.

However, the President's most immediate problem was not posed by the Republicans but by one of his own Democratic colleagues, Senator David I. Walsh, the irascible Chairman of the Senate Naval Affairs Committee. He was particuarly determined to thwart White House plans to aid Britain. When he learned that Roosevelt intended to hand over the twenty torpedo boats to the British, for example, he had Congress pass a law prohibiting the transfer of any equipment unless the various service chiefs were willing to certify that the material was 'not essential to the defence of the United States'. The Walsh Amendment, as it was called, not only killed the transfer of the torpedo boats, but also proved to be somewhat of a stumbling block later that summer when Roosevelt sought to comply with Churchill's continued requests for destroyers following the fall of France.

The British were virtually alone in the fight against Germany and Italy, with the result that ships were needed desperately. But the Walsh Amendment seemed to tie Roosevelt's hands. Since the United States navy needed the destroyers being sought by Britain, White House advisers were convinced that Congressional authorisation was necessary to hand over the ships, and it seemed unlikely that this approval would be forthcoming.

In mid-July 1940 a pro-Allied group of Americans began a propaganda campaign for the transfer of destroyers, arguing that the President should exchange them for bases in British possessions in the Caribbean. Since this could be taken as strengthening American defences, they contended that the President could hand over the vessels without first securing Congressional approval.

Soon the pros and cons of such an arrangement were being argued both inside and outside the halls of government. Some Irish-American elements were in the forefront of the isolationist opposition. The Irish-American owned *Chicago Daily Tribune* took a firm stand against the proposed deal, warning: 'The sale of the Navy's ships to a nation at war would be an act of war.

If we want to get into the war, the destroyers offer as good a way as any of accomplishing the purpose.'

While opposition from the *Chicago Daily Tribune*, with its strong ties to the Republican Party, was one thing, the opposition of Senator Walsh, a staunch Democrat, was something else, especially as he had already demonstrated considerable Congressional strength by killing the transfer of the torpedo boats. On 13 August 1940 he delivered an impassioned radio address over the Columbia Broadcasting System (CBS), explaining that he was 'utterly and irrevocably opposed to this destroyer proposal'. He warned that 'The transfer of naval destroyers from our flag to the British flag, no matter by what method or device, makes mockery of our declared policy of neutrality and non-intervention. It is an act of belligerency and of war.'

In a letter to the President, the following week, Walsh explained that while the American people abhorred the conduct of the European dictators, the 'vast majority think practically and realistically that it is too late to endanger American safety by committing ourselves as saviours of surrendered France and Great Britain and can have no other result than war for ourselves.'[3]

By this time, however, a deal handing over fifty destroyers in return for the lease of certain bases was almost finalised, and Roosevelt was determined to press on. The Attorney-General had assured him and the Naval Chief of Staff that they could conscientiously certify that the destroyers were not essential for American security, because the bases being leased actually enhanced the country's defence posture. As a result the President did not need the approval of Congress. Moreover with public opinion polls indicating that a majority of the people of the United States were in favour of stringent measures to protect the American hemisphere, north and south, the President was assured of a measure of popular support for the deal by depicting it as strengthening the defensive posture of the United States in the Caribbean. Nevertheless he was very uneasy about the possible opposition, so he wrote to Walsh in a vain effort to enlist his support.

Roosevelt explained that Hitler would not attack the United States over the arrangement. If the Führer wanted to declare war, the President argued, he would 'do so on any number of

trumped-up charges.' Concluding with a strong appeal to the
Irish-American Senator, Roosevelt wrote: 'I do hope you will
not oppose the deal which, from the point of view of the United
States, I regard as being the finest thing for the nation that has
been done in your lifetime and mine.'[4]

While drafting a message to Congress announcing the deal
that was formally concluded on 2 September 1940, the President
spoke to his secretary, Grace Tully. 'Congress is going to raise
hell about this,' he said, 'but even another day's delay may mean
the end of civilisation. Cries of "warmonger" and "dictator" will
fill the air, but if Britain is to survive, we must act.'

Roosevelt did act, of course, and it quickly became apparent
that he had overestimated the strength of his opposition. He had
simply outmanoeuvred his critics. When news of the deal was
released, the general reaction in the United States was enthusiastic. Hitler's quick victories had frightened the American
people, and there was tremendous apprehension that once he
had conquered Europe he would turn to Latin America before
eventually waging war on the United States. As a result Americans welcomed the destroyer-base deal on the grounds that it
strengthened their country's defences against possible Nazi en-
croachment in the hemisphere.

Although the United States was still supposedly neutral, no
one with any sense of reality could fail to appreciate that the
agreement greatly aided Britain's war effort. It was, in the words
of Churchill himself, 'a decidedly unneutral act'.

Realising that it was an historic arrangement, David Gray,
who had by then taken over as Minister to Ireland, sent Roosevelt a short congratulatory note that seemed to echo the sentiments of the President's own letter to Walsh:

> The deal . . . for bases seems to me the most important thing
> that has happened to our nation in my lifetime. Of course it
> is far more than what it appears to be on its face. If you can
> lay the foundations for an Anglo-American control of the
> world on the principles of Democracy and Justice you will
> have achieved the most that any man has done since
> Octavianus.[5]

The destroyer-base deal was a particularly bold move in an
election year, especially when Roosevelt was trying to become

the first American President ever to win a third term. Although an in-depth analysis of that election campaign is beyond the scope of this study, it is necessary to examine the role played in it by some Irish-Americans.

Serious cracks were beginning to show in Roosevelt's Irish-American support in 1940. James A. Farley, who had managed both of his earlier Presidential campaigns, broke with him over the third-term issue and had his own name put forward at the Democratic Party convention. An astute politician, Farley knew that he would not be able to wrest the nomination from Roosevelt, but his gesture in opposing the President was an indication of the intensity of his feeling.

After Roosevelt won the nomination, Alfred E. Smith announced that he was going to support Wendell Willkie, the President's Republican opponent. Smith was only one of many Irish-Americans anxious to see Roosevelt defeated. Hans Thomsen, the German *Chargé d'Affaires*, reported that Irish-Americans were helpful in his efforts to defeat the President.

One of Thomsen's tactics was to distribute some 50,000 copies of *Country Squire in the White House*, a book extremely critical of Roosevelt, written by an Irish-American economist, John T. Flynn. Thomsen described the book as a 'vitriolic attack on President Roosevelt and his administration', and he noted that the *New York Times* had portrayed Flynn's work as more damaging to Roosevelt's reputation than anything previously published. The *Chicago Daily Tribune* actually published extensive excerpts from the book in the days immediately before the election, thereby contributing to German efforts to discredit the President.

Working behind the scenes the German *Chargé d'Affaires* and his staff played a significant part in stirring up a controversy around foreign policy issues in the campaign, even though there was really very little difference between Willkie and the President on foreign policy. Both men were outspoken proponents of aid for Britain. But Willkie played into the hands of the Germans by ridiculing Roosevelt's promises to preserve neutrality. He even suggested that the President might already have committed the United States to war on Britain's behalf.

'Who really thinks that the President is sincerely trying to keep us out of war?' Willkie asked, before going on to suggest that there might be an 'international understanding to put America in the war that we citizens do not know about.'

Willkie's tactics seemed to be paying off as the President's lead in the polls was slipping badly. By mid-October party regulars were inundating the White House with pleas for the President to refute Willkie's charges and to assure the American people that he would not abandon neutrality if re-elected. Suddenly, less than two weeks before the election, there were rumours that Willkie was going to receive some Irish-American help that could prove decisive.

Ambassador Kennedy, who was known to be unhappy at his post in London, was reported to be returning home, and it was rumoured that he intended to endorse the Republican candidate. The rumour, which was apparently well-founded, was widespread and taken very seriously by all concerned. In Dublin, for instance, the British representative told the American Minister that Kennedy was indeed going to denounce the President.

Roosevelt was very uneasy. He called Senator James F. Byrnes, a friend of Kennedy, and asked him to get in touch with the Ambassador to make sure that he made no pronouncements before visiting the White House. For if Kennedy spoke out, it could have been disastrous for the President, as the Ambassador had been privy to much of the secret correspondence between Roosevelt and Churchill.

Upon his arrival in Washington, Kennedy refused to endorse the President. But after the latter had a chance to turn on his charm, give an assurance that he only intended to aid Britain short of war and, according to some reports, promise to support Kennedy for the Democratic Presidential nomination in 1944, the Ambassador relented and agreed to make a radio address supporting the President as a peace candidate.

Kennedy then created great drama and further excited the rumours by announcing that his speech was being paid for by himself and not the Democratic National Committee. People were thereby encouraged to believe that the Ambassador had broken with the President and that he was about to make an important announcement. As a result there was a very large audience for the speech, which was carried nationwide on radio exactly one week before the election. In it Kennedy endorsed Roosevelt as a peace candidate, contending that he was helping

Britain so that the United States would have time to build up
her own defences. If any secret commitment had been made to
lead America into the war, Kennedy argued that he would
know about it himself. And assuring his audience that there was
no such commitment, he declared that Roosevelt had no intention of abandoning neutrality, unless the United States were
attacked first.

The address had a tremendous impact. 'As a vote-getting
speech, it was probably the most effective of the campaign',
according to *Life* magazine, 'for more than anything else it
allayed fear that Roosevelt would take this country into war.'

The President had by this time already set out on a campaign
tour, stopping in Boston next day for probably the most celebrated speech of the whole campaign. The ties with Kennedy
were greatly stressed. At the railroad station, the President's
train was met by the Ambassador's father-in-law, John 'Honey
Fitz' Fitzgerald, a former Mayor of Boston, who was accompanied by his grandson, the future President, John F. Kennedy.

During his speech to a large gathering Roosevelt spoke in the
most complimentary terms of Ambassador Kennedy and then
went on to make his famous promise not to involve the United
States in the war. 'I have said this before', he declared, 'but I
shall say it again and again and again, your boys are not going
to be sent into any foreign wars.'

According to the President's biographer, James McGregor
Burns: 'The pursuit of victory had exacted a heavy price. In
the last desperate days, Roosevelt made some fearsome concessions to the isolationists.' For months his foreign policy had been
based on the belief that fascism was a danger to democracy
everywhere—including the Americas—and the fascists were bent
on dividing the whole world between themselves. But the Boston
speech appeared to tie the President's hands and firmly commit
him to neutrality.

By his actions, nevertheless, Roosevelt had effectively split
the Irish-American vote. Privately he had convinced people like
Kennedy and John Cudahy that he was determined to remain
neutral, and they then actively campaigned for him.

Shortly after the war began Cudahy had actually written to
the President from Dublin urging him to seek re-election. 'I am
sure', he wrote, 'the overwhelming mass of Americans have my

conviction that you are the only man in point of training, experience, and demonstrated judgment capable of handling the Presidency during this war.' Of course, Cudahy was convinced that Roosevelt was determined to keep the United States out of war at that time. He was therefore prepared to support him.[6]

By early August 1940, however, the former Minister to Ireland was diverging from White House policy by being openly critical of Britain. During a visit to London while on his way back to the United States following the closing of the American embassy in Brussels, for instance, he stunned a press conference by criticising reports about the conduct of German troops occupying Belgium. He described the troops as better behaved than American soldiers had been while in Europe during the First World War. But the most important aspect of the press conference was a charge by Cudahy that Britain's recently instituted blockade of the continent was going to lead to the starvation of millions of innocent people in Belgium.

The State Department was disturbed by the remarks because they played into the hands of one of Roosevelt's most influential critics, former President Herbert Hoover, who had been waging what was called the 'Starving Europe Campaign' against Britain's blockade of the continent. When a State Department spokesman issued what amounted to a rebuke by announcing that Cudahy had been ordered home immediately, London newspapers reported that the Ambassador was going to resign from the administration. But after a meeting with the President, the former Minister to Ireland—still harbouring ambitions of securing another important ambassadorial position—announced his support for the President and campaigned for him as a peace candidate.

Yet many people did not place any faith in the President's promises to keep America out of the war. And in an effort to undermine public confidence in these promises the German *Chargé d'Affaires* had the *New York Enquirer*, an Irish-American owned weekly newspaper, publish a captured Polish document purporting to show that Roosevelt intended to lead the United States into the war.

Dated 7 March 1939, the document was a report in which the Polish Ambassador to the United States, Count Jerzy Potocki, gave details of a conversation in which the American Ambassador to France had assured him, with Roosevelt's apparent approval, that the White House was prepared to give the Allies 'all-out support in a possible war'.

News of the report had actually been released by the Germans several months earlier, but Thomsen hoped that by resurrecting it in the form of a major news story in the *New York Enquirer*, the only Sunday evening newspaper in New York, enough people would be influenced to vote for Willkie to help him carry the state, which was then the most populous state in the union with more electoral votes than the combined total of the country's twelve smallest states. The Germans put up the money to bring out an extra large edition of a quarter of a million copies, the weekend before the election, with a bold front-page headline:

'ROOSEVELT'S PREPARATIONS FOR AMERICAN ENTRY INTO THE WAR.'

Although the article did cause a brief flurry, Roosevelt and the Secretary of State both disavowed Potocki's statement. There the matter rested, as election day was too close for the affair to become much of a campaign issue.

Most American newspapers were actually opposed to Roosevelt's re-election, among them Irish-American owned dailies with large circulations, such as the New York *Daily News, Chicago Daily Tribune*, and *Washington Times-Herald*. While some of the ethnic Irish-American newspapers did not actually take an open stand editorially, there could have been no mistaking their lack of enthusiasm for the President. In its last pre-election issue, for example, the *Gaelic-American*, which had for some weeks been carrying a mast across its front page, 'Keep U.S. Out of Foreign War', had a story underneath it headlined, 'Re-election of Roosevelt Would Undoubtedly Jockey United States into War.' About the same time the San Francisco *Leader* warned that the very existence of the republic depended on the defeat of Roosevelt.

Even though the election was much closer than either of his two earlier victories, Roosevelt managed to win. He even carried the state of New York in spite of a strong vote for Willkie in areas with large Irish-American concentrations.[7]

American policy appeared to drift in the month following the

election, but on 8 December 1940 Churchill sent what was probably his most important message to the President. In it he
explained that Britain was in dire financial straits because the
war had dislocated her trade. The country was on the verge of
bankruptcy, so he asked Roosevelt to devise a plan whereby the
United States would give, rather than sell, the much needed
supplies to Britain. If the United States provided the tools, the
Prime Minister wrote that Britain would provide the manpower
to defeat Hitler.

Determined to help, Roosevelt drew up 'lend-lease'—in accordance with which the United States would loan Britain the necessary war supplies. Since this amounted to repeal of the 'cash and
carry' legislation passed the previous year, Congress had to
approve the plan.

The President moved cautiously. His first step was to send
up a trial balloon to measure Congressional and public sentiment. On 17 December 1940 he told a press conference that
America's best defence would be a British victory and that the
United States should therefore 'do everything to help the British
Empire defend itself'. Thus, he suggested leasing war material to
the British. Illustrating the proposal, he explained that when a
neighbour's house was on fire, one would loan the neighbour a
garden hose to fight the fire, if only to ensure that the conflagration did not spread to one's own home.[8]

Soon there was a full scale debate in both Congress and the
American press on the 'lend-lease' proposal. Fearing that Roosevelt was moving dangerously close to war, many Irish-Americans
were in the forefront of those opposing the bill.

The United Irish Societies in New York, Philadelphia,
Chicago, and San Francisco all passed resolutions condemning
the plan. In Congress Senator Walsh was one of the leaders
in the fight against the bill. Among those who spoke against it
at Congressional hearings was Joseph P. Kennedy, who had
earlier caused a sensation by telling a newspaper reporter that
democracy was dead in Britain.

The attitude of the ethnic Irish-American press ranged from
indifference to outright hostility. But even more important was
the opposition of the large Irish-American owned dailies such as
the New York *Daily News*, which had the largest circulation of
any newspaper in the United States, the *Washington Times-*

Herald, and the *Chicago Daily Tribune.* Roosevelt was so disturbed by their opposition to his policy that he eventually referred to their publishers as the 'Dover House Set', comparing them to Brtain's infamous group of appeasers, the Cliveden Set.

As had happened during the debate over repeal of the arms embargo in 1939, many Irish-Americans supported the President. John McCormack of Massachusetts, the majority leader of the House of Representatives, and Senator James F. Byrnes of South Carolina were among the bill's principal sponsors in Congress. It was actually McCormack who first introduced the legislation.

A representative from Missouri expressed surprise that McCormack should support the bill. 'I never knew I would live to see the day when a good Irishman like John McCormack from Massachusetts would openly admit that Great Britain is our first line of defence.'

McCormack responded next day, thanking the Congressman for paying him a great compliment by characterising him as an Irishman. 'There is', McCormack added, 'one greater compliment that he could give me—by characterising me as "The American of Irish descent from Boston"!' This response really typified the attitude of most Irish-Americans. They were now Americans and the Irish prefix was indicative only of their ancestry, not of their allegiance.

The 'lend-lease' bill was easily passed in the House of Representatives, where Congressmen with Irish surnames like Buckley, Byrne, Delaney, Fitzgerald, Flannagan, Kelley, Kennedy, McCormack, McGranery, O'Brien, O'Toole, Russell, and Sullivan—to mention only some of the more than seventy Congressmen with Irish names—voted in favour of the bill by a three-to-one majority. In the United States Senate the overall voting was much closer, but a majority of Irish-Americans still supported the legislation.

No sooner was 'lend-lease' passed into law on 11 March 1941 than widespread speculation began that Roosevelt would soon introduce United States convoys to ship the 'lend-lease' material to Britain. Churchill had actually asked the President for such assistance in his December message, but Roosevelt was afraid to move so boldly at the time. He explained publicly that American convoys would lead to shooting and, he added, 'shooting comes awfully close to war'.

During the spring of 1941 Roosevelt became very concerned about the 'Starving Europe Campaign' which had been gathering momentum as ex-President Hoover continued to speak out. Although many people undoubtedly supported Hoover for purely humanitarian reasons, his campaign had a great attraction to isolationist and anglophobic elements in view of its implication that the British were no better than the Nazis because they were starving innocent people with their blockade. In late March 1941 the campaign received a boost from John Cudahy, when *Life* published the first of a number of articles from the former diplomat who had returned to Europe as a journalist.

In the article he blamed Britain for causing a state of famine in such countries as Spain, France, Belgium, and Poland. Conditions were especially bad in Spain, where, he wrote, the British blockade had been responsible for grave shortages. He added that Germany, unlike Britain, had made no effort to coerce the Spanish.

Shortly after the magazine came on the news stands, William Cardinal O'Connell, the Primate of the United States, headed a list of twenty Roman Catholic prelates (three archbishops and seventeen bishops) announcing support for Hoover's efforts to lift the British blockade. The cardinal also talked with a reporter of the Boston *Traveller*.

'I can't understand', he said, 'why any power should prohibit the sending of food to old women and little children.' In the course of the interview he also charged that 'some sort of secret manoeuvres are bringing us nearer war all the time'. The allegation was similar to one made earlier by the Mayo-born Archbishop of Cincinnati, John T. McNicholas, who had declared that a minority of ten per cent of the American people was forcing the United States 'subtly and cleverly into the world conflict and the majority of ninety per cent favouring peace is standing by silent and helpless.'

Against the backdrop of such opposition Roosevelt's next move was to impound all German and Italian vessels in United States ports. Interventionists like Stimson and Knox pressed him to go further and introduce convoys. But the President was still reluctant to move that far, especially as the America First Committee, the most influential isolationist organisation, had recently been strengthened by the addition of Charles Lindbergh, the renowned flyer, who began touring the country supporting isolationist policies. In the face of the America First opposition, Roosevelt was unwilling to begin convoying. He decided instead to introduce naval patrols in waters up to three hundred miles off the coast of the United States. These patrols would shadow any Axis vessels in the area and would report their location to the British.

When the cabinet was informed about the decision, some members were obviously disappointed that the President had not been prepared to go further. 'Well', said Roosevelt trying to placate them, 'it's a step forward.'

'I hope', Stimson interjected in disgust, 'you will keep on walking, Mr President. Keep on walking.' The cabinet erupted in laughter. The Secretary of War was disappointed that Roosevelt was only prepared to walk, rather than stampede, the American people into the Second World War.

Critics of Roosevelt realised what was happening, but they seemed virtually powerless to do anything about it. 'Do not let Churchill run this country', cautioned James F. O'Connor, the Democratic Congressman from Montana, who wrote to the President reminding him of his Boston speech promising that Americans would not be sent into any foreign wars. 'I am deeply concerned about the future of this country if you take us into this war', he added. Having learned a lesson in the First World War, the American people now wanted peace, so if the United States became involved because of the President's actions, the Irish-American Congressman warned that it 'would be the worst blow to democracy that could happen'. The best of the nation's manhood would be destroyed and the country would be bankrupted. He predicted that 'British diplomacy, intrigue and the financial oligarchy of England will see to it that the United States will be the prime sucker Nation of the world again.'[9]

Roosevelt was obviously not influenced by the arguments. 'When will you Irishmen ever get over hating England?' he asked O'Connor in reply. 'Remember that if England goes down, Ireland goes down too. Ireland has a better chance for complete independence if democracy survives in the world than if Hitlerism supersedes it.'

Of all Irish-Americans, John Cudahy probably went to the greatest extreme in his efforts to stop Roosevelt's drift towards war. Fearing that the United States navy would soon begin convoying duties, he advised the German Foreign Minister to warn Roosevelt that Germany would sink any American vessels escorting North Atlantic convoys.

The Germans actually found Cudahy useful in their efforts to retard the growth of United States aid to Britain. Josef Goebbels, the Nazi Propaganda Minister, noted that Roosevelt had been able to increase the aid by exciting American fears that, after the conquest of Europe, Hitler's next objective would be South America. Goebbels, therefore, arranged a meeting between Hitler and Cudahy so that the Führer could give an assurance that he would respect the Monroe Doctrine and keep his hands off the American hemisphere.

Cudahy had the rather dubious honour on 23 May 1941 of being the last American correspondent to have an interview with Hitler. During the meeting he urged the Führer to warn the United States that Germany would sink any ships attempting to convoy material to Britain. Of course, Cudahy did not mention in his highly publicised account of the interview that he had himself suggested that the Germans should threaten to sink American ships. He simply reported that Hitler harboured no hostility towards either North or South America, and that the Führer intended to respect the Monroe Doctrine, but would nevertheless sink any American ships in Atlantic convoys. Cudahy's actions were an example of the pains to which at least one Irish-American was prepared to go in order to prevent further American aid to Britain, for fear that it would lead to American involvement in the war.

Ironically, the same day that Cudahy met Hitler, there was a cabinet meeting in Washington from which many of the participants came away convinced that the President was hoping for an incident that would involve America in the war. Churchill also came to the same conclusion, and he was, of course, anxious to implicate the Americans in such an incident. On 28 May 1941, for example, the Prime Minister wrote a top secret memorandum to the First Sea Lord of the Admiralty, suggesting the desirability of bringing about a confrontation in which a German vessel would fire on an American patrol. He advocated that a German pocket battleship which was believed to be in the Atlantic, should, if possible, 'be located by a United States ship, as this might tempt her to fire upon that ship, thus providing the incident for which the United States government would be so thankful.'[10]

It was some weeks before such an incident occurred. In the interim there were some important developments. In July 1941 Roosevelt extended the United States security zone to Iceland, where he stationed American troops. Then in early August he met Churchill off the coast of Newfoundland. Following their discussions they announced what amounted to Anglo-American war aims in the form of the Atlantic Charter, which outlined the kind of world they wished to see after 'the final destruction of Nazi tyranny'. That a supposedly neutral country should join a belligerent nation 'in making such a declaration was astonishing', according to Churchill. He noted that the inclusion of the phrase referring to 'Nazi tyranny' 'amounted to a challenge which in ordinary times would have implied warlike action'. The Americans were gradually moving closer to war.

On 4 September 1941 there was an incident for which Churchill had long been hoping. The *Greer*, a United States destroyer, was making towards Iceland when a British aeroplane reported a U-boat in the vicinity. The destroyer located the submarine and began shadowing it, reporting its location to the plane, which waited for almost an hour before dropping four depth charges and returning to base. The destroyer continued to follow the U-boat for a further two hours, before the submarine fired two or three torpedoes at it. The *Greer* then dropped a number of depth charges of her own before losing contact with the U-boat. A further two hours passed before she located the submarine again and dropped eleven more depth charges. Having failed to destroy the U-boat, the American vessel trailed it for a while longer and then handed the task over to British destroyers and aircraft in the area.

Conveniently overlooking the American harassment, Roosevelt used the incident as an excuse to take the next step towards stopping Hitler. 'From now on', he told the American people, 'if German or Italian vessels of war enter the water the protection of which is necessary for American defence, they do so at their own peril'. American ships were ordered to shoot on sight at Axis vessels within the American defence sphere, and they were also instructed to allow foreign vessels to sail in American convoys as far as Iceland. This amounted to taking over half the Admiralty's convoying duties in the North Atlantic, with the result that Britain was able to transfer forty destroyers and corvettes for duty elsewhere.

In early October 1941 Roosevelt asked Congress to repeal the last vestige of the neutrality laws so that American merchant ships could be armed and enter the war zone. While Congress was debating the issue, there was a further incident in the Atlantic.

On 16 October eleven American sailors were killed when a U-boat torpedoed the United States destroyer, *Kearney*, which was engaged in convoying duties near Iceland. The United States was now a belligerent in everything but name, and it was testimony to the President's political skill that he brought the American people along with him.

Public opinion polls taken the previous April, for instance, showed that only thirty-one per cent of the people of the United States favoured the introduction of American convoys against sixty-one per cent who disapproved. But by the end of September, those figures had changed to forty-six per cent in favour, with forty per cent disapproving, and the remainder expressing no opinion. Three weeks later a full majority of fifty-four per cent actually favoured United States convoys.

The President's critics were being reduced to impotent frustration. On 30 October 1941 Cudahy and John T. Flynn joined Lindbergh on the platform at a large rally in Madison Square Garden, New York, denouncing White House subterfuge. They wanted the President to face the issue of war or peace honestly and ask Congress for a declaration of war so that the representatives of the people could determine constitutionally whether or not the United States was to go to war.

Events were running against the isolationists however. The big news story next day was not concerning the America First rally, but about the torpedoing of the United States destroyer, *Ruben James*, in which more than a hundred American sailors lost their lives. The next public opinion poll showed that sixty-one per cent of the American people favoured the introduction of American convoys all the way to Britain.

There was therefore little surprise when, on 13 November 1941, Congress voted to amend the remaining neutrality laws. But the vote in the House of Representatives was much too close for comfort for the White House. According to two of America's foremost authorities, William L. Langer and S. Everett Gleason, Roosevelt would have been beaten that day if he had asked for a declaration of war. Yet less than a month later Congress passed such a declaration with only one dissenting vote, following the Japanese attack on Pearl Harbour.

American historians have long disputed whether or not Roosevelt deliberately provoked the Japanese attack. Shortly after the war two distinguished historians, Charles A. Beard and Harry Elmer Barnes, argued that the President had deliberately provoked the assault, but the consensus of more recent scholarship seems to be running against them.

In his biography of Roosevelt, James MacGregor Burns argued persuasively that even though Roosevelt wanted to get into the war against Hitler, he hoped to avoid a conflict with Japan, because he did not want a two-ocean war. Consequently, he took a hard-line with the Japanese, trying not to make the mistake of appeasement that had previously proved so unsuccessful with the Nazis. The fact that his policy led to war with Japan was not planned.

For the purpose of this study, however, it is important to note that David Gray, the United States Minister to Ireland, was an astute judge of the events covered. Shortly after Japan joined the Rome-Berlin Axis in September 1940, for instance, he predicted in a letter to Roosevelt that the United States would become involved in the war as a result of a surprise Japanese attack in the Pacific. It was then more than fourteen months before Pearl Harbour was attacked.[11]

A year later Gray was still writing on the same lines. 'Before you get this', he wrote to the President on 21 October 1941, 'Japan may have touched things off. You have handled that situation as miraculously as every other as far as I can see.' He seemed to be congratulating the President for bringing the United States to the point at which Japan was going to attack, even though the assault was still more than six weeks off.

Gray was certainly not upset when the attack did occur. In fact, he was so happy that the United States was in the war that he seemed oblivious to the terrible defeat suffered in the Pacific. 'Our first reaction to the news that Japan had attacked us was', he wrote on 17 December 1941, ' "Thank God! the country is now behind the President." I think any number of wars are easier to fight than what you have been through for two years.'

3. David Gray, The USA and Partition

DE VALERA REFUSES TO BARGAIN WITH
IRISH NEUTRALITY
March—July 1940

BEFORE the war John Cudahy urged President Roosevelt to use his influence to settle the partition question in Ireland in order to remove the last barrier to complete Anglo-Irish rapprochement. Such a settlement, he believed, would mollify the Irish-Americans and would thus open the way for closer Anglo-American co-operation. 'An Ireland friendly to Great Britain', he explained, 'means the approval by a great share of American public opinion of closer American-British relations.'[1]

Although Roosevelt did intervene discreetly, his action was not sufficient to end partition. Within little over a year, however, the need to remove the Irish-American barrier to closer Anglo-American relations assumed greater importance with the outbreak of hostilities in Europe. David Gray understood this when he was appointed to replace Cudahy as United States Minister to Ireland in February 1940.

Before proceeding further, it is necessary to look at Gray's background as he was to become the central figure in relations between the United States and Ireland during the remainder of the war. A reputed hunting and shooting expert, he had an interesting and diverse career.

Gray was born in 1870 in Buffalo, New York, where his father owned a newspaper. He received a bachelor's degree from Harvard University before going into the newspaper business himself as a reporter and editorial writer in Rochester, New York. After acquiring some experience he moved to his father's newspaper and became one of the country's youngest managing editors. But he was not destined to make a success of his newspaper career. According to himself, he was very precocious and sure of himself, with the result that he initiated changes in the newspaper that were not accepted by the reading public. Consequently he lost subscribers and was forced to sell the newspaper.

In 1899 Gray passed the bar examination and began to prac-
tise as a rather unsuccessful criminal lawyer. 'All my clients went
to jail in spite of my defence', he later recalled.[2] After three years
he quit his legal practice and tried his hand at writing short
stories. At this he was a success. He had a number of sporting
stories published in *Century Magazine* and received the sure
stamp of success by having contributions published in the prestigious *Saturday Evening Post*. He also wrote a number of novels
and one play, *The Best People*, had a successful run in New
York, Chicago and London.

When the United States entered the First World War, Gray
served with the signal corps of the American Expeditionary
Force. Acting as a liaison officer with the French, he received the
Croix de Guerre and became Chevalier of the Legion of Honour.

Following the war he returned to his writing and spent considerable time travelling. It was during his travels that he made
his first visit to Ireland in the summer of 1933. He became so
enthralled with the hunting and fishing possibilities that he spent
the winter in Castletownshend, County Cork. He subsequently
made two further visits to Ireland, but neither was connected
with diplomatic or political activities.

Since he was without diplomatic experience and had a Scot-
tish Presbyterian—rather than Roman Catholic Irish—background, the sixty-nine-year-old Gray probably owed his appointment to the Dublin post to his close ties with the Roosevelt
family, with whom he was connected by marriage. His wife
Maud was an aunt of Eleanor Roosevelt, the President's wife.*
As a result Gray, whose personal relationship with Franklin D.
Roosevelt went back many years, had direct access to the White
House.

Before leaving to take up his position the new Minister had
some definite ideas about the role that the United States should
play in the European war. He wanted to give as much help as
possible to Britain. When making final arrangements for his

---

*Maud was the youngest sister of Eleanor Roosevelt's mother, who died
when Eleanor was a child. Subsequently Eleanor was reared by her grand-
mother in the same home as Maud, who was only six years her senior, with
the result that the relationship between them was more akin to that between
younger and older sisters than between aunt and niece.

departure, he found that even his bank manager in Sarasota, Florida, whom he described as a typical isolationist Republican, had come to realise that the United States would lose almost all of her foreign trade if the Germans overcame the British navy. When relating the story to Roosevelt, Gray left little doubt that he concurred with the banker's views, especially when the latter concluded that Washington would be foolish not to arm and finance the British seeing that they were willing to do the fighting for America.[3]

Knowing that Roosevelt held similar views on the international situation, Gray was anxious to help the President to aid Britain. He was therefore quick to realise that his new appointment afforded him an opportunity to be of assistance. It was not that neutral Ireland with her three million people was so important; rather, it was because of the influence that Irish affairs exerted over those Irish-Americans who were imbued with such a deep hatred of Britain that they bitterly opposed Roosevelt's pro-British policies.

It was in order to mollify this Irish-American opposition to the President that Gray first thought of trying to settle the Ulster question by ending partition. If he could secure such a settlement he believed that many Irish-American critics of the President could be won over. Roosevelt concurred with the idea and authorised him to do some spadework on the question before assuming the Dublin post.

Gray first went to the Vatican to talk with Pope Pius XII in order to get an assurance that the Roman Catholic Church would have no objection to the complete separation of church and state in Ireland, if this would help to end partition. On 21 March 1940 he had an audience with the Pope and explained that he was exploring the possibility of securing an Irish settlement because 'The Irish question had maintained an abnormal and almost continuous pressure on American foreign relations which the great majority of Americans resented, without being able to do anything about it.' Although they never did get around to discussing the possibility of a separation of church and state in Ireland, the Pope made it clear that he had no objection to the principle as it operated in the United States. Gray was therefore satisfied that he had obtained the assurance for which he had gone to the Vatican.[4]

Before meeting some British leaders in London, where he remained for a week, Gray had discussions on the Ulster question in Rome with Michael MacWhite and William B. Macauley, the respective Irish representatives to Italy and the Vatican, and in Paris with Seán Murphy, the Irish Minister to France. Then upon his arrival in London he talked with John Dulanty, the Irish High Commissioner to Britain. Each time he was careful to stress that his interest in partition was because of the abnormal un-American pressure that it was exerting upon American politics and policy.

'I am exploring the facts of the situation in order to report them to my government', Gray told Dulanty. 'I am not conducting a negotiation or proposing a mediation.'

As far as Dulanty was concerned, however, any settlement was likely to take years. For the immediate future, he said that a joint commission on roads, or an all-Ireland football team, was about the best that could be expected, but he nevertheless encouraged Gray to continue his explorative talks. 'For heaven's sake', he said, 'explore away and if you turn up any chance tell us.'

Following the discussions with various Irish representatives, Gray was well-prepared for his talks with such British leaders as Anthony Eden, the Dominions Secretary; Harold Nicolson, the head of the British Broadcasting Corporation; David Margesson, the Conservative whip; and Duff Cooper, the Minister for Information. All of them seemed to want an Irish settlement, but they were anxious that Northern Ireland should not be coerced.

On 3 April 1940 Gray met Winston Churchill, who was rapidly establishing himself as the real war leader in the Chamberlain cabinet. Churchill was insistent that there could be no coercion of the majority in the Six Counties. What was more he was particularly bitter about the refusal to allow Britain to use Irish ports. He 'roared' that he was sick of the Irish, that Britain had given them 'a generous settlement' in 1921, but they immediately violated the agreement and were now 'stabbing Britain in the back'.

Obviously briefed on the principal facets of the controversy over the Anglo-Irish Treaty, Gray told Churchill that although what he said might be true, London had failed to understand that what the Irish had really been seeking was a generous recognition of the 'contention that Irish sovereignty derived from the Irish people and not from the British Crown'. This, he added, the British had refused to concede.

While supposedly only exploring the facts of the situation, Gray was already thinking of a plan to end partition. He was hoping that de Valera could be persuaded to abandon neutrality in return for the Six Counties. But since this would also involve Lord Craigavon, the Northern Ireland Prime Minister, agreeing to unity in return for Dublin's co-operation, Gray was anxious to find out how far the British would go to persuade Craigavon to accept such an agreement.

The answer was simple. Churchill said that Britain would not coerce Belfast and that such a proposal would, therefore, be strictly a matter for Craigavon. As a result Gray was convinced as he set out on the last leg of his journey to Ireland that the settlement of partition was up to de Valera and Craigavon, and that neither Pope Pius XII nor the British government was likely to object to a settlement mutually acceptable to Dublin and Belfast.[5]

On 8 April 1940, two days after his arrival in Dublin, Gray got a chance to discuss the Ulster question with de Valera, who produced a map of Northern Ireland demonstrating that there was strong support for ending partition in south Down, south Armagh, and particularly large areas of Fermanagh and Tyrone. He also declared that a majority in the latter two counties were against partition but were, in effect, being coerced to remain in Northern Ireland. 'That is his line', Gray reported. 'The British refuse to coerce Belfast but connive at the coercion of these two counties and elements in the others.'

When asked if he would demand the recall of the German legation and give Berehaven to the British in return for a guarantee of unity, de Valera was adamant. 'No,' he replied without hesitation. 'We could never bargain with our neutrality.'

The American representative, however, was not prepared to quit. He still hoped that he might be able to make some progress with Craigavon and possibly help to bring about some agreement —any kind of agreement—between Dublin and Belfast that the British would be able to endorse publicly. In this way the Irish-Americans might be somewhat appeased and President Roosevelt would, at least, be in a little better position to take drastic action in support of Britain, should such help be needed. 'And that is of course the real reason why I want to see Craigavon', Gray wrote. 'It is evidently a hundred to one chance but it ought to be taken. It's too important all round not to be explored.'

Gray was able to derive some encouragement from his conversation with the Taoiseach in that the latter had no objection to him meeting Craigavon. 'I would see him myself,' de Valera said, 'but he will not see me.' The Taoiseach also made it clear that he concurred both with Gray's bitter opposition to Hitler and his sympathy with the Allies but added that many Irish people did not see things the same way, especially IRA elements which—although small in number—were a force to be reckoned with because 'they appealed to something very deep in the Irish heart.'

Subsequent discussions with other members of the de Valera government only confirmed the American Minister's original assessment. The following week he reported that he had talked with five or six government people and 'ALL' had given him the impression of 'being definitely anti-German and pro-ally'. But while they had 'no illusions as to where they would be in case Britain goes down', they were afraid to give public expression to their real sentiments for fear of provoking trouble with the IRA.[6]

It was some weeks before the American Minister got a chance to meet Craigavon. In the interim the international situation changed drastically following the German invasion of the Low Countries on 10 May 1940. In Britain, Churchill replaced Chamberlain as Prime Minister, but he was unable to save the situation on the continent. Within little more than three weeks the Allied forces were routed in Belgium, and the British were forced to withdraw their army. While they were fortunate to be able to retreat behind the English Channel, the French were not so lucky. There was no channel to protect them. Consequently France lay virtually prostrate before the advancing Germans.

De Valera watched these developments with growing alarm. Realising that without adequate weapons Ireland could hardly put up anything but a token resistance if the country were invaded, he turned to the United States for help. On 16 May he asked Gray to use his influence to secure American protection for Ireland.

During the conversation the American Minister explained that he had a meeting arranged with Craigavon for the following week. He asked the Taoiseach if he could think of any line of compromise that would at least secure a measure of co-operation between North and South.

In reply de Valera said that he had already accepted External Association with the British Commonwealth as a compromise to satisfy Stormont, so he was not going to compromise further. The only solution to partition, he said, was for Northern Ireland to agree to unity and accept neutrality.

Gray suggested that the time was right for a compromise with Belfast. If the Taoiseach helped during the war, he explained, it might produce some progress towards unity that might otherwise take many years. De Valera agreed with this in principle but was still unwilling to compromise. 'I fear the common view of him is true that he is incapable of compromise,' Gray wrote. 'He has got out on a limb and he is lonely there but does not know how to get back.'[7]

The American Minister eventually learned, however, that the Taoiseach had absolutely no desire to get back. Indeed it also became apparent that leaders in the Six Counties were not very enthusiastic about compromising with de Valera.

On 22 May 1940 Gray went up to Belfast to see Craigavon, only to find that the latter had been called to London for urgent talks. The American Minister had therefore to content himself with a discussion with Sir John Andrews, the Minister of Finance, and Sir Basil Brooke (later Lord Brookeborough), the Minister of Agriculture. Both men—each of whom later became Prime Minister of Northern Ireland—were adamantly opposed to any suggestion of Irish unity.

Although his efforts to promote an Irish settlement seemed to have run aground at this point, Gray's hopes were again raised two weeks later when de Valera asked him to support Irish efforts to purchase arms in the United States. The Taoiseach explained that he was terrified that the Germans were about to invade Ireland through the Six Counties, so he needed the arms for defence.

Gray saw the Irish difficulties as a chance to acquire some real influence for himself in Dublin by getting the desired equipment for the Irish army. He therefore urged the State Department to

c

do what it could to comply with the bulk of the Irish requests so that he would be in a better position to urge Dublin to co-operate with Britain.* This was especially important at the time because he was worried that if Ireland were not brought into the war soon, the British might seize Irish ports. Only the previous week, for example, he warned Roosevelt that there was a 'possibility of events shaping so that the British have to occupy Berehaven to combat the submarine menace when it starts up again'.[8]

What Gray was most concerned about, however, was not the possible violation of Irish neutrality, but the effect that such a violation would have on American public opinion. He was so worried about this, in fact, that he wrote to Duff Cooper, the British Information Minister, warning that if it became necessary to seize the ports, the British government should make one of two claims for propaganda purposes. It should either declare that the action was undertaken in order to ensure the continued delivery of export quotas to Ireland, or else should assert that at the time the ports were handed back, de Valera had made a gentleman's agreement with Chamberlain, guaranteeing Britain use of the bases in case of an emergency.[9]

While either of these pronouncements might have conciliated many people, Gray realised that the best way to satisfy the American public was to avoid a British seizure by getting Dublin to give up the facilities voluntarily in order to make progress towards ending partition. He therefore decided to seek again for a meeting with Craigavon. With the help of the Duke of Abercorn, the Governor of Northern Ireland, a meeting was duly arranged for 7 June 1940 at Government House in Hillsborough.[10]

Before leaving for the Six Counties Gray was visited by Sir John Maffey who told him that Craigavon had recently been called to London where he had been given 'merry hell' and all but ordered to 'end partition on the best terms he could.' Although the Northern leader remained very obstinate, he was supposedly told that Ireland would have to defend herself as a unit.

*Only at the request for four destroyers did Gray balk. He wrote that 'the Irish government has no more use for one destroyer than I have for a white elephant. To defend this coast with a navy would require, in the opinion of experts, a fleet of submarines and fast torpedo boats, entirely beyond the means of the nation.'

When Gray reached Hillsborough, therefore, he was sure that Craigavon's stand on partition would not be as inflexible as the attitude adopted by his two colleagues earlier. But such was not the case. The Prime Minister seemed unmoved by anything that might have transpired during his visit to London. 'I never would have known', Gray wrote, 'that he had been crushed by the Downing Street steam roller.'

The American Minister reported that he 'got along fine' with the Stormont leader, but he was unable to make any headway with him. 'I became satisfied that he intended to do nothing or learn nothing', Gray wrote. 'He was a perfect Bourbon but very pleasant.'[11]

Craigavon explained that the people of the Six Counties were a different race and were not interested in the rest of the island, which had been disloyal and had taken down and burned the Union Jack. Although he seemed pleasantly surprised when Gray assured him that de Valera was making serious preparations to prevent Germany from using Ireland as a back door to Britain, Craigavon absolutely refused to compromise.

What would happen if the Nazis should invade Northern Ireland and proclaim that they were liberating the area? Gray asked.

'Oh,' the Prime Minister replied, 'we'll take care of them.'

Next, when the American Minister suggested that Belfast and Dublin should establish a united defence front for the whole island, Craigavon replied that it was a good idea but it was a matter for the General Staff in London. According to Gray, the Northern Irish leader 'absolutely refused to take any step that would recognise the South in any way that differentiated Ulster from Britain'.

Back in Dublin the American Minister could only look on in frustration as the Allied position continued to crumble on the continent. France was on the verge of collapse and Britain was virtually powerless to help. Then, on 10 June 1940, Italy declared war on the Allies. Gray wanted to help them from Ireland, but he was getting nowhere because, for one thing, the Northern Ireland Prime Minister seemed oblivious to what was happening. 'The interview with Craigavon at Government House', he wrote, 'showed the old man utterly unwilling to make any compromise and utterly ignorant of what was going on in the world and in the south of Ireland.'

Believing that somebody should try to do something to bring about Irish co-operation with the Allies, Gray threw diplomatic caution to the wind and went out on a limb by calling on colleagues of both de Valera and Craigavon to use their influence to get the two leaders to compromise with one another.

On 12 June, for instance, he suggested to Joseph P. Walshe, the permanent Secretary of the Irish Department of External Affairs, that he and some of his colleagues should try to use their influence to persuade de Valera to compromise with Craigavon. Gray reported that he told Walshe that 'Dev is sure not to compromise and they have got to put pressure on him from within his own party if they are going to act quick.'

Yet even if the Taoiseach could be won over, there would still be the problem of how to cope with the strong public reaction that would undoubtedly arise in Ireland in opposition to an alliance with Britain under existing circumstances. The American Minister realised that 'There would need to be some dramatic gesture of at least military unity for the duration of the war by Craigavon.' Since such an arrangement would recognise special ties between the Six Counties and the rest of Ireland and would, in effect, demonstrate that Northern Ireland was no longer an integral part of the United Kingdom, Gray believed that de Valera might accept the arrangement as a first step towards ending partition.

There was also the problem of persuading Craigavon to offer to establish a united defensive front with Dublin, as he had already made it clear to the American Minister that he was not willing to accept any modification of the ties between the Six Counties and Britain.

On 14 June, therefore, Gray wrote to the Duke of Abercorn, urging him to exert his influence on Craigavon to make a 'striking gesture' towards Irish unity for defence, at least. There was no time to waste, he warned, as each Allied setback on the continent was making it more difficult for Dublin to co-operate. 'If this situation be allowed to drift, even for another week,' the American Minister added, 'it will very likely be too late to do anything.' Explaining that he realised that what he was asking Craigavon to do was tantamount to political surrender, Gray warned that this appeared to be the only alternative to 'a break-down of Irish defence with the consequence of opening Britain to attack from the rear, which might well prove fatal'.[12]

While waiting for a response from Belfast, Gray continued his efforts to bolster United States influence in Dublin by getting Washington to accede to Irish requests for arms. Writing to Roosevelt he explained that he had 'been telegraphing frantically' for arms because 'the time may come soon when the most useful thing I can do for you is strongly to urge compromise with Ulster on Mr de Valera and I want to be thought of as helpful to them and well disposed.'

The delay in responding had been due to a State Department decision to consult the British. Secretary of State Cordell Hull wanted to find out if London would have any objection to the United States supplying weapons to Ireland. After making some enquiries Ambassador Kennedy reported that the British approved of the Taoiseach being assisted 'as far as possible in obtaining the material desired provided it does not interfere or postpone delivery of any similar material ordered by the British government'. Gray was therefore informed on 21 June 1940 that de Valera's requests would be met, at least, in part.

Next day the American Minister was able to pass on the news to de Valera personally, but there was no sign that this softened the latter's resolve to remain neutral. When Gray asked if there had been any word from Craigavon, the Taoiseach replied that there had not.

'If I were you,' Gray said, 'I would sit tight and wait for it, but when it comes I think you would do well to make compromises and meet them more than half way.'

'There is only one solution of this thing,' de Valera replied, 'and that is for the North to join us in our neutrality until we are invaded. We could be more useful that way.'

This would be impossible, Gray argued. The British could not be expected to give up their bases in the Six Counties, he said, because it was imperative that they should control both sides of the North Channel.

De Valera suggested that such control would not be necessary if the United States would guarantee Irish neutrality. He hoped that this might now be possible in view of Roosevelt's recent inclusion in his cabinet of the two interventionists, Stimson and

Knox, but Gray replied that Washington would not be able to give any guarantee of protection to Ireland.

'If America came in it would alter our situation overnight,' de Valera said, 'but as it is I can't throw in with Britain now.' He explained that he could not ask a virtually unarmed country to go to war, even if he were sure that the people would follow him.

'Perhaps if you would throw in now, England would share her arms,' Gray suggested.

'Why doesn't she do it now?' the Taoiseach asked. 'When the Germans land they are going to announce themselves as liberators and call on us to help them free Ulster.'

The American Minister could not dispute that. He thought it was a distinct possibility.

'I think you are doing everything that can be done at present,' Gray said. 'I haven't met a single person of any school of political opinion who does not applaud you and say that you are the only man for this terrible job.'

Even though Gray's own report of this meeting clearly showed that de Valera was determined to remain neutral, the American Minister still remained optimistic that a deal would be possible. Immediately following the meeting he cabled the State Department to rush delivery of the promised equipment. Then, in a letter to Roosevelt that evening he explained that anything that Washington could do to place de Valera 'under obligations to us will help very much when this Ulster situation comes to a head as it is very likely to do soon. If he balks at a reasonable compromise which will save Ulster's face we'll have to tell him that American public opinion will not stand for it.'

Next day in a letter to Under Secretary of State Sumner Welles, Gray went into a little more detail on his reasons for wanting to put de Valera 'under all the obligation possible immediately' :

One of two things will probably happen soon. There will be a change in the attitude of the Ulster government recognising the geographical unity of the island at a minimum for purposes of national defence or England will take over some of the ports by *vis major*. If Ulster makes a gesture which is to be hoped for devoutly we must be ready to put all the friendly pressure we can on this Government to prevent the premier from insisting on too much and muffing the situation completely as the Opposition and some members of his own government fear he might do.

If Ulster makes no gesture and England insists on preventative occupation of some of the ports the fat will be in the fire for fair and we shall have to do what we can to keep Mr de Valera in line.

By even thinking that the United States might be able to influence de Valera to abandon neutrality in favour of a united defence arrangement, the American Minister was obviously allowing his own enthusiasm for a settlement to get the better of his judgment, because he had already reported on three separate occasions that the Taoiseach had refused to consider abandoning neutrality even in return for an end to partition. In fact, Gray actually mentioned one of these occasions in his letter to Welles:

> My own belief is that if Ulster would consent to the ending of partition under suitable guarantees, De Valera could capitalise [on] it politically and bring Éire into the war, that is invite England to come in and defend the island at once. But De Valera won't say he will do it. He told me a month ago, when I was exploring the possibility, 'The neutrality of Ireland is not for sale' and with some heat.[13]

Gray's continued optimism was based on his belief that there was no hope that Irish neutrality would be respected by the belligerents. He believed, and found that de Valera and some of his government colleagues also believed, that the Germans would occupy Ireland if Britain went down. 'Accepting this premise', the American Minister reasoned, 'the Government can only choose between making such a result less likely by joining up with Britain at once or pursuing neutrality without hope that it will be respected or by joining the Germans. In no one of the alternatives can she hope to escape being a battlefield.'

Among the alternatives outlined, however, Gray did not mention the possibility that Britain might actually respect Irish neutrality and still win the war. It was not that he ever seemed to doubt that Britain would ultimately be on the winning side, but he thought that the British were going to get their hands on the ports, one way or another—either by force or by agreement. He therefore felt that de Valera would accept a compromise offer from Belfast, because it would provide some measure of compensation, whereas Ireland would have nothing if Dublin just waited for one of the belligerents to attack.

With no compromise offer from Northern Ireland forthcoming, Gray was becoming very impatient. He apparently thought that he was the only one trying to do anything to get de Valera into the war. On 24 June 1940 he began writing a letter to Maffey, warning that it was probably too late anyway but Britain's only hope of securing Irish bases without suffering serious distractions, depended on Craigavon's willingness to compromise. For if Britain took the ports by force, the American Minister predicted that there would be a hostile majority in the Twenty-Six Counties, not to mention a division of opinion in the United States that would 'embarrass American efforts to aid Britain'.[14]

Gray never did finish this letter because Maffey visited him while he was still writing. The American Minister therefore began complaining forcefully about Craigavon's failure to act.

Maffey assured Gray, however, that London had been working on de Valera, but the latter was insisting on neutrality. The British representative was most uneasy about the situation. Now that France had fallen he thought the Germans would intensify their submarine campaign in the Atlantic and he was afraid that Churchill would respond by seizing Irish bases.

Gray cautioned against any such move on account of the probable public reaction in the United States. 'I warned him again', he wrote to the President, 'against forcible action on the score of its effect upon American opinion and the opportunity it would give enemies of Britain to score.' Before the British should attempt to move against Ireland, Gray wanted Craigavon to make a compromise proposal because, if the British seized the ports after Dublin had rejected an offer from Belfast, de Valera would not be able to secure as much public sympathy in the United States, as he would if no compromise were offered.

Although Maffey did not go into detail about the efforts being exerted to persuade de Valera, it is necessary to consider them here because they actually paralleled Gray's own efforts. On 16 June 1940, following a suggestion from his country's High Commissioner in Britain, for instance, William Lyon Mackenzie King, the Canadian Prime Minister, sent similar telegrams to de Valera and Craigavon warning of the danger of an invasion by the Germans. 'There is', he noted, 'little doubt that their forces will be directed against Ireland, because of its tempting value as a prize in itself and a base for immediate operations against Great Britain.' Mackenzie King went on to propose that the two Irish leaders should 'meet and work out a basis upon which united and effective resistance could be offered in the event of invasion or attack'.[15]

Craigavon did not show any more enthusiasm for the Canadian Prime Minister's suggestion than he had when Gray had proposed it two weeks earlier. On 19 June the Northern Ireland leader replied to Mackenzie King that 'any question of rendering assistance to Mr de Valera to guard against enemy invasion is one for His Majesty's government in the United Kingdom in consultation with Mr de Valera'.

Although de Valera never did reply to the Canadian telegram, he showed absolutely no interest in the defence proposal during some secret talks with a British emissary. These talks were being directed by Neville Chamberlain on behalf of the war cabinet. After failing to get de Valera to come to London, he sent Malcolm MacDonald, then Minister of Health, to Dublin instead. The war cabinet hoped that the combination of Chamberlain and MacDonald would be able to persuade de Valera to abandon neutrality, as they were the two men most responsible for the 1938 agreement surrendering the ports.[16]

On meeting de Valera on 17 June 1940 MacDonald suggested that a united defensive front be established with Northern Ireland, but the suggestion was offhandedly rejected on the grounds that it would be a violation of neutrality.

In a second meeting with MacDonald three days later de Valera made it clear that Dublin would not even consider abandoning neutrality until Irish unity was actually established. The Taoiseach said that the only solution to partition was for Northern Ireland to withdraw from the war, declare neutrality, and then agree to unity with the rest of the island. In return, the new, united Irish parliament would consider whether or not to declare war on Germany and Italy. Although de Valera did not rule out the possibility that such a declaration would carry, he warned that it would probably be defeated, even if he supported it himself. MacDonald tried to get the Taoiseach to give a commitment to abandon neutrality if partition were ended, but he was unsuccessful.

Maffey reported that the Irish government would have freely made such a commitment two or three months earlier, but recent German successes had scared them. Nevertheless, he added, some members of the de Valera government might yet bargain.

'I suggest that we should test this', Chamberlain said on 25 June as he presented the war cabinet with formal proposals that he advocated offering to de Valera. The former Prime Minister wanted to make a firm offer to end partition in return for Irish co-operation. He advocated that the war cabinet should tell Craigavon that 'the interests of Northern Ireland could not be allowed to stand against the vital interests of the British Empire.'

Although the cabinet accepted the formal proposals, it did not agree to abandoning Craigavon. It was decided, instead, that the proposals would only be tentative and that Belfast would have a veto over them, but that they would nevertheless be presented to de Valera as if they were a firm offer. If he accepted them, which was thought unlikely, then Craigavon would be consulted.

The proposals were handed to de Valera by MacDonald next day. If Dublin would 'enter the war on the side of the United Kingdom and her allies forthwith', the British offered to accept 'the principle of a United Ireland'. A joint body of representatives from Belfast and Dublin would then work out the constitutional and practical details of the arrangement. De Valera was also given a fairly elaborate list of weapons that the British promised to hand over if he agreed to their terms.

The following afternoon MacDonald discussed the proposals with the Taoiseach, who was accompanied by Frank Aiken and Seán Lemass, the Minister of Supplies. Although the latter showed an inclination to seriously consider the proposals, his two colleagues cut him off. Doing most of the talking, Aiken was insistent that Ireland should be both united and neutral. De Valera also made this point. He noted in addition that the terms of the offer were too vague. The Belfast crowd would sabotage the whole thing by making impossible demands on the committee drawing up the new constitution, he said.

MacDonald gave an assurance that once declared, the principle of a united Ireland would be categorical. But the Taoiseach was unconvinced, as there was still no guarantee that Belfast would actually co-operate.

In his report of the meeting, the British emissary suggested that Dublin might be given further assurances, but he added that there was very little hope of getting the Irish government to hand over bases. He explained that he was 'definitely' of the opinion that Dublin would reject the plan.

Next day, 28 June, Maffey showed Gray the proposals and briefed him on the negotiations. What he did not tell the American Minister at the time, however, was that the proposals were not a firm offer but only tentative terms that would ultimately need Belfast's approval. As a result Gray jumped to the conclusion that London was willing to go behind Craigavon's back and guarantee unity 'lock, stock and barrel'. Nevertheless, he explained to Roosevelt that de Valera appeared determined to remain neutral.

'You cannot blame him for thinking that he will fare better if he doesn't dip in', Gray added. 'In all this it must always be remembered that while the government wants Britain to win there are enough people whose hatred of Britain has been kept alive by the present regime for political advantage to make it difficult for the government to throw in with Britain before being attacked by Germany.'

There was also another problem. Gray advised Roosevelt that the Irish would question the sincerity of the British offer and that the United States should therefore 'wait a bit and not give the impression that we [are] helping Britain get them into a trap'.[17] Some weeks later the American Minister reported that he subsequently learned that the British were really only promising to use their 'utmost influence to bring Ulster into a conference to devise a new all Ireland constitution'.[18]

Chamberlain stressed this point in a letter to de Valera on 29 June 1940. 'I would remind you', the former Prime Minister wrote, 'that the whole plan depends on our obtaining the assent of Northern Ireland. I cannot, of course, give a guarantee that Northern Ireland will assent, but if the plan is acceptable to

Éire we should do our best to persuade Northern Ireland to accept it also in the interests of the security of the whole island.'

During a speech in County Down, that same day, Craigavon left little doubt about his attitude. He complained that there was 'sinister evidence that something serious is afoot'. He therefore declared that he would 'be no party, directly or indirectly, to any change in the constitution conferred upon Northern Ireland, which assures us of full partnership in the United Kingdom and British Empire'. Although the Northern Ireland Prime Minister did agree to the estabishment of a united defensive front with the rest of Ireland, his offer was couched in terms that minimised its significance as a political surrender.

In the interest of all of Ireland, Craigavon said that he was prepared 'to enter the closest co-operation with Mr de Valera on matters of defence provided he takes his stand, as we are doing, on the side of Britain and the Empire, clears out the German and Italian representatives from Éire and undertakes not to raise any issue of a constitutional nature'.

Under the circumstances, Gray reported that de Valera and William T. Cosgrave each believed that even if they combined with one another they would not be able to lead the country into war on the strength of the British proposals. Richard Mulcahy, a member of the Fine Gael shadow cabinet, concurred with that assessment. He actually estimated that de Valera would only be able to command the support of about half of the members of Fianna Fáil.[19]

James Dillon, the deputy leader of Fine Gael and the only member of the Dáil to openly advocate abandoning neutrality during the war, told the American Minister that Dublin had no choice in the matter. The Taoiseach would be defeated if he tried to abandon neutrality in response to the British offer. Dillon explained that neither the Dáil nor the country at large would tolerate an alliance with Britain at the time because they believed that the British were going to lose the war.[20]

This could hardly have been surprising, as even Churchill himself was not very confident at the time. The following year, for instance, he told the House of Commons that 'Every high authority that I know of, if asked in cold blood a year ago how we could get through, would have found it impossible to give a favourable answer.'[21]

De Valera formally rejected the British offer on 4 July 1940. 'The plan would involve our entry into the war', he explained to Chamberlain. 'That is a course for which we could not accept responsibility. Our people would be quite unprepared for it, and Dáil Éireann would certainly reject it.'

4. Threatening the Belligerents

THE SMALL NEUTRAL AND THE GREAT POWERS
April—November 1940

THE problems facing the Irish government in the spring of 1940 were certainly great, for the country was beset with domestic problems at a time that the international order was being rent asunder. Probably no incident so dramatised the dangers of remaining neutral as the misfortune that befell Norway.

The British struck the first blow on 8 April 1940 when they mined Norwegian coastal waters. Then early next morning the Germans invaded claiming that their action was being taken in order to prevent Allied occupation of the Scandinavian country. Although Adolf Hitler and his colleagues were not renowned for their veracity, in this case they were telling the truth. Their occupation had been a reluctant one, provoked by the Allies who had indeed planned an invasion of their own.[1]

Having argued for the occupation of Norway ever since the previous September, Churchill had finally won over his colleagues, only to have the Germans land their troops first. Yet he was apparently not disappointed by this outcome because he told the House of Commons, two days later, that 'the strategic blunder into which our mortal enemy has been provoked' had 'greatly advantaged' the Allies. He was confident that the Allies, with their naval superiority, would be able to defeat the Germans. Yet it soon became apparent that he had miscalculated, because with the aid of fifth columnists headed by Vidkun Quisling—whose name was to become synonymous with treasonous perfidity—the Germans quickly established control of Norway and repelled all Allied efforts to eject them.

In Ireland the censored press provided extensive coverage of the Norwegian invasion, and David Gray found the Taoiseach deeply interested in the situation. But de Valera was also profoundly troubled by internal developments in Ireland as six IRA men, who had been on hunger strike since late February, were approaching death. Among them was Jack Plunkett, whose brother Joseph had been one of the executed leaders of the 1916 Rising. Tension was running so high that the annual celebration commemorating the Easter Rising had to be cancelled. And when de Valera laid a wreath at the burial ground of the 1916 leaders, he was vociferously abused by Plunkett's sister, who called him a traitor.

It was an extremely trying time for the Irish government. Having previously surrendered in the case of Patrick McGrath some months earlier, de Valera believed that he had to take a strong stand this time, or else lose all control of the situation. The American Minister reported that the Taoiseach was very troubled by the whole affair and 'spoke with a good deal of feeling' about the strikers, explaining that he had been in jail with Plunkett's brother after the Easter Rising.[2]

When Gray offered to intercede with the hunger strikers in an effort to get them to call off their campaign, de Valera politely rejected the suggestion. Such intercession, he said, would only be viewed as a sign of governmental weakness by the IRA, which would be convinced that the Taoiseach had instigated the move. Nevertheless de Valera did ask the American Minister to tell anyone broaching him on the question that the government was not bluffing and that it was determined to see the matter through to the bitter end, if necessary.

Gray did just that on 19 April 1940 when Plunkett's parents asked him to intervene on behalf of their son.[3] In reply he told them that he would only help if they got their son to give up the hunger strike and agree to oppose the government in a constitutional manner. This, the Plunketts absolutely refused to do.

'That would give the whole cause away,' said Plunkett's mother.

Later that night the hunger strike was called off and Plunkett was saved, but one of his colleagues was already dead and another soon died. The government had won, but at a price. De Valera was becoming more estranged than ever from his former colleagues.

In the aftermath of the hunger strikes there were widespread rumours that the IRA was planning to stage a rebellion with help from Germany. Although the organisation was numerically weak, it could not be dismissed lightly because its sympathisers were in all walks of life. As a result it could strike virtually anywhere in Ireland.

The previous December the IRA had demonstrated this by the raid on the Magazine Fort. Then on 25 April 1940 it demonstrated it again by setting off a bomb in Dublin Castle, the headquarters of the Irish police force. This was only one of a number of outrages. In Dublin on 7 May IRA gunmen fired on and wounded two policemen who were believed to be carrying mail for the British representative. It was certainly no time to provoke the British, especially with the international situation coming to a head.

Three days later the last hope of avoiding a conflict on the scale of the First World War suddenly vanished with the German invasion of Belgium and Holland. The Taoiseach was particularly alarmed that the rights of two more neutrals had been blatantly violated. He publicly denounced the invasion. 'Today', he said, 'these two small nations are fighting for their lives and I think I would be unworthy of this small nation if, on an occasion like this, I did not utter our protest against the cruel wrong that has been done them.'

That the German advance posed new dangers for Ireland could hardly have been doubted, but it was not the only disturbing news. From Britain there was word that Churchill had taken over as Prime Minister. He had never shown any sympathy for Irish independence, and many Irishmen held him responsible for igniting the spark that started the Civil War. In addition, his vociferous opposition to the agreement handing over the Treaty ports was an indication of the importance that he attached to them and would now give rise to Irish fears that he might decide to take them back by force, if only to ensure that the Germans would not be able to get a foothold in Ireland from where they could easily strangle Britain's trade.

Maffey approached de Valera informally about the possibility of Ireland joining the anti-Nazi alliance but, he reported, de Valera immediately 'invoked the old bogey of partition'. The Taoiseach explained that there was no sense in asking the Irish people to fight on behalf of freedom when part of the island was being denied that freedom. He added that he could not understand why London 'does not tell Lord Craigavon to fix up his difficulties with us and come in. That would solve the trouble.'

In this interview de Valera displayed a naïvety about the northern situation. He did not seem to realise that Craigavon would no more have been able to lead the Northern Ireland majority into a united, independent Ireland than he himself would have been able to lead the majority in the Twenty-Six Counties back into the United Kingdom. When Maffey asked if Ireland would become an active ally of Britain if partition were ended, de Valera said that she eventually probably would, but he was not willing to make any commitments, nor was he prepared to try to influence public opinion so that he would be in a position to lead the country into war.

'Unfortunately', Maffey wrote, 'he is a physical and mental expression of the most narrow-minded and bigoted section of the country. In all circumstances great difficulties surround the path of the leader here, but Mr de Valera is not a strong man and his many critics here know that fact well. Nothing is more characteristic than his tendency to surrender always to the extremist view and to the extremist menace.'

As of that time the Taoiseach had taken few steps to deal with the international threat; he was hoping that the United States would be willing to protect Ireland. On 16 May 1940 he asked Gray to 'inquire confidentially' if Roosevelt would be willing to proclaim a deep interest in the preservation of the status quo in regard to Ireland, on the grounds that Irish bases commanded North Atlantic trade routes by sea and air. De Valera admitted that he was really looking for a United States pledge to preserve Ireland's independence, but he realised that America's traditional policy of keeping out of European affairs precluded the President from making such an overt commitment.

The Irish request was quickly rejected in Washington. Secretary of State Cordell Hull explained on 22 May that such a 'declaration would imply that we are departing from our traditional policies in regard to European affairs, and would inevitably lead to misunderstanding and confusion in the United States and abroad'.

There was even more distressing news for the Irish leadership that day. Indeed the government was thrown into a near frenzy following a police raid on the Dublin home of Stephen Karl Held, a member of the IRA. The police had found unmistakable evidence that Held had been harbouring a German spy. Although the spy, Herman Goertz, was not apprehended at the time, his equipment was seized, including a radio transmitter and receiver, in addition to a file containing information about Irish airfields, harbours, roads, bridges, landing places, and the distribution of Irish defence forces. Also found were some crude plans outlining a German invasion of Northern Ireland to be conducted with IRA support from the Twenty-Six Counties.

Irish authorities feared that an invasion was imminent. The Taoiseach privately admitted that he was terrified that the Germans were going to invade Northern Ireland and enlist the support of the IRA and other nationalist elements by announcing that they were liberating the area from the British.

The danger of a German attack also gave rise to the possibility of a British assault. Paradoxically, in a telegram to Berlin just before he learned of the Held affair, the German Minister noted that the Irish did not fear Britain because the British were so concerned about American public opinion that they would not dare to invade Ireland except 'in an emergency, e.g., suspicion of being forestalled by Germany'. That reason for such suspicion existed following the arrest of Held could hardly have been doubted.

De Valera was therefore confronted with the apparent danger of invasion by either of the belligerents. He was certainly in an unenviable position as the leader of an unarmed and bitterly divided country. On the one hand, he was being denounced as a traitor by the IRA, which was anxious to overthrow his government and enter into an alliance with Germany in order to end partition. And on the other hand, Fine Gael and many of its staunch supporters had not forgiven him for his role in events leading to the Civil War.

The manner in which the Taoiseach was to confront his challenge unfolded during the following weeks. At the very essence of his policy was the necessity to present a united front at home and convince the belligerents that the Irish government would use everything in its power to resist invasion. He made it clear that if Germany invaded, he would enlist British help, and if Britain invaded, he would enlist German help. At the same time he left no doubt that he would appeal to American public opinion to condemn the invader.

In view of the Held affair, however, it was first necessary to assure the British that they had nothing to fear that would necessitate a pre-emptive strike. On 23 May 1940, therefore, de Valera promised the British that he would immediately seek their assistance if the Germans attacked, and he even went so far as to suggest the holding of staff talks between British and Irish military people to co-ordinate plans for repelling the Germans. These talks began three days later in Dublin and their initial progress was to the satisfaction of the British military, a committee of whose leaders reported to the war cabinet on 30 May that Irish authorities had 'shown a genuine desire to co-operate'.

On the home front de Valera sought to bolster Ireland's defence posture in a number of ways. First, the internment of members of the IRA was intensified. Next, an earnest recruiting drive for the Irish army was launched, and efforts were made to secure adequate arms from both Britain and the United States. At the same time an inter-party Defence Conference was established, consisting of three members of Fianna Fáil, three from Fine Gael, and two from the Labour Party.* The conference, which was to meet regularly in order to advise the government on defence matters, was designed primarily as a show of solidarity that would allow a united Dáil to call on the Irish people to support neutrality. Now, for the first time since the Civil War, men with deep personal animosities began to share the same platforms at public meetings in support of the government's defence policy.

On 1 June 1940 de Valera went on Radio Éireann to warn the Irish people that they should 'recognise that when great powers are locked in mortal combat the rights of small nations are as naught to them: the only thing that counts is how one may secure an advantage over the other, and, if the violation of our territory promises such an advantage, then our territory will be violated, our country will be made a cockpit, our homes will

---

*The members of the Defence Conference were Frank Aiken as chairman, Gerald Boland, and Oscar Traynor of Fianna Fáil; James Dillon, Richard Mulcahy, and T. F. O'Higgins of Fine Gael; and William Norton and William Davin of the Labour Party.

be levelled and our people slaughtered'. He added that 'internal division would be our greatest danger; for assuredly in this hour if we do not in our several sections hang together we shall indeed hang separately'.

The German Minister fully realised that de Valera sympathised with the Allied cause. In a telegram to Berlin in late May 1940, for example, he predicted that the Taoiseach would 'maintain the line of friendly understanding with England as far as it is at all possible, on account of geographical and economic dependence, which will continue even in the event of England's defeat, as well as his democratic principles, even in face of the threatening danger of Ireland becoming involved in the war'.

Although disturbed that de Valera's sympathy with Britain appeared to become even stronger following the Held affair, Hempel was initially unwilling to give, or to seek from his own government, any commitment not to invade Ireland. On 17 June 1940 he told Joseph Walshe that it would be impossible for Germany to promise to respect Irish neutrality under existing circumstances.

Next day the Taoiseach, who had made no secret of his fear that the Held affair portended a German invasion, told Hempel that the Irish government was determined to use all means at its disposal to preserve neutrality. According to the German Minister, de Valera 'regarded determination to resist any attacker to the uttermost as the only possibility to reduce the danger'. And to this end the Taoiseach was prepared to call for outside help. 'In an English invasion', Hempel predicted, 'we would fight with Irishmen against the English, in a German invasion the English would fight along with the Irish.'

Although Dublin had failed to get a German commitment to respect Irish neutrality at this stage, de Valera and the Department of External Affairs manoeuvred adroitly and, by exploiting both the Held affair and the MacDonald talks, managed to secure the desired assurance from the Germans.

The first step was taken by Walshe and Frederick H. Boland, the Assistant Secretary at the Department of External Affairs. Together they managed to convince Hempel that the MacDonald talks constituted a British threat to Ireland. Next, de Valera told the Italian Minister that the Held affair had so shattered his confidence in the Axis powers that he needed a commitment from them to respect Irish neutrality in order to resist British threats. Since the Italians never posed any real danger to Ireland, de Valera was obviously using the Italian Minister, knowing that he would pass on to his German colleague what amounted to a warning that the Irish government might not be able to resist British pressure unless Germany was prepared to promise not to attack Ireland.

The ploy obviously worked, because on 1 July 1940 the German Minister advised his government to promise not to violate Irish neutrality. Ten days later Foreign Minister von Ribbentrop ordered Hempel to stress in 'all' his conversations 'that in connection with Ireland we have exclusively the single interest that her neutrality be maintained. As long as Ireland conducts herself in a neutral fashion it can be counted on with absolute certainty that Germany will respect her neutrality unconditionally.'

Although the Irish had been primarily concerned about the danger of a German attack following the Held affair, the possibility of a British invasion also began to loom as a menacing prospect for the Dublin government during late June and much of July.

The British war cabinet actually discussed what to do about Irish neutrality on 16 June 1940. At the time the cabinet had before it a message from Jan Christiaan Smuts, the Prime Minister of South Africa, proposing that 'the Irish Atlantic ports should be seized at once, even in the face of Irish opposition to prevent them suffering the same fate as the Norwegian ports.'

Churchill was not willing to go that far however. He summed up the discussion that day by rejecting the South African leader's proposal because of the possibility of antagonising public opinion in the United States. 'Although as a last resort we should not hesitate to secure the ports by force,' he explained, 'it would be unwise at this moment to take any action that might compromise our position with the United States of America, in view of the present delicate developments.'

The cabinet decided instead to go ahead with efforts that Neville Chamberlain was directing in order to secure further Irish co-operation. The former Prime Minister explained that Malcolm MacDonald was going to Dublin for talks in which he would insist on internment of the IRA. 'If this precipitated a rebellion, as it well might, so much the better,' he added. 'The Éire army would then be fighting the IRA and upsetting the German arrangements.'

The British were so concerned about their own plight that even Chamberlain, who was regarded in Dublin as a friend of Ireland, did not care if an Irish civil war were provoked. What was more, Churchill was primarily opposed to attacking Ireland only on account of American opinion, not because of the moral implications involved. The record of this cabinet meeting presents a vivid picture of the problems facing the Irish government in its relations with Britain.

Nothing ever came of Chamberlain's idea about interning members of the IRA, because de Valera was able to tell Mac-Donald that as many of them as possible had already been interned. Since the talks that followed have already been discussed in the previous chapter, there is no need to dwell on them further, except to mention that there was grave concern in Dublin that Britain would seize the treaty ports once the proposals brought by MacDonald were rejected.

Some wild press reports emanating from London actually gave impetus to this concern. One account, for example, claimed that de Valera had gone to London for talks with Churchill and Craigavon, while another asserted that the Taoiseach had entered a military pact with Britain. Such reports gave rise to suspicions that the British were trying to provoke a German attack on Ireland so that Britain would have an excuse to intervene herself. And this was an understandable fear in view of British actions in the case of Norway.

There were also other reports, either critical of Irish neutrality, or warning of the danger of a German invasion. The *Daily Express* reported that the German press was contending that Ireland was not maintaining strict neutrality. One German source was actually quoted as warning that 'Sooner or later, Germany may have to act in consequence as in the case of other small European neutrals.'[4]

The British public no doubt looked on this report as an indication that the Germans might be about to invade Ireland, seeing that they were now making claims similar to those put forward to justify their invasions of Norway, Belgium, and

Holland. The Irish leadership, on the other hand, was afraid that such reports might be designed to persuade public opinion that a British move against Ireland would be justified in order to forestall a German attack.

What neither London nor Dublin knew at the time, however, was that Berlin was deliberately creating the false impression that Germany was about to invade Ireland. General Walter Warlimont, who held a key position in the supreme command headquarters in Germany, wrote in his memoirs that on 28 June 1940 Hitler ordered 'all available information media' to indicate that a German invasion of Ireland was imminent.[5] This, no doubt, helps to explain such reports as that carried by the *Daily Express*. In addition, the Germans leaked bogus information to British intelligence about an upcoming assault on Ireland.

The British fell for the German ruse and began intensifying preparations to use troops stationed in Northern Ireland to help the Irish army in the event of an attack. But these preparations caused a near state of panic in Dublin, especially when Irish authorities got their hands on a British plan for an invasion of Ireland, and also when they arrested a British army officer who had come down from the Six Counties to gather information to be used by British troops in the Twenty-Six Counties.

Although both these matters were viewed in Dublin as proof of a British invasion in the offing, the London government had no such intention. The invasion plan was really only one of a number of contingency plans drawn up in case Britain ever decided to invade; while the army officer was only gathering information. Possibly the uneasiness in Ireland could have been avoided if Churchill had given an assurance that Britain would respect Irish neutrality, but the British never were willing to make such a commitment, with the result that Irish authorities were left on edge.

On 4 July 1940, the day that de Valera formally rejected the proposals brought by MacDonald, Churchill increased the tension with a speech concerning the British attack on the French fleet at Oran that had taken place only hours earlier. He explained that the British navy had attacked French ships in order to make sure that they did not fall into German hands. He then went on to state that 'every preparation in our power' was being made 'to repel the assaults of the enemy whether they be directed upon Great Britain or upon Ireland—which all Irishmen without distinction of creed or party, should realise is in imminent danger'. If the British had been willing to attack the French fleet to prevent it falling into German hands, there could be little doubt that they would also be willing to attack Ireland to prevent the Nazis getting a foothold there.

Following the speech Ambassador Kennedy cabled the State Department from London that Churchill was despondent and seemed to fear that 'de Valera and his crowd' were going over to the Germans. At the same time Gray reported from Dublin that the Irish government was extremely apprehensive.

In fact, the Irish army was put on alert, and de Valera issued a statement that there was no intention of abandoning neutrality. 'The government is resolved', the statement added, 'to maintain and defend the country's neutrality in all circumstances.'

In order to lessen the danger of a British incursion, the Irish used American public opinion for protection. Frank Aiken, the Minister for Co-ordination of Defensive Measures, gave an interview to Denis Johnson of the National Broadcasting Corporation (NBC), the American radio network. In it he mentioned that Ireland had been scrupulous in observing its neutrality and had 'avoided doing a lot of things' that were legally permitted. The country would not abandon its neutrality, he said, even if offered a guarantee of unity with the Six Counties. But he made it clear that if Ireland were attacked, there would be no question of just surrendering. Ireland would fight and would call for help. 'You know how the old Irish saying goes,' Aiken said, ' "God likes a little help." and we are going to try to give him all the help we can.'[6]

Next day, 5 July 1940, de Valera stressed the same theme in an interview with Harold Denny of the *New York Times*. 'We do not have the slightest intention of abandoning our neutrality,' he said. 'We intend to resist any attack, from any quarter whatever.'

This interview and the Aiken one which preceded it were designed to deter a British invasion by reminding the American people that the Irish, like themselves, were determined to remain neutral. Thus, under the circumstances, a British attack would make Churchill look little better than Hitler and would thereby give impetus to isolationist sentiment in the United States, which, in turn, could undermine American aid to Britain and also damage Roosevelt's chances for re-election.

In Washington Secretary of State Hull was greatly disturbed by the whole situation. He warned the British Ambassador on 8 July against any attack on Ireland on the grounds that it would seriously embarrass the Roosevelt administration. In reply the Ambassador assured him that Britain would undertake no such venture unless the Germans attacked first.

The British were genuinely worried that Germany was going to attack Ireland. But on 15 July 1940 when Sir John Maffey warned the Irish Department of External Affairs that a German invasion, which had supposedly been originally planned for earlier in the month, was set for the following day, Joseph Walshe was more concerned about the intentions of the London government. He protested about both the press campaign and the conduct of the British officer caught spying. Although Maffey had apparently been unaware of the officer's activities and was therefore unable to put up any defence of the affair, he did admit that the British Ministry of Information had probably had a hand in some of the press reports.

On meeting Maffey two days later to discuss means of repairing the damage done to Anglo-Irish relations, de Valera explained that after the outbreak of the war the Irish army had concentrated their defence preparations for a German attack, but in recent weeks they found it necessary to take the British danger into account also. In fact, he admitted that Ireland was now more worried about the British than the Germans.

Of particular annoyance to the Taoiseach was the capture of the British spy. He explained that Irish army officers were perplexed by the affair. They had already shown Irish defences to representatives of the British army and had also revealed their plans for coping with a German attack. As a result they could not understand why the spy had been sent, unless it was to prepare for a British assault.

Explaining that the officer had only been seeking information to be used in case British troops were invited into the Twenty-Six Counties, Maffey apologised for the whole affair and said that it did not have the blessing of the War Office in London. He added that steps had been taken to ensure that the same thing would not happen again, and he asked for the release of the officer.

Satisfied with the explanation, the Taoiseach agreed to free the man. He then proceeded to make a moving appeal for weapons. 'Give us help with arms and we will fight the Germans as only Irishmen in their own country can fight,' he said. 'There is no doubt on which side my sympathies lie. Nowadays some people joke about my becoming pro-British. The cause I am urging on you is in the best interest of my own country and this is what matters most to me.'[7]

Maffey's report of this meeting made a good impression on the Dominions Office, which suggested to the war cabinet that it should clamp down on the press campaign, supply the Irish with arms, and promise not to invade Ireland. Although the cabinet rejected the latter suggestion, it did authorise the transfer of some arms before the end of the month, and these weapons brought about a noticeable relaxation in the Irish government's fear of Britain.

Gray watched the deterioration of Anglo-Irish relations with disquiet, because Irish authorities were indicating publicly that they feared the British just as much as the Germans, thus giving the impression to Americans that the Irish government thought the British were no better than Nazis. This was only likely to harden the attitude of Irish-Americans towards Roosevelt's pro-British policy.

Some Irish authorities, however, were apparently emphasising their fear of Britain—not so much because they were afraid that the British were going to invade, but in an effort to win favour with the Germans. The American Minister learned from private discussions with two members of the de Valera's cabinet, Seán T. O'Kelly, the Tánaiste (Deputy Prime Minister), and Seán Mac-Entee, the Minister for Industry and Commerce, that there was a tremendous feeling within government circles in Dublin that Britain was going to lose the war. One of them explained that the Irish government was so nervous that it seemed to be formulating its policy as if the German Minister were present, evaluating its performance. Nevertheless Gray was still convinced that the Taoiseach was 'acting in good faith but is in a very nervous state of mind and the ready host to the suspicions which the anti-British elements in his government plant in his mind'.[8]

Walshe was one of the people about whom Gray was worried. Although the former personally disliked the Nazis, he had been careful to conceal his attitude because he was convinced that Germany was going to win the war. In private meetings with diplomatic representatives he usually sought to stress aspects of Irish policy that were in line with policies being advocated by the representative with whom he was in conversation. While such a practice was understandable, he nevertheless carried it to questionable lengths at times.

With the German Minister, for example, Walshe stressed his fear of Britain. Even at the time he was most intimately involved in organising the secret Anglo-Irish military talks, Walshe told Hempel that he was afraid that the Held affair might have been the work of British intelligence. Later when the Germans were sweeping through France, Hempel reported that the Secretary of the Irish Department of External Affairs had spoken in very congratulatory tones about German successes.

When prospects for an Allied victory seemed to almost vanish following the fall of France, Walshe went so far as to express hope that Germany would not abandon Ireland to the British. This was a very subtle tactic. He was, in effect, contending that Irish neutrality had been so favourable to Germany that he was afraid that the British would retaliate against Ireland unless Germany were willing to protect her after the war. In late July 1940 Walshe went a step further and led the German Minister to conclude that 'The Irish government apparently believes that if the Irish element in the United States is properly used, it could constitute a powerful influence in our favour, likewise the Irish-American press.' Here Walshe was only alluding to an obvious fact; he was not advocating that the Germans should intervene in American politics. In fact, he warned Hempel that such intervention might actually do more harm than good. The suggestion should really be seen in the context of a way of telling the German Minister that Irish-Americans could be used to Germany's advantage as long as Berlin did not antagonise them by violating Irish sovereignty.

In a conversation with the American Minister on 6 August 1940 Walshe freely admitted that he believed that Germany was in an unbeatable position.[9] Wondering if the Irishman was actually hoping for a German victory in the belief that Hitler would end partition, Gray asked about a rather preposterous story to the effect that the Germans had supposedly promised the

IRA that they would unite the thirty-two counties of Ireland and also throw in two English counties for good measure.

'I don't think I believe that,' Walshe replied. 'But', he added with a laugh, 'on the basis of Irish majority we ought to have Liverpool.'

Even though the Germans had told various representatives of the IRA that they would end partition, de Valera never sought any such commitment. In fact, on 18 June 1940 he told the German Minister that he could only adhere to a peaceful solution of the problem. In other words, he did not want the Germans to sever Northern Ireland's ties with Britain by force.

Any doubts about the Taoiseach's attitude towards the Nazis were dispelled by his stern handling of the IRA, in spite of that organisation's close ties with the Germans. Following a shooting incident in which two detectives were killed and another wounded in Dublin on 16 August 1940, for example, two members of the IRA Patrick McGrath and Thomas Green (alias Francis Harte), were captured, summarily tried by a military court, and sentenced to death.

Gray observed first-hand some of the domestic bitterness towards the Fianna Fáil government when IRA sympathisers tried to get him to intervene on behalf of the two condemned men. On 23 August he was visited by Father Michael O'Flanagan, a former vice-president of Sinn Féin; Cattie Maloney (née Barry), sister of Kevin Barry; and a Dublin barrister named Mullane. They predicted civil war and reprisals against Dáil Ministers if the executions were carried out.

Seeking to avoid involvement in the execution controversy, Gray told his visitors that it would be diplomatically improper for him to interfere in an internal Irish matter, but at the same time he tried to reassure them by explaining that the Taoiseach was not a vindictive person.

'It's nonsense to pretend that Mr de Valera likes to execute people,' Gray said. 'He is a very humane man.'

'Yes,' replied Mullane, 'he forgives and forgets. He forgives his enemies and forgets his friends.'[10]

Gray explained to Roosevelt that the IRA people had previously served with and supported de Valera during the Civil War. 'They are bitter now', he added, 'because he condemns them for doing just what he did for many years, that is, insisting on the right of the minority not to bow to majority rule.'

On 5 September 1940 Seán MacBride, counsel for the condemned men, telephoned Gray to have him use his influence to get the executions postponed. Mrs Maloney, who was with MacBride at the time, said that the IRA command had decided to call 'a truce' in order to get the sentences commuted, but she warned that there would be civil war otherwise. They wanted the American Minister to pass on the offer, or ultimatum, to the government, as they had been unable to get in touch with any members of the cabinet—all of whom were refusing to answer their telephones. But there was really nothing that Gray could do. The Irish government had already decided to direct the military to execute the two men.[11]

They were duly executed next day. After trying to avoid an irreconcilable break with the IRA, Gray believed that de Valera had 'now crossed the Rubicon'. There could be no going back.[12]

In the tension-filled days before the executions, Ireland's defence plight was dramatised when a German aeroplane bombed a creamery in County Wexford, killing three girl workers. Although the British had supplied some weapons the previous month, the country was still virtually defenceless, especially against an air attack. Consequently de Valera again tried to secure American arms.

The State Department had agreed to supply some equipment the previous June, but since then there had been a change in policy, because President Roosevelt had become disillusioned with Irish neutrality. On 15 August 1940 he wrote to Gray that the Irish people 'must realise that in the end they will have to fish or cut bait'. In other words they were going to have to help Britain.

Next day the President had an Irish arms request on his desk when he marked a consignment of 80,000 rifles 'O.K. for Canada,' even though it was more rifles than the Canadians had requested. He then ordered that Robert Brennan, the Irish Minister to the United States, be told to contact authorities of the British Purchasing Commission, which was in charge of Anglo-Canadian purchases, about securing the excess rifles.

In order to keep up the appearance of being helpful, Gray

pretended to support subsequent Irish requests, but he really agreed with the White House approach. He had originally sought arms for the Irish because he thought that the gesture would make de Valera more amenable to British efforts to obtain bases in Ireland, but now this seemed to be out of the question. 'I shall go on protesting and telegraphing for Mr de Valera', Gray wrote to the President, 'but you are quite right to take the line you are taking.'[13]

Gray liked the President's approach because it was compelling de Valera to rely on the British and was thereby helping to promote friendlier Anglo-Irish relations. When the British handed over 20,000 American rifles in October 1940, for instance, the gesture was greatly appreciated.

Unlike many of his fellow countrymen, Gray had a deep appreciation of the international danger confronting the United States. On 2 October 1940 he wrote a prophetic letter to Roosevelt explaining that although the United States might just drift into the war, it was 'more probable' that Japan would attack American forces in the Pacific without warning, thus leaving Washington with no option but to declare war on the Axis powers. Should this happen, he believed that the United States would want to establish bases in Ireland, but he was not sure that de Valera would hand them over.

Some months earlier the Taoiseach had indicated that American involvement in the war would change the whole complexion of Irish policy. This, Gray took to mean that 'Ireland could safely abandon and probably would abandon its neutrality.'[14]

But was de Valera prepared to abandon neutrality under such circumstances? Gray, of course, had no way of knowing, but he was virtually certain that Washington would not be able to change the Taoiseach's mind, whatever his decision might be. 'I am pretty well convinced that no one can "bargain" with de Valera,' he wrote. 'You trust him or you don't.'[15]

In a letter to Ambassador Kennedy on 15 October 1940 Gray wrote that he doubted that Dublin would be prepared to abandon neutrality even if the United States became a belligerent. His conviction was based on the manner in which press censorship was being enforced. Believing that the censorship had been unfavourable to Britain in that some pro-British news from the United States had been played down, Gray reasoned that if there were any desire to abandon neutrality, de Valera would at least prepare the Irish people by allowing the press to win them over to the Allied cause.

Although Gray would later be able to point to some unfair censorship practices, his charge was rather harsh in the autumn of 1940. The censor was only attempting to ensure an unbiased press by insisting that Allied and Axis accounts of international developments be accorded what amounted to equal coverage. This could have been considered unfavourable to the British in as much as it put them on the same plane as the Nazis. Conversely, of course, it could also have been argued, as in the case of Norway, that the British descended to the level of the Nazis. Yet Irish newspapers displayed no sympathy for the Germans, while in many subtle ways even de Valera's own newspaper, the *Irish Press*, favoured the Allies—notwithstanding its reputation of being the least favourable of the Irish national dailies.

During the early months of the war, for instance, editorials in the *Irish Press* commended the Poles for fighting gallantly and mentioned that the Germans had introduced the practice of bombing civilian centres. On 30 September 1939, following the partitioning of Poland by Germany and the Soviet Union, the *Irish Press* remarked that 'to all intents and purposes, Russia and Germany are now in the closest alliance.' Yet this did not prevent the editor from being blisteringly critical of the Soviet Union's invasion of Finland. Then again, following the German invasion of Denmark and Norway, the *Irish Press* mentioned that while the Germans used the British mining of Norwegian waters to justify their invasion of Norway, Britain had not made any move against Denmark, and the Germans had made scarcely any attempt to justify their Danish attack on moral grounds. Although the editorial stopped short of actually denouncing the Germans, no reader could escape the conclusion that the editor was critical of Berlin.

On 3 September 1940 during the height of the Battle of Britain, the *Irish Press* published on its front page a photograph of de Valera, Maffey, and Gray, who had been pictured together at the all-Ireland hurling final the previous afternoon. In this case the picture was worth the proverbial thousand words. The Taoiseach had not accorded such an honour to the German Minister, so the prominent publication of the photograph in a newspaper—many of whose readers admired de Valera's every move—was tantamount to endorsement of support for both Britain and the United States.

The German Minister found, however, that members of the Irish government seemed to be hoping for Roosevelt's defeat in the Presidential Election of 1940. Hempel thought that they were afraid that the President's re-election would mean that Ireland would no longer be able to rely on American public opinion to protect Irish neutrality. Because if the President were elected for another term, the British would be able to act against Ireland, knowing that their friend was safely in power for another four years.

Gray did not detect any anti-Roosevelt feeling in Dublin before the election, but he grew suspicious soon afterwards. He reported on 30 November 1940 that he had received congratulations on the President's victory from many private individuals and most of the foreign representatives in Ireland but 'not one word from any member of the government'. Consequently, he suspected that there might have 'been some dirty work at the cross-roads'.

He never found any evidence to indicate that the Irish government had in any way tried to influence the election. Indeed it was most improbable that any such effort was ever made, for the *Irish Press* had predicted that Roosevelt would win and had also mentioned in two separate editorials that there was little difference between the candidates on foreign policy issues. In addition, the day after the election the same paper carried an editorial that was very favourable to the President, who was praised for tremendous domestic achievements in the United States and also for being one of the first to perceive the international danger.

5. The Screws are Tightened

IRISH PORTS AND THE BATTLE OF
THE ATLANTIC
November 1940—March 1941

THROUGHOUT much of the autumn of 1940 the Irish did not have to worry about a British attack. It seemed unthinkable that London would consider an invasion, at least until after the American elections.

As the people of the United States were going to the polls on 5 November, however, Churchill gave vent to his frustration at the Irish refusal to surrender the ports. He told the House of Commons that British forces had just won the Battle of Britain but now an even more important battle—the Battle of the Atlantic—was about to begin, and Britain was being forced to fight under unfavourable conditions.

'The fact that we cannot use the South and West Coasts of Ireland to refuel our flotillas and aircraft and thus protect the trade by which Ireland as well as Great Britain lives', Churchill said, 'is a most heavy and grievous burden and one which should never have been placed on our shoulders, broad though they be.'

Although the Prime Minister made no actual threat in his speech, he did cause uneasiness in Dublin. The German Minister was particularly disturbed, as he saw the outburst as an indication that 'England was now shedding her fear of unfavourable repercussions in the United States.'

Joseph P. Walshe tried to reassure Hempel by explaining that there were a number of reasons militating against a British attack on Ireland. Firstly, Britain could not afford to risk antagonising Irish-Americans because Roosevelt still needed their support in Congress. Secondly, the advantages to be gained by seizing Irish bases would not amount to much because Ireland's southern ports were overly vulnerable to German attack from the French coast. Thirdly, Walshe contended that whatever advantage the British might gain would be more than offset by the disadvan-

D

tages of having to cope with Irish resistance and unfavourable repercussions in the United States.

The German Minister's uneasiness was not altogether allayed. He thought that Walshe's optimism was possibly an effort 'to play down the matter' in order to ease tension. Hempel was especially disturbed by the reaction of British newspapers. In a report to Berlin he concluded that 'The comments in the British press after the debate in the House of Commons indicate, in my opinion, that at least attempts are being made or are yet to be expected, to put pressure on Ireland in order to obtain certain concessions.'

It was the press reactions to Churchill's speech which troubled de Valera most. He was afraid that it might be the start of a propaganda campaign to convince world opinion that Britain would be justified in seizing Irish ports on the grounds that they were vital to her survival. And the attitude of the American Minister could hardly have been reassuring.

Gray suggested to Walshe on 7 November that the Irish government should allow Britain to use the ports. In reply Walshe explained that while Dublin could allow Americans to use them, if the United States entered the war, it would not be possible to give facilities to the British because they would never give them back.

Unwilling to accept this, Gray warned that the United States would support the British if they took the ports. 'I told him', he reported, 'that I thought his government must be prepared for support of Great Britain in the American press in case Churchill moved by what he considered to be a necessity, announced that he would occupy the ports by force after presenting publicly his brief which would probably include what is reported to be Chamberlain's undocumented understanding at the time he surrendered them, that in case of need the harbours would be available.'[1]

The reference to Chamberlain's understanding must have been particularly disturbing to Walshe, as there never had been one. What was more, he had explained as much to Gray previously. In fact, he had gone to the trouble of writing a letter to the American Minister, quoting Churchill's speech denouncing the Anglo-Irish agreement of 1938 on the grounds that the return of the ports was unconditional.[2]

Following the meeting between Gray and Walshe, de Valera responded publicly to the British Prime Minister's latest speech. He told the Dáil that there could be no question of handing over or leasing the ports. 'Any attempt to bring pressure to bear on us by any side', he said, 'could only lead to bloodshed.' As long as his government remained in office, he declared that it would defend the country's rights in regard to the ports against any attacker.

Much to de Valera's chagrin, the British press campaign had begun to find an echo in the United States. The same day as his speech in the Dáil, for instance, the influential *New York Herald Tribune* carried an article by its military correspondent, claiming that 'The denial of Irish bases is a serious handicap to Britain.' The article continued that it was feared that there were German agents in Ireland, 'where they can, of course, find many ways of aiding the operations of their U-boats and aircraft'. The author concluded by explaining that 'American opinion, highly regarded always in Ireland, might be of some service in urging a change of attitude at Dublin.'

Worried that the British really intended to ask Roosevelt to use the full weight of his influence to persuade Dublin to give up the ports, the Taoiseach instructed Robert Brennan in Washington to give the State Department a copy of his latest speech and to explain that any American efforts to get the Irish government to give bases to Britain would be fruitless.

De Valera also sent a telegram to Brennan for John J. Reilly, president of the American Association for Recognition of the Irish Republic—an organisation that the Taoiseach had himself helped to establish while in the United States during the Black and Tan war. The telegram requested the association 'and all friends of Ireland to organise and put the Irish case, including partition, clearly before the American public'. It would be an 'inhuman outrage', de Valera explained, to force Ireland into the war when the country was virtually defenceless. He added that the Irish had the same right as Americans to keep out of the war and were determined to 'defend that right to the utmost'.[3]

The Fine Gael leader was no less resolute in his determination to remain neutral. Even if the government wanted to side with the British 'or finesse the ports to them', Cosgrave warned his colleagues, 'the complete lack of aerial defence for Dublin, etc., would prevent us supporting them—apart altogether from the question of getting the people to support such a line of action.'[4]

Nevertheless de Valera's bellicose statements disturbed Fine Gael leaders, who noted that Churchill had not threatened any action against Ireland. They thought the Taoiseach was simply creating a bogus crisis for selfish political ends. And they were especially annoyed that he had not bothered to consult the Defence Conference. In fact, he had told the press that he was going to make an important address before he even intimated his intention to the opposition.

T. F. O'Higgins, one of the Fine Gael representatives on the Defence Conference, wrote to Cosgrave complaining that the political truce on defence matters was allowing de Valera to make 'any reckless statement' with Fine Gael appearing to condone it. He therefore suggested that Cosgrave should insist that the Taoiseach consult the Defence Conference in future before making any important defence pronouncements. Otherwise, O'Higgins wrote, members of Fine Gael might just as well merge with Fianna Fáil and accept de Valera as their leader. 'Such a position in practice or in fact,' he added, 'I could not tolerate for one hour.'[5]

The distrust of de Valera within opposition ranks was so intense that when Cosgrave prepared a formal complaint that he intended to transmit privately, Dillon dissuaded him by explaining that the Taoiseach would use the formal protest as a pretext for dissolving the Defence Conference and accusing Fine Gael of trying to stab the government in the back in the midst of a crisis. 'If there is to be a breach, we must break with de Valera,' Dillon advocated. 'Under no circumstances must we take any action which will give him an excuse for breaking with us.'[6]

Dillon's advice was accepted and the formal protest shelved. The Fine Gael members of the Defence Conference simply complained informally that they had been ignored by the government. In response, the Taoiseach promised to consult them in future, if possible.[7]

Although the Fine Gael leadership did not share the Taoiseach's concern over Churchill's address, de Valera was certainly justified in fearing that the British intended to enlist

American help in order to secure Irish facilities. Churchill intended to do so. On 8 November 1940 he told his war cabinet that he planned to cable Roosevelt on the following lines:

> It will be at least two years before America can give us any effective help since she is only now laying out her armament factories. The question is whether Great Britain can hold out for so long without the Treaty ports. Anything which can be done to get for us the use of the Treaty ports would thus be in defence of American interests.[8]

Before this message was sent, however, the Americans were already thinking on the same lines. Next day, for instance, Frank Knox, who as Secretary of the United States Navy was an influential member of Roosevelt's cabinet, was reported to be wondering whether a systematic campaign among Irish-Americans would encourage de Valera to hand over bases to Britain. Also that same morning, when Brennan called at the State Department to deliver the copy of the Taoiseach's speech, Sumner Welles told him that the Dublin government was jeopardising its own security by not co-operating with the British and handing over the ports. He added that Ireland's democracy and freedom would be dead if the Nazis won the war.

Since Welles said that the Roosevelt administration had not been approached by Britain on the subject (and indeed was not until almost a month later), it was clear that American diplomatic authorities had little sympathy for Irish neutrality. But de Valera did find support elsewhere in the United States, especially in the Irish-American press.

The San Francisco *Leader* was greatly impressed by the Taoiseach's speech: 'The Irish leader never expressed the sentiments of his race at home and abroad more thoroughly than in the manly, courageous and uncompromising pronouncement.' Charlie Connolly, editor of the *Irish Echo* (New York) called on 'all people interested in assisting Ireland in preserving her neutrality' to meet on Sunday, 24 November 1940, at a New York city ballroom.

More than 2,500 people attended the subsequent meeting, which was presided over by Paul O'Dwyer, a Mayo-born, New York lawyer. In order to counter the propaganda being directed against Irish neutrality, the meeting decided to establish a new organisation, the American Friends of Irish Neutrality, with O'Dwyer as national chairman. During the following months, new chapters of the organisation were established in many cities throughout the country.[9]

The Taoiseach also found strong support among politicians. In Washington, Senator Rush D. Hold of Virginia had an editorial from the *New York Enquirer* inserted into the *Congressional Record* accusing Churchill of talking like Hitler and being 'eager to commit the crowning blunder of his career by making an assault on Ireland'. A copy of this editorial along with a goodwill message signed by eighty senators, one hundred and eighty-eight members of the House of Representatives, and nineteen governors was also sent to de Valera.[10] Such support was certainly significant, as Roosevelt was in no position to ignore Congressional sentiment.

Churchill's speech had been a tactical error, as far as Gray was concerned. The latter was convinced that de Valera was not going to be persuaded to give up the ports. 'As we see it here', he telegraphed Washington on 10 November 1940, 'any attempt by Churchill to negotiate for the ports will be hopeless. He has the choice between seizing them and paying the price in possible bloodshed and certain hostility and doing without.' Even though London could still use economic coercion against the Irish by refusing to allow British ships to supply them, the American Minister was afraid that de Valera would probably use such pressure to 'his own political advantage'.

Much of de Valera's political power, according to Gray, was based 'on his genius for engendering and utilising anti-British sentiment'. The Taoiseach supposedly clouded his political and economic failures on the domestic front by exploiting the emotions of the Irish people on problems with Britain. Such anti-British sentiment was still easily excited, seeing that the wounds of the Black and Tan days were still deep. The American Minister went on to explain that de Valera was

> probably the most adroit politician in Europe and he honestly believes that all he does is for the good of the country. He had the qualities of martyr, fanatic and Machiavelli. No one can outwit him, frighten or brandish him. Remember that he is not pro-German nor personally anti-British but only pro-de

Valera. My view is that he will do business on his own terms
or must be overcome by force.

While Gray thought that Churchill had made the mistake of
trying to frighten de Valera, it seems more likely that Robert
Brennan was nearer the truth when he contended that the
outburst had been prompted by distressing news from the
Atlantic.

On the afternoon of Churchill's speech a distress call was picked
up from a convoy being attacked by a German pocket battleship
in mid-Atlantic. This was followed by radio silence. Since the
British had not known that there were any German battleships
loose in the Atlantic, the convoy was escorted only by a lightly
armed merchant cruiser, the *Jervis Bay*, which was no match for
a vessel the size of the German raider. As a result there were
fears at the Admiralty for the safety of the whole convoy of forty
ships. And these fears were exacerbated some hours later, when
Berlin announced that the convoy had been 'wiped out'. All
further sailings were suspended for what transpired to be the
longest delay of the war.

A certain amount of recrimination followed concerning the
failure to provide sufficient protection for the convoy. But after
four days the Admiralty was able to give a ray of hope by
announcing that in spite of the German claims, 'A number of
ships successfully eluded the raider.' Three days later ships began
straggling into port and they continued to arrive for the next
twelve days during which the story of Commander Fogarty Fegen
and his crew was flashed around the world.

Fegen, who was from Ballinunty, County Tipperary, had been
in charge of the *Jervis Bay* when the German raider attacked. He
immediately turned his ship and made a suicide run, holding off
the Germans long enough for the bulk of the convoy to make
good its escape. Instead of sinking the whole convoy, the raider,
the *Admiral Scheer*, only managed to sink four of the thirty-nine
ships being escorted by the *Jervis Bay* at the time of the attack.
Fegen, who went down with his ship, was posthumously awarded
the Victoria Cross, Britain's highest award for gallantry. He
became the third of eight Irishmen, born in the Twenty-Six
Counties, to be so honoured during the war. It was indeed
ironic that, while Churchill was, in effect, denouncing Ireland

for not helping to protect the trade of the British Isles, an Irishman was playing the leading role in averting what could easily have been the greatest maritime disaster of the war for Britain.

Meanwhile the press campaign concerning Irish neutrality and the ports continued. The *Economist*, which enjoyed a large and prestigious international readership, criticised de Valera's speech and suggested that Britain should seize bases if they became vital to her defence. An editorial in the *Observer* was equally critical of the speech and referred to the Taoiseach derogatorily as the 'Irish Führer', before going on to note that he was 'giving, if not positive, at any rate negative, aid to the enemy'. In Canada the *Montreal Gazette* called on the Taoiseach to give the ports of Britain, while Richard Hanson, the leader of the Canadian opposition, went somewhat further and asserted that de Valera's failure to co-operate was 'a valuable contribution to the Axis powers'.

John H. Kelly, the Canadian High Commissioner in Ireland, was disturbed by the trend of the propaganda. He warned his government that the press campaign was based on the erroneously held view that Ireland was anti-British because the government refused to hand over the ports. 'Although Ireland is neutral', he explained, 'public opinion is certainly not pro-German and sympathy with Britain is constantly increasing. Any anti-Irish campaign can do no good and may prove detrimental.' He therefore suggested that the fewer press comments made about the ports, the better.[11]

Sir John Maffey sent essentially the same message to the Dominions Office. In a subsequent letter to Churchill he warned of the danger that 'Mr de Valera and his extremists will exploit at once all the resources of the old tribal hatred. Whatever Mr de Valera may be in Geneva, here, in Ireland, he has never in essentials moved from the track he has consistently followed—the narrow avenue of hate.'[12]

Although the Canadian government took steps to suppress the propaganda campaign in Canada,* Churchill was unwilling to act. He sent an explicit memorandum to the Dominions Secretary,

---

*In December 1940 Prime Minister Mackenzie King approved of the actions of the Canadian Department of External Affairs in killing a proposal whereby a group of Irish-Canadians from Winnipeg would make a radio appeal to de Valera to give bases to Britain.

on 22 November 1940, rejecting Maffey's suggestion that the ports question be soft pedalled :

> I think it would be better to let de Valera stew in his own juice for a while. Nothing could be more harmless or more just than the remarks in the *Economist*. The claim now put forward on behalf of de Valera is that we are not only to be strangled by them, but to suffer our fate without making any complaint.
>
> Sir John Maffey should be made aware of the rising anger in England and Scotland, and especially among the merchant seamen, and he should not be encouraged to think that his only task is to mollify de Valera and make everything, including our ruin, pass off pleasantly. Apart from this, the less we say to de Valera at this juncture the better, and certainly nothing must be said to reassure him.

With the British government unwilling to give any reassurance, the attitude of the Roosevelt administration in general, and Gray in particular, only had made matters worse for the Irish.

On 19 November 1940, for instance, Welles instructed Gray to tell de Valera, as Brennan had already been told ten days earlier, that Irish freedom and democracy would be dead if Britain did not win the war and that 'The utilisation of Irish ports apparently was imperative to the success of the British Navy under present conditions.' The Under Secretary of State added that these views coincided with those of 'virtually the entire American press and the vast preponderance of public opinion as well'.

Before Gray could arrange a meeting, however, de Valera gave another widely publicised interview to an American press correspondent, emphasising his determination to stay out of the war. For one thing, he explained that Ireland—unlike the United States which could influence the course of the war by intervening—was too small to be of any real significance. When asked if it would make any difference if Washington requested him to give the ports to Britain, the Taoiseach replied that it would not be proper for the United States to make such a request, because the Americans were trying to stay out of the war themselves.

Gray was too determined to aid Britain to be put off by the apparent contradiction of urging Ireland to go to war, while his own government was protesting its determination to remain neutral. On 22 November 1940 when he spoke to the Taoiseach in accordance with his instructions from the State Department, he adopted a rather minatory tone. Ireland's survival depended on the British, Gray said, and if the Irish government did not at least explore the possibility of further co-operation with Britain, then there might be a deterioration in relations between Dublin and Washington.

De Valera would have none of this. There could be no discussion of leasing as much as an inch of Irish territory to anyone, he replied. And he added, somewhat pointedly, that it was not a war of Ireland's choosing and that it was rather strange that the United States, a neutral power, should deny the right of neutrality to a small country.

'I replied', Gray reported, 'that we were not denying any right but that as all right ultimately depended on power he might be relying on the power of American public opinion to support him and that he might fail to receive this support.'

According to the Taoiseach, Gray claimed that 'Americans could be cruel if their interests were affected and Ireland should expect little or no sympathy if the British took the ports.' De Valera's record of this conversation actually showed that the American Minister's report was not really complete.[13] The latter had omitted that he had said that the United States were going to be in the war soon and would therefore require Irish bases. At the time Gray was arguing that Ireland might just as well anticipate that moment by allowing Britain to use the ports immediately. He was, of course, assuming that Ireland would be willing to give the facilities to the United States, as Walshe had indicated two weeks earlier.

The discrepancy between the two reports is really easy to explain. When Gray mentioned that the United States was going to enter the war, he was, in effect, speaking off the record. The statement had not been part of his instructions from Welles and, as it was not official policy, he did not take the chance of mentioning it in his routine report to the State Department. The United States was then supposedly determined to remain neutral, or so the American people were being told. But Gray was sure that Roosevelt felt otherwise. Hence, while he was willing to give full details in his letters to the President, he was not willing to take a chance with the career people in the diplomatic service,

and misrepresentations being carried by the American press, often in influential newspapers.

These distortions were in four main areas. First, Ireland was supposedly infested with Axis agents; second, the Axis legations in Dublin were reported to be retaining excessively large staffs; third, Ireland was reputed to be affording refuelling facilities to German U-boats; and fourth, the lights of Irish cities were supposedly being used by German pilots to get their bearings on British cities. Although these rumours were often authoritatively denied, they persisted throughout the war.

The *Christian Science Monitor* asserted, for instance, that the German legation in Dublin had a staff of sixty people. This was refuted by the *New York Times,* which reported that the Germans had only a Minister, secretary, press attaché, and two clerks in Dublin, and a consul in Limerick. *The Times* of London declared that the behaviour of the German legation had been 'uniformly correct and the stories of its activities as a vast centre of espionage are without foundation'. Nevertheless such newspapers as the *New York Herald Tribune, Fort Worth Star-Telegram,* and *PM,* to mention only a few, subsequently carried statements to the contrary.

In late November the *Washington Evening Star* carried an article which asserted that Galway was being used as a U-boat base. Only the previous month, however, Lord Snell, the Deputy Leader of the House of Lords, had denied on behalf of the British government that there was any evidence that Ireland was affording facilities to U-boats. This would really have been virtually impossible, because U-boats used a heavy oil which could only be carried to Ireland in surface vessels. Since any German tankers could be easily detected, the British were sure that Ireland could not refuel U-boats seeing that Britain herself supplied all Ireland's oil. Nevertheless the rumours that there were U-boat bases in Ireland were often repeated in the American press.

Having promised that Irish neutrality would not be used against Britain, de Valera was anxious to scotch the inaccurate stories. In an interview with an American reporter on 11 December 1940 he denounced the rumours, not only about the U-boat bases and the size of the Axis legations, but also concerning the Germans being able to use the lights of Irish cities as beacons for bombing purposes. He explained that the lights were cowled in order to prevent a sky glow and that the British government were apparently satisfied because they had made no objections. But some years after the war, Gray was to resurrect the story and cite it as an example of how Irish neutrality was used against Britain.

The Taoiseach actually went out of his way to avoid giving even the appearance of assisting the Germans. In November 1940, for instance, he rejected a German offer of arms. He explained that Britain might use the transfer of equipment as a pretext for attacking Ireland. Then the following month when the Germans announced that they were transferring some of their diplomats from the United States to Ireland, the Taoiseach insisted on impossible conditions. He refused to allow the Germans to fly directly to Ireland. Instead, he demanded that they should travel by the normal commercial route, which was from the United States to Portugal, and from there through Britain to Ireland. This, of course, killed the project.

Nevertheless Churchill was not satisfied with anything less than being allowed to use Irish facilities. On 8 December 1940 he finally sent a message to Roosevelt seeking to enlist the aid of 'the good offices of the United States and the whole influence of its government' in order 'to procure for Great Britain the necessary facilities upon the southern and western shores of Éire for our flotillas, and still more important, for our aircraft, working to the westward into the Atlantic'. He hoped that if the United States proclaimed that it was in America's interest that the Atlantic trade route be kept open and Britain's resistance prolonged, then 'The Irish-American elements might impress on de Valera the need which the democracies had for the Irish ports.' In return, the Prime Minister contended that Northern Ireland would probably agree to some form of Irish unity after the war, though he added that the British government would not be willing to force Belfast to do so.[16]

In his next message on 13 December 1940 Churchill explained that Britain intended to cut down on shipments of feeding stuffs and fertilisers to Ireland. 'We need this tonnage for our own supply,' he wrote, 'and we do not need the food which Éire has been sending us.' Ireland would still have plenty of food to meet the country's needs, he declared, but Britain was going to have to cut down on the trade, because she needed the shipping space. 'I am sorry about this,' he added, 'but we must think of our own self-preservation, and use for vital purposes our own tonnage brought in through so many perils.' The Prime Minister hinted that this was only to be a first step towards cutting off all British shipping to Ireland. He asked, for example, what Roosevelt's 'reactions would be if and when we are forced to concentrate our tonnage upon the supply of Great Britain'. And he then explained that 'Our merchant seamen, as well as public opinion generally, take it much amiss that we should have to carry Irish supplies through air and U-boat attacks and subsidise them handsomely when de Valera is quite content to sit happy and see us strangle.'

A few days later the British informed Dublin that they were cutting back on petrol supplies to Ireland, in spite of what Irish authorities believed had been an understanding to maintain the level of such supplies in return for the seven tankers turned over at the start of the war. The Taoiseach saw the cut back as an indication that the British intended to use economic pressure to force him to give up the ports. He therefore tried to bolster Ireland's shipping capacity by using his annual Christmas address to the United States to ask the Americans to sell Ireland, not only arms, but also ships that could be used to transport food. He explained that Ireland was facing serious shortages as a result of a blockade by the belligerents.

Coming barely a week after Roosevelt hinted at the introduction of lend-lease with his garden hose analogy, administration officials in Washington were annoyed that de Valera's address appeared to give a boost to the President's critics at a crucial time by linking Ireland with the 'Starving Europe Campaign' being waged by former President Hoover, who had recently made a highly publicised speech calling on Britain to lift her blockade of the continent. Since Americans could hardly avoid noting that Britain was in control of the seas around Ireland, it appeared that de Valera's address was implying that Britain was trying to starve Ireland. Moreover, in the version of the speech released by CBS and published in the *New York Times*, the Taoiseach was attributed with having said that 'the overshadowing anxiety' of the Irish government was the 'possibility of incitement which would force our people once more to do battle against Britain and the British'. Actually he had not mentioned either Britain or the

British by name, but it was some days before CBS corrected the misquotation and explained that the error was due to atmospheric conditions.

In the meantime the White House was apparently so upset by the speech that Roosevelt took time to ridicule Irish neutrality during a radio address on 29 December 1940. He asked what would happen if Britain were defeated. 'Could Ireland hold out? Would Irish freedom be permitted as an amazing exception in an unfree world?' There could be no doubting what the President meant: Ireland was acting as a parasite, while the British were fighting for her freedom as well as their own.

In Dublin Gray, too, was irate over the Taoiseach's address. He complained to de Valera that the speech 'appeared to be an attempt to put the pressure of the Irish-American vote on the government'. Oblivious to his own attempts to influence Irish officials, the American Minister said that de Valera would resent it if the United States went over his head in Ireland. Gray added 'that it was not so much Irish neutrality that was causing the sympathies of our two countries to diverge as the impression American newspaper men got that the Irish *wanted* Britain to be beaten even if they went down too'.[17] Instead of speaking directly to the American people, therefore, he suggested that the Taoiseach should send an emissary to the United States to explain the Irish government's problems. But when this suggestion was eventually adopted, it only led to further complications.

In view of the circumstances surrounding de Valera's Christmas appeal for arms and ships, it was little surprise that the United States government did not respond favourably. Nevertheless the Irish persisted in their efforts through diplomatic channels.

The need for arms, especially, seemed greater than ever following aerial bombings of various Irish localities during the first three days of the new year. Although the bomb fragments were identified as German and a strong diplomatic protest was lodged by the Irish *Chargé d'Affaires* in Berlin, this did not make the Irish government any more receptive to British efforts to secure bases, because the Irish people still distrusted Britain so much that many feared that the British had dropped the German bombs. Gray learned that the IRA was 'certain' that the British were responsible, and he also noted that 'a general majority' of the Irish people 'appear to think it probable'.[18]

With at least a German feint toward Ireland a distinct possibility, the British concentrated troops in Northern Ireland in order to respond to such an attack. This, together with some editorial comment in the British and American press, coupled with Churchill's continued refusal to promise that Britain would not attack, gave rise to renewed fears in Dublin that the British might invade without waiting for the Germans to attack first. The *Economist* declared, for example, that 'If the Irish-ports question becomes a matter of life and death, the only thing to do, as the *Economist* has remarked before, is to seize them. There will be plenty of moral justification for the act.'

The German representative in Washington reported that the United States press had 'for a considerable time been preparing the American public' for British seizure of the ports. Consequently the Irish ability to excite American public opinion was beginning to lose its potency as a deterrent to a British attack.

Although it is not possible to determine what proportion of the American people would have supported British seizure of Irish facilities, a Gallup poll published in January 1941 revealed that sixty-three per cent of the American people believed that Dublin should allow Britain to use the ports, and only sixteen per cent opposed the proposition, with the remainder undecided. Of first generation Americans whose fathers were born in Ireland, a majority of only fifty-two per cent opposed the suggestion, with 40 per cent favouring it, and eight per cent undecided. These figures, which Gray gleefully passed on, could hardly have been reassuring to de Valera, who so obviously relied on American opinion as his trump card against a British attack.

The British representative noted that de Valera was upset by the trend of American opinion. In a report to the Dominions Office on 20 January Maffey explained that the Taoiseach was 'more uneasy today than he had ever been in any stage of his political career'. It was now the 'soul of England' that was stirring Americans, not the Irish under their 'chosen tribal leader', de Valera. 'His feelings today when he hears the courageous speeches of President Roosevelt can be imagined,' wrote Maffey. 'These Irish-Americans are the pillars of Mr de Valera's temple. They created him, preserved him, and endowed him.'

De Valera complained to Maffey about Britain's recent policy towards Ireland. Previously Irish authorities had regarded Germany as the probable aggressor, he said, but now they also feared Britain, with the result that a German attack might not be met with the same spirited resistance that it would have met six months earlier. The Taoiseach was particularly critical of the British refusal to arm Ireland.

Maffey concluded his report by suggesting that military leaders in London should consider providing arms. 'Mr de Valera', he wrote, 'is telling the truth when he says that if we arm Éire we shall create a most powerful weapon against a German invasion and establish a good friend on our flank.'

But unless the Irish were prepared to make arrangements to enter the war, Churchill would not hear of handing over any more weapons. 'Until we are so satisfied', he explained in a note to Cranborne on 31 January, 'we do not wish them to have further arms, and certainly will not give them ourselves.' Nor was the Prime Minister prepared to provide an assurance to respect Irish neutrality. 'I could under no circumstances give the guarantee asked for,' he wrote. Two weeks earlier he had written to the Dominions Secretary that Britain would actually seize Irish facilities if such a move became necessary. 'Should the danger to our war effort through the denial of Irish bases threaten to become mortal, which is not the case at present,' Churchill wrote, 'we should have to act in accordance with our own self-preservation.'

Meanwhile some of the European news media were encouraging rumours of an imminent British or German invasion of Ireland. The Swedish *Social-democraten*, for instance, contended that the Germans had information indicating that 'the British government have the intention of carrying out the military occupation of Ireland during the coming weeks, or at least occupying the western ports.' Reports such as that, which were probably planted by the Nazis, were also carried on German radio. One broadcast asserted that the British were about to invade Ireland and that in such an event 'Berlin is determined to respond in the same way as in the case of Norway and Belgium.'

De Valera was greatly troubled by Germany's recent interest in Ireland. First there was the offer of arms, then the attempt to enlarge the legation in Dublin, which was followed by the bombings and the obvious efforts to create an invasion scare.

On 22 January 1941 he told Gray that he was convinced that the Germans were going to invade, and he explained that Ireland was in desperate need of arms from the United States in order to ensure that the Irish army would be able to hold out until British help could be secured.

This was not enough for Gray. He wanted an assurance that if Germany attacked, then Ireland would ally with Britain and hand over naval and air facilities for the duration of the war, but de Valera replied that he would be unable to commit himself until the occasion arose. At this point the Taoiseach could have told Gray that certain military arrangements had already been made with Britain, but he apparently was so uneasy about the American Minister's lack of discretion that he was unwilling to confide in him.

Earlier in the month, for example, Gray had talked about some confidential matters during an interview with an American correspondent. The Defence Conference was informed that an AP correspondent reported that Gray had told him that following the German bombing incidents, de Valera threatened Hempel with expulsion if the incidents did not cease. If Irish authorities had wanted to release news of the de Valera-Hempel interview, that was for them to do; it was certainly not for the American Minister. To make matters worse, the account was subsequently distorted and there were reports in the American press that the Irish government had actually expelled Hempel.[19]

In view of Gray's apparent role in the whole affair it was hardly surprising that the Taoiseach was reluctant to confide in him. Consequently the American Minister knew little about Anglo-Irish military co-operation. He told de Valera that unless the Irish government were willing to give a commitment to co-operate fully with Britain in the event of an attack on Ireland, then he would not recommend that Dublin be allowed to purchase American equipment.

Gray had received no authority from the State Department to make such a statement, so in his report to Roosevelt he suggested that the President should warn him to be 'careful' if it appeared that he was going out on a limb. 'I feel that I only can be helpful to you and to Ireland by trying to interpret your policy AND ITS IMPLICATIONS to this government,' Gray explained. 'It is better that they get their feet on the ground even if they blame me for the shock than that they should go on in the world of unreality in which they are existing.'[20]

In the same letter the American Minister was particularly critical of the quality of the Irish cabinet which, except for one or two members, he said was of the same timbre as the Board of Supervisors of Dutchess County, New York. 'The Dáil', he added, 'makes me think of the Supervisors meetings that I used to report in Monroe County when I worked on the *Rochester Union and Advertiser*.'

Roosevelt had no objection to Gray interpreting American policy. In a short cryptic reply the President assured him that he 'need not "be careful".'

At the same time the President was, if anything, more critical of the Dáil and its executive than was Gray. 'I think', Roosevelt wrote, 'you are unfair to the Board of Dutchess County or of Monroe County. Almost all of them were highly practical people.'[21]

Although de Valera's authorised biographers have written that the American Minister had by this time shown a powerful dislike of the Taoiseach, such was not the case. In contrast with Maffey who, in his report of 20 January, characterised de Valera as a vain, ambitious, 'petty leader raking over old muck heaps', Gray credited the Taoiseach with having some excellent policies, especially in the field of social legislation. In a letter to Eleanor Roosevelt on 10 February 1941, for example, the American Minister wrote that 'The great thing the de Valera government has done and is doing, is to govern in the interest of the under-privileged as far as possible. They have a real new deal here.' In the area of foreign policy, however, he complained that de Valera 'lives in a dream-wish world'. The Taoiseach and his colleagues could not grasp the fact that a small country like Ireland, without mineral resources, could not 'be free and independent in a sense that a continent wide state or federation of states can be independent and free'. Yet, in spite of what he saw as shortcomings, Gray still had a genuine personal affection for de Valera. 'I like him very much', he wrote, 'though I despair of coping with him.'

Since Gray was not making any headway, other Americans tried. On 4 February 1941 Wendell Willkie visited Dublin.[22] At the time it was generally assumed that he was on a mission for

Roosevelt, but he really made the trip on his own initiative because he was being criticised by Irish-Americans for being too pro-British. The visit was supposedly to assure Irish-Americans that he was not ignoring Ireland. Willkie also saw it as an opportunity to persuade de Valera to allow Britain to use the ports, even though Churchill had personally told him that all efforts to persuade the Irish leader would be a waste of time.

In Dublin Willkie had what he described as a 'brutally frank' discussion with de Valera. He told the Taoiseach that the Irish were making fools of themselves by thinking that they could remain neutral. Hitler would attack whenever it suited him, he contended, so Ireland might as well join the British at once and give them the ports.

De Valera, of course, refused, saying that he was afraid that Dublin would be bombed. At this, Willkie did not conceal his contempt. 'American opinion', he said, 'will not be with you.' He added that American sentiment had been responsible for Irish freedom, and Ireland would stand condemned in the United States if Britain were defeated.

After the meeting Frank Aiken accompanied Willkie to the airport, so Gray had only the briefest of opportunities to find out how the meeting with the Taoiseach had gone.

'Did it go all right?' he asked Willkie when they were momentarily alone.

'I handed him a couple of jolts,' Willkie whispered in reply.

Four weeks later Colonel William J. Donovan, who later won fame as the organiser of the Central Intelligence Agency (CIA), visited Dublin in an effort to acquire Lough Swilly, County Donegal, for an American base. His visit was in connection with secret Anglo-American talks being conducted in Washington. It had been decided that the United States would build a base in Northern Ireland and station troops there, if America became involved in the war. But when it came to selecting a site for the base, it was found that Lough Swilly was more suitable than any ports in the Six Counties. Donovan therefore tried to persuade de Valera to give up the port, but his efforts were in vain. The Taoiseach made it clear that he was not about to jeopardise Irish neutrality by giving up any territory. The American base was subsequently built on nearby Lough Foyle in Northern Ireland.

Ironically some weeks later Secretary of State Hull, who was conceivably unaware of the exact nature of Donovan's mission, denied that the United States had ever asked for the Irish base. 'Lough Swilly', Hull said, 'would be scarcely any improvement over Lough Foyle, twenty miles away over the border in Northern Ireland and already being used by the British.'[23]

6. The Aiken Mission to USA

THE SEEDS OF FUTURE DISCORD
March—June 1941

IN February 1941 relations between the United States and Ireland seemed stalemated. On the one hand, the Americans had failed to persuade de Valera to allow Britain to use the ports. While on the other hand, Ireland had been unable to secure either arms or ships from the United States.

The need for ships was becoming quite serious at the time because the British were deliberately cutting back on supplies to Ireland, and to make matters worse, the Irish, who had never possessed adequate vessels of their own, had lost nine ships since the start of the war. Even though Churchill had assured Roosevelt the previous December that trade cuts would be reluctantly instituted on account of a need for shipping space, the British government really had ulterior motives.

Churchill and his colleagues were annoyed that de Valera had been unwilling to help in protecting British shipping and also that the Irish did not seem to appreciate the hardships under which supplies were being delivered to them. In fact, the Irish people appeared to be under the delusion that Britain was dependent on Irish trade, rather than the other way around. By cutting back on supplies and thus demonstrating that Britain did not need to trade with Ireland, London hoped to shake the Irish out of their complacency and possibly even make them more ready to co-operate. But it was decided to try to avoid giving the appearance that the measure was punitive.

Churchill rejected a plan whereby virtually all shipping to Ireland would be cut off. Instead it was decided to change British export licensing laws in order to prohibit the export to Ireland of various items, such as feeding stuffs, fertilisers, spare parts, various metals, paper, chemicals, and electrical products. In addition the British decided to terminate the informal understanding whereby they provided Ireland with shipping space equivalent to forty whole-time ships in return for an Irish agreement to refrain from chartering neutral ships. That arrangement, which had been requested by the British, was designed to keep chartering rates down by eliminating Anglo-Irish competition from the market for neutral shipping. By the beginning of 1941, however, Britain no longer had to worry about such competition because she already had control of Greek and Norwegian ships. As a result the Chancellor of the Exchequer estimated that the Irish would be lucky if they could charter enough ships to fulfil quarter of their needs.

On 2 January 1941 Churchill told the war cabinet that British authorities would cut back the supplies gradually, pretending that they were taking the action only out of 'dire necessity' and telling the press that 'the government viewed this measure with profound regret'.[1]

De Valera quickly realised what was happening. On 30 January he told Richard Mulcahy, a Fine Gael member of the Defence Conference, that although the British had previously dealt with Ireland 'with extraordinary generosity', there were signs that they had begun to exert economic pressure. As evidence, he cited that Head Line, a Northern Irish shipping company, had been ordered not 'to take stuff for Ireland' in the United States.[2]

Faced with an ever increasing need for ships, Irish authorities were convinced that the Roosevelt administration was deliberately frustrating their efforts to purchase American vessels. In early February 1941 de Valera told the Defence Conference that Gray, who he believed was representing Roosevelt's views, had been distinctly unhelpful. As a result the Taoiseach announced that he was sending Frank Aiken to the United States to deal with the Americans directly.[3]

Gray had actually suggested such a mission the previous month. It was not that he thought that it would be a better way for the Irish to fulfil their needs, but because he saw it as a means of educating the Irish government, which he believed was woefully uninformed not only about Roosevelt's determination to help Britain, but also about how little Irish neutrality really mattered to Americans. 'It has seemed impossible', Gray wrote on 4 February 1941, 'to make any of these people realise what was going on in the USA or that the American people had very little understanding or sympathy with Mr de Valera's academic contentions.' The American Minister therefore welcomed the Aiken mission as an opportunity for the Irish cabinet to get a first hand report on conditions in the United States from one of its own members.

From the Irish standpoint, however, the choice of Aiken could hardly have been worse, because Gray had been very critical of him in letters to the White House. He thought that Aiken, who was in charge of Irish censorship, had not only been playing down the assistance that the British were giving Ireland, but was also preventing anything being published that was critical of the Nazis.[4]

When asked by the Dominions Office whether the British government should comply with an Irish request to allow Aiken to travel through Britain on his way to the United States, Sir John Maffey gave enthusiastic approval. He realised that the mission would not be successful and that it was only likely to help British policy. 'Aiken is anti-British', he wrote, 'but certainly not pro-German. He is not impressive. . . . I hope that every assistance will be given.'

The British representative, who concurred with Gray's assessment of the educational value of the proposed visit, explained that 'Personal contact with outside opinion will do immense good here where views are narrow and insular.' Maffey noted, in addition, that facilitating Aiken would be a show of goodwill which would make more credible the British contention that the cut back of supplies to Ireland was not punitive.[5]

In his conversations with Irish authorities, Maffey had been insisting that British economic measures were not designed to put pressure on the Dublin government, but he did not rule out the possibility that Britain might eventually use pressure. Indeed, on 14 March 1941 he warned the Taoiseach not only that Britain could not guarantee to respect Irish neutrality, but that he believed that the time would probably come when Britain, or the United States, or both, would bring strong pressure to bear on Ireland.[6]

De Valera was in a serious predicament. If all imports were cut off, much of the country's industry would grind to a halt, and there was a danger of serious food shortages, especially as a foot and mouth epidemic was causing many cattle to be slaughtered at the time. The only way out of the predicament was to bolster Ireland's shipping capacity so that the country would be able to undertake the transportation of its own supplies. Preparations were therefore made to establish Irish Shipping Limited, a nationally owned shipping company.

In his St Patrick's Day address to the United States, which was broadcast over 126 CBS radio stations, the Taoiseach explained his plight. He declared that 'serious shortages' were being felt in the past two months as a result of a blockade by both sides in the war. In trying to blockade each other, he said, the belligerents were blockading Ireland. He therefore asked the United States to facilitate Aiken's efforts to purchase arms and ships.

As far as administration officials in Washington were concerned, however, this speech was badly timed. De Valera had again implied that the British were no better than the Nazis and, as with his Christmas address, he could hardly have picked a less opportune moment even to imply such a charge, especially in a speech directed at the American people. Because, even though Congress had recently passed lend-lease, Roosevelt had only just launched what was apparently a trial balloon measuring the possible repercussions to the introduction of American convoys to bring supplies to Britain.

Two days before de Valera's speech, the President told a dinner for White House correspondents that 'the survival of the vital bridge across the ocean' depended on the will and determination of the American people, and that the great task of the day was 'to move products from American factories to the battle lines of democracy'. The address, which was prominently reported on both sides of the Atlantic, was widely interpreted as an indication that Roosevelt hoped to introduce American convoys to help Britain. As a result de Valera's subsequent remarks were ill-timed, and they created a most unfavourable climate for the Aiken mission.

When Roosevelt was asked at a press conference, following the Taoiseach's speech, whether the United States would be willing to sell food and arms to Ireland, he brushed aside the inquiry with a pointed question of his own. 'How are they going to get them in?' he asked.

Although the German Minister in Dublin was delighted that de Valera's speech was strictly neutral, Gray was very annoyed that the Taoiseach had again, in effect, told the American people that Britain and Germany were equally guilty for Ireland's plight. This implied that those two countries shared responsibility for the nine Irish ships lost since the start of the war, even though there was absolutely no evidence that the British had been involved in any instance, while there was proof that the Germans and Italians had been responsible for a number of sinkings. It also denied any credit to British seamen who were risking their lives in bringing supplies to Ireland. Of course, Gray did not know that the need for shipping space was not the real reason for the cut in British supplies, but even if he had known, it probably would not have affected his attitude, because he believed that the British had a perfect right to refuse economic assistance to Ireland, when Dublin was refusing military help to them.

Gray complained to James Dillon, who subsequently spoke out in the Dáil. On 3 April 1941 in the course of a bitter attack on the government's censorship policies, the Fine Gael man denounced de Valera's speech as unfair, because Britain had not tried to blockade Ireland. In fact, Dillon said that trade with Britain had decreased very little since the start of the war, and he cited statistics supporting his charge.

Gray wrote to Roosevelt, next day, that he had been avoiding de Valera since the St Patrick's Day speech in order to get time to cool off, but he added that he did tell Seán T. O'Kelly that the Taoiseach apparently 'had no idea of what was going on in America and that the speech was as well calculated to prevent Ireland getting what she wanted as was possible'. The American Minister went on to report that he had been adopting a very cheerful attitude towards Irish authorities and was saying in effect: 'Well boys this is your show, only if you find that our things are available only for those doing their bit for Democracy, don't be surprised. You can't have it both ways.'

Even though Aiken was accorded the courtesy of a hearing by all the leading officials in the Roosevelt administration, including the President, Vice-President, Secretary of State, Secretary of the Navy, and various State Department representatives, he found it extremely difficult to make any headway. At first he apparently associated mainly with supporters of Roosevelt and shied away from the White House's many Irish-American critics.

According to the *New York Daily Mirror*, Aiken avoided Irish-Americans in Washington who had opposed lend-lease, but 'hobnobbed' with such supporters of the bill as John McCormack and James McGranery, the Pennsylvania Congressman. The newspaper also reported that the Irish emissary had been eloquent in praise of both British courage and Roosevelt's policy of making the United States the 'arsenal of Democracy'.

Nevertheless there was a limit to Aiken's willingness to show sympathy for Britain. He was not prepared to give any details of the secret Anglo-Irish military talks, even to State Department officials. On 2 April 1941 when Dean Acheson, the Assistant Secretary of State, asked him if any arrangement had been made with the British to repel a possible German invasion of Ireland, Aiken replied that there had not. Explaining that there could be no such preparations for fear of actually provoking the attack, the Irish emissary contended that the best way that Dublin could help the British would be to have a strong Ireland, fully prepared to resist a German invasion. If he could get adequate arms from the United States, he said that Ireland could increase five-fold the 50,000 men already under arms and since these men would be defending their homeland, they would be worth a further three to four times their number in foreign troops.

In making his argument, Aiken actually dismissed the value of the ports to Britain. According to Acheson, the Irish emissary 'insisted that the British had greatly exaggerated the utility of Irish ports, since the convoy routes were around the north of Ireland instead of the south of the island as had been the case in the last war'. Although the American Chiefs of Staff would themselves argue this way, a couple of years later, the State Department obviously failed to appreciate the validity of the contention at this time.

On 7 April 1941 Aiken met Roosevelt in the White House. Robert Brennan, who was also present, later gave an account of the meeting in an article for the *Irish Press* in which he related that Roosevelt had begun by charging Aiken with having said that Ireland had nothing to fear from a German victory. After Aiken denied the charge, the President launched into a

long oration on Britain's need for Irish help. The emissary had
hardly had a chance to speak by the time a presidential aide
entered the office, which was the prearranged signal to terminate
the meeting. But Aiken was not about to be brushed aside that
easily. Instead he tried to persuade the President to accede to
Irish requests, and he was not to be put off even when a servant
came in and arranged a table cloth and cutlery on the President's
desk for lunch.[7]

At one point Roosevelt suggested that some aircraft might be
furnished for submarine spotting, but Aiken replied that he was
not concerned about submarines. He said that he was worried
about the danger of an invasion and he assumed that if one
took place, Ireland could anticipate having the President's
sympathy.

'Yes,' responded Roosevelt. Ireland could expect his sympathy
against German aggression.

'Or British aggression,' added Aiken.

Enraged, Roosevelt said that there was no danger of a British
attack.

'If that is so,' Aiken interjected, 'why cannot they say so. We
have asked them.'

'What you have to fear is German aggression,' argued Roosevelt.

'Or British aggression,' Aiken brazenly maintained.

The President suddenly lost his temper. 'I have never heard
anything so preposterous in all my life,' he said as he jerked
the table cloth from his desk, sending the cutlery flying and
effectively ending the discussion.

Before leaving, Brennan suggested that much of the Anglo-
Irish tension would be eased if the President could get a commitment from the British not to invade Ireland. Roosevelt replied
that he would get one in the morning, but he never did.

Four days later Secretary of State Hull met Aiken and found
him 'strongly anti-British'. He therefore made it clear that the
United States was fervently opposed to the Nazis. 'All countries
alike', Hull said, 'are now in danger from Hitler, whether they
are peaceful or otherwise. Hitler has no friends and is not a
friend of anybody, and he would sacrifice any of his most loyal
followers or sympathisers just as quickly as he would an enemy,
if it would serve any small purpose for him to do so.'[8]

Administration officials were upset with Aiken's attitude, which they considered fanatically anti-British. This was compounded following his departure from Washington when he began touring the United States, associating with some of Roosevelt's most bitter critics and addressing Irish-American groups, many of which were actively opposing the President's aid to Britain. The administration therefore decided not to do business with him.

Apparently desiring to avoid incurring a charge of deliberately permitting the Irish to starve, Roosevelt decided to sell two ships to Ireland. On 25 April 1941 the State Department instructed Gray to tell de Valera that the United States would negotiate the transfer of the ships with him personally, but not with Aiken. The department explained that since Aiken's attitude was one of blind hostility toward Britain—on whom Ireland's freedom rested—the United States would not do business with him 'unless and until the Irish government is prepared to adopt a more co-operative attitude'. The telegram, which had been drafted by Welles, added that although the United States did not wish to question Ireland's right to remain neutral, 'there is a clear distinction between such a policy and a policy which at least potentially provides real encouragement to the German government.'

Gray called on de Valera on 28 April and delivered the message during a somewhat stormy meeting. Having come prepared for a showdown, he read from some notes drafted for the occasion. First, he warned the Taoiseach that the United States was determined to aid Britain until the fascists had been defeated. Consequently, he said, referring to de Valera's Christmas and St Patrick's Day addresses to the United States, the Irish government's policy of depicting Britain as being equally guilty as Germany for Ireland's shortage of supplies, was antagonistic to the policy of the United States government. What was more, the Irish charge was untrue, because the British had been supplying Ireland. Using the same statistics quoted by Dillon in the Dáil, Gray pointed out that during the first full year of the war the value of Irish imports from Britain had been greater than before the outbreak of hostilities. And he noted that the latest British imports were running at three-quarters of the previous year, despite British shipping losses. Furthermore, he continued, the

British, unlike the Germans, had not attacked Irish property nor sunk Irish ships.

The American Minister went on explaining his government's problem with the Irish stand :

> Unless therefore there is some interpretation of your statement other than its plain meaning it is difficult to avoid the conclusion that ... in framing your statement as you did you intended to put a responsibility on Great Britain for Irish privations equal to that imposed on Germany and to withhold credit from Great Britain for her services in supplying you in the measure that she has. The effect of creating such an impression on your American audience as you must see, whether or not it was so intended, could only be to excite antagonism against that nation which it is our national policy to aid, and thus to weaken popular support in America for that policy. It is obvious that in the present emergency policies antagonistic to the British war effort are antagonistic to American interests.

The Taoiseach flushed angrily and shouted that it was impertinent to question his statement. But the American Minister complained that he should not expect to go unchallenged as the St Patrick's Day speech to the United States appealed mainly to anti-British elements, who had opposed Roosevelt, his lend-lease programme, and who were 'now engaged in sabotaging' American aid for Britain.

What seemed to have troubled de Valera most was that Gray had not objected for more than a month and so much of his case was based on Dillon's criticism in the Dáil. The Taoiseach explained that the real intention of his government was to let the British know that he believed they were considering a blockade of Ireland by making it impossible for the Irish to get ships. And he also hinted that Gray was acting more British than the British and that he would do well to watch over American interests.

Gray did not let pass the opportunity to restate his position. For the rest of the war, he said that he 'considered British interests the same as American interests'.

While the American Minister hoped that his blunt approach would have a 'sobering' effect, he warned the State Department that henceforth relations with de Valera would likely be much less amicable. 'I no longer hope to get anything from him by generosity and conciliation,' Gray wrote. Nevertheless he was convinced that it had been his duty to impress on the Taoiseach the gravity of the situation. It was necessary, he explained, to make him realise that 'if it be essential to survival his ports will be seized with the approval of the liberal sentiment of the world,' and he would have only the choice of fighting on the side of Britain or Germany.

Disturbed by what amounted to a lecture from the American Minister, de Valera instructed Robert Brennan to reject the offer of the two ships, on the grounds that its acceptance would be tantamount to assenting to the validity of the criticism of both his government's position and Aiken's actions. The Irish government could not accept the ships, he explained, even though it really needed them.

The Taoiseach also protested that there was some apparent misunderstanding about Ireland's attitude toward Britain. 'For the first time in several centuries', he contended, 'Britain whilst engaged in a continental war has not had to reckon with a hostile Ireland.' In fact, Ireland had helped the British in many ways. 'Our neutrality', de Valera continued, 'has been a benevolent one, and consequently we have leaned on the side of helpful and sympathetic understanding.'

Ignoring the Irish rejection, Roosevelt announced publicly the offer to sell the two ships on 20 May 1941 at a press conference. He also said that he had instructed Norman Davis, president of the American Red Cross, to get in touch with Brennan and inform him that Washington was willing to give Ireland $500,000 worth of food and medical supplies. When asked about arms, however, the President stated that American weapons could only be spared for 'those nations which are actively waging war on behalf of the maintenance of Democracy, and there isn't anything left over'.

As there was no overt criticism of Aiken or Irish policy in the President's remarks, the Irish government accepted the offer. Some months of negotiations followed as arrangements were made for the selection and transfer of the two ships.

Initially the Americans tried to give Ireland two of the impounded Italian vessels. But Dublin balked at this.[9] Later the sale ran into legal complications that were skirted only by chartering the *West Hematite* and *West Neris* to an American shipping company, which in turn chartered them to Irish Shipping Limited. The vessels were then renamed *Irish Pine* and *Irish Oak* respectively.

The United States had given Ireland some much needed help, but the manner in which it was given was not characteristic of a generous gesture. The Americans were simply too annoyed to be magnanimous.

To understand the reaction of Washington, one must look to the broader implications that the Irish government's attitude had for the American political scene and the potential effect which that attitude could have had on the war situation. At the time there was a strong wave of anti-British sentiment sweeping the United States as the 'Starving Europe Campaign' was gathering momentum with the help of Cardinal O'Connell, Cudahy, and other Irish-Americans. Not only did de Valera's St Patrick's Day address fit neatly into that campaign, but Aiken also contributed by frequently reiterating the same theme in his speeches in the United States.

In addition the Irish emissary made other charges against the British. On 23 April 1941, for instance, he contended at a press conference in New York that the Irish people were suffering from food shortages because the British were breaking a trade agreement with Ireland. 'England has not been giving us a fair share of goods from overseas,' he said. 'There is no acute shortage of petrol in England.'[10] The charge fitted into the anti-British picture particularly well because it was made only hours before a large anti-war rally in the city.

It was Lindbergh's first rally in New York since joining the America First Committee. As a result there was an overflow crowd of about 25,000 people to greet him. According to various accounts, the crowd was mainly Irish-American.[11] Thus, given the make-up of the crowd and the fact that other speakers at the rally included Senator Walsh and John T. Flynn, Aiken's statement was somewhat untimely, at least as far as Washington was concerned.

At the time Aiken was actually encouraging opposition to United States aid for Britain. Immediately after the New York rally, for instance, he was a guest of honour at a dinner given

E

by Flynn, who was anathema to President Roosevelt. Lindbergh was also present and he had a discussion with Aiken, who declared that he was in complete agreement with the famous flyer's views. The Irish emissary also explained that Britain's position was really much worse than was commonly believed in the United States because British shipping losses were greater than was generally reported.[12]

Aiken's assessment of Britain's position was correct, but this explains all the more Washington's reaction to him. Britain was really on the verge of defeat during the spring of 1941 because the Germans were sinking British ships twice as fast as the combined building output of the United States and Britain.[13] At that rate it was obvious that Britain could not survive for long without some further assistance, such as the introduction of United States convoys.

In view of the war situation it was important that Irish representatives in the United States should tread carefully on issues likely to exacerbate the anglophobia of Irish-Americans, many of whom tended to view Anglo-Irish relations in the context of centuries of feuding. These people seemed to think that Ireland was still living in the age of the infamous Black and Tans.

The Irish-American press still referred to the Black and Tan period with monotonous regularity. In fact, in May 1941 the San Francisco *Leader* began running a series of scathing excerpts from the 1920 report of an Irish-American commission which, following an enquiry into conditions in Ireland, condemned the Black and Tans.

De Valera was obviously aware of the need to choose words carefully, because in his American addresses he avoided referring to the British by name when mentioning the danger of invasion or blockade. He simply said that Ireland would resist any attacker, or that in the process of blockading each other, the unnamed belligerents were blockading Ireland.

Frank Aiken, however, was not as discreet in the wording of his speeches and this accounts in part for the animosity of the Roosevelt administration toward him. He harped on the grievance of partition and often made imprudent references to the British by making over-simplified and exaggerated charges. He not only accused them of occupying Northern Ireland and blockading the rest of the island, but also touched a nerve by referring to the Black and Tans, and even worded some remarks so vaguely that they could be interpreted as questioning Britain's motives in fighting the Germans.

The *Irish World* reported on 12 April 1941, for example, that in justifying Irish neutrality Aiken had said that a quarter of a million Irishmen had fought for democracy in the First World War and had been rewarded only by having Britain foist the Black and Tans on them. In Chicago on 27 April he referred to the Twenty-Six Counties as 'the free portion of Ireland',[14] thereby implying that the people of Northern Ireland were being kept in subjugation—notwithstanding the fact that a clear majority of those people actually favoured Britain's presence. The following week in San Francisco Aiken not only scorned Britain over partition and warned that Ireland would fight if the British invaded, but he reiterated the charge that Ireland was the most blockaded country in Europe. Indeed, he then went a step further and accused the British of introducing the blockade first. The Germans had only followed, he said.[15] Two days later during a speech in the same city he remarked that Ireland intended 'to remain neutral even in the face of economic warfare with England'.[16]

When the possible introduction of conscription in Northern Ireland was being mooted in late May, Aiken denounced the British. He said in New York that they had 'no right to occupy six counties of Ireland and then go on to commit the monstrous outrage of conscripting men into an army they allege is fighting for freedom and democracy'.[17]

White House officials were not interested in the merits of Aiken's contentions. Rather, they were bitterly resentful of the references to Anglo-Irish disputes in which the United States was not involved, especially when those references were likely to harden the attitude of some Americans towards Roosevelt's pro-British policies. From various remarks Americans could hardly be blamed for thinking that Aiken was more afraid of the British than the Germans. This was certainly the impression he gave Charles Lindbergh on 24 May when the two of them had dinner together. What was more, Aiken seemed undisturbed that he was infuriating authorities in Washington by his tactics. Alluding to the two ships and the $500,000 worth of non-military supplies that the United States had offered Ireland, he commented sarcastically to Lindbergh. 'I'd hate like hell to think our nuisance value was only half a million dollars,' he said.[18]

The Irish emissary was obviously not worried that he was making a nuisance of himself in the eyes of the Roosevelt administration. Actions such as his tour addressing Irish-American groups, most of which were opposed to Roosevelt, or his associating with such people as Lindbergh, Flynn, Walsh and Cudahy (with whom he shared a reviewing platform during an Irish-American parade in mid-June) were certainly not calculated to win friends in the White House.

There was little doubt that Aiken was deliberately involving himself in domestic American politics by appealing directly to Irish-Americans over the head of their government. This was not the conclusion of the Americans alone; both Hempel and Vincenso Berardis, the Italian Minister to Ireland, were of the same opinion.[19] While such undiplomatic conduct may have been sound strategy in view of the international situation, it was certainly not good statesmanship, and American authorities were bitterly resentful of the foreign interference in their affairs.

Fine Gael leaders complained that Aiken was antagonising Washington by his actions. They warned that serious damage was being done to the traditionally cordial relations between the United States and Ireland. Richard Mulcahy privately asked that Aiken be recalled, but the Taoiseach rejected the suggestion. In fact, de Valera blamed the American Minister for the growing tension and said that he would demand Gray's recall if it were not for the latter's relationship with Roosevelt.[20]

De Valera's support of his own emissary could hardly have been surprising seeing that Aiken was obviously in line with government policy. Even members of the government with strong Allied sympathies like O'Kelly and Lemass had been warning of the danger of famine in Ireland on account of the supposed Anglo-German blockade, and de Valera himself had made essentially the same charge in his Christmas and St Patrick's Day addresses to the United States.

The Fianna Fáil government was exaggerating the dangers. From a purely Irish standpoint this was understandable because it lent an urgency to the need for increased agricultural production at home. Moreover, when conditions did not deteriorate to the extent forewarned, people tended to credit the government with having saved the situation.

The Fine Gael front bench was irate, however, over the charge that Britain was blockading Ireland. The accusation was false. Even though the British were exerting economic pressure, they had made no effort to introduce an actual blockade. Opposition leaders thought that de Valera was simply stirring up an anti-British issue in order to conceal his government's economic mismanagement. Yet when they tried to explain the situation, they found their efforts frustrated by the censor.

In a public speech on 19 May 1941, for example, Mulcahy criticised Aiken's actions in the United States and berated the government over its policy of accusing Britain of blockading Ireland. But when the *Irish Times* tried to report the speech, the censorship office ordered that most of the account should be deleted.

Although Mulcahy held the Taoiseach personally responsible for the rigidity of the censorship, Robert Smyllie, editor of the *Irish Times* explained that the 'long fellow'—as de Valera was often called—had been eager to be fair. The routine censorship duties, for which Aiken was nominally responsible, were undertaken by three men, Mike Knightly, a newspaperman; T. J. Coyne, who had been drafted from the Justice Department; and Joe Connolly.* Smyllie wrote that he had found 'Knightly reasonable, and even sympathetic, Coyne casuistically helpful, Joe Connolly a bitter anglophobe and Aiken unintelligently impossible. Whenever I have appealed to Caesar—and I have done so more than once—I have found the long fellow more than anxious to be fair.'[21]

---

* A fellow Ulsterman and a close friend of Aiken, Connolly was seconded from the Board of Works to head the censorship organisation. Coyne, who had been responsible for drafting the shadow plan of the organisation while at the Justice Department, acted as Connolly's assistant in overseeing the large staff engaged in the press, radio, and postal censoring, while Knightly, who had been drafted from the editorial staff of the parliamentary debates, took charge of the specific section dealing with the press.

7. Neutrals at Odds

US-IRISH RELATIONS IN THE MONTHS
BEFORE PEARL HARBOUR
May—December 1941

THE confrontation over the St Patrick's Day address marked the beginning of Gray's almost total disenchantment with de Valera. Henceforth he would hold the Taoiseach in contempt and made no further references to having any personal admiration for him. Yet the American Minister did not want the Fianna Fáil government to collapse, even though he was confident that Fine Gael would be more favourable to British and American interests.

Convinced that the Irish leader's political strength was based on an ability to exploit anti-British sentiment, Gray realised that de Valera would have to temper such exploitation while in power because of Ireland's economic dependence on the British. 'In my opinion and that of the leaders of the opposition,' Gray wrote to Duff Cooper, 'it would be very unfortunate if his government should fall, as in opposition he would be more difficult to deal with than at present.'[1]

Nevertheless the American Minister was most anxious to prevent de Valera from strengthening his political position at the expense of Fine Gael because, as he explained to Roosevelt the previous November, he wanted the Irish opposition strong enough to split the country, if the British ever delivered an ultimatum for the ports. Thus, it was to keep de Valera as politically weak as possible that Gray intervened in May 1941 when Churchill announced that the British government was thinking about extending compulsory military service to Northern Ireland.

In a telegram to the State Department Gray explained that conscription would probably have harmful repercussions for American interests, because de Valera would exploit the situation to his own political advantage, which would be at the expense of Fine Gael. 'It will seriously hamper the opposition on which we

must rely', the American Minister predicted, adding that he
could 'discover no reason why Ulster conscription should not
wait for several months'.

After sending his telegram he became even more convinced
about the danger involved, following discussion with Fine Gael
leaders. They outlined the disadvantages of the policy and fore-
cast that nationalists would resist conscription, draft dodgers
would be proclaimed as heroes, and the IRA would foment
trouble. James Dillon predicted that de Valera would rouse
anti-British feelings and would use the crisis to escape from
economic and political realities by enlisting the support of the
Roman Catholic cardinal for 'a Holy War'.

'All classes of opinion here unite in condemning the move as
calamitous', Gray explained in a further telegram to the State
Department. 'It appears to be a repetition of the same fatal
blunder made during the last war. The weak and failing Ulster
government is probably seeking to sustain itself by provoking a
crisis. Unless Great Britain is prepared from a military point of
view to seize the whole country it appears to be madness. So
little can be gained and so much lost.'

The American Minister noted that there would be few
nationalist conscripts, while thousands of Irish volunteers in the
British forces would become disaffected. In addition, the Irish
government, a majority of the Irish people, and the Irish army,
all of which had hitherto 'been inclined to be friendly' towards
Britain, would become definitely hostile and possibly give active
support to Germany. But what was 'most important of all', as far
as Gray was concerned, was that in the process Fine Gael would
be undermined 'and the opportunity for dividing the country on
the question of the ports will be lost for the duration' of the war.

The attitude of the island's only cardinal was, of course, of
great importance, especially since Joseph Cardinal MacRory was
himself from Northern Ireland. On 24 May 1941 he issued a
statement declaring that Ireland, which had been 'made one
by God, was partitioned by a foreign Power against the vehement
protest of its people'. He added that 'Conscription would now
seek to compel those who still writhe under this grievous wrong to
fight on the side of its perpetrators.'

There were demonstrations throughout Northern Ireland, with
public gatherings in Derry, Armagh, Newry, Omagh, Dungan-

non, Enniskillen, and Belfast. On 25 May a crowd of between five and ten thousand people gathered in Corrigan Park, Belfast, to voice their disapproval.

There was also an amount of disquiet in the British press. 'Our experiences in the last war proved the folly of seeking to conscript unwilling Irishmen,' warned the *News Chronicle*. 'The number of men conscripted would have to be offset by a considerable number of troops required to keep order.' The *Daily Express* predicted that if the measure were introduced, moderates in Northern Ireland would join the IRA, the people of the Twenty-Six counties would sympathise with them, border clashes would follow, and Britain would eventually find it necessary to re-occupy the whole island. *The Times* questioned whether enough men would be involved to justify the policy. It explained that there were 1,280,000 people in the Six Counties, of whom 623,000 were males and 200,000 of those were of draftable age. But this did not take into consideration either those who had already volunteered, or those who were working in defence plants. Consequently, it concluded that probably less than 100,000 men would be involved. The *Daily Telegraph* was more specific; it estimated that only 60,000 men would be eligible.

In the United States the controversy received extensive publicity. In fact, the *New York Times* afforded it more attention than did any Irish newspaper. Paul O'Dwyer, national chairman of the American Friends of Irish Neutrality, deplored the whole affair. 'It is a political move by the Churchill government to intimidate the Irish people into giving up their ports and bases, thus inviting destruction by German planes,' O'Dwyer asserted. 'Following the Axis pattern, provocative incidents undoubtedly will be created to provide an excuse for aggressive action against the Irish.'

According to the Belfast correspondent of the *New York Times*, 'The opposition to conscription has brought about almost complete unanimity between the various factions in Southern Ireland, as well as Nationalists and those with Nationalist tendencies in Northern Ireland.' For one of the few times since the Anglo-Irish Treaty was signed in 1921 the various segments of the Irish nationalist movement were in agreement—there could be no conscription in the Six Counties. Even the *Irish Times*, one of the last bastions of unionism in the Twenty-Six Counties, was opposed to the move. 'Writing as Irishmen who always have stood for the British connection,' the newspaper explained, 'we would appeal to the British government not to persist in its plan. The effect of conscription in the North to our domestic relations would be deplorable; in the long run its effect on British interests would be equally bad.'

Irish diplomats worked quietly behind the scenes in an effort to have the proposal dropped. In London on 22 May John Dulanty talked with Churchill, but to no avail. Next day in Ottawa John J. Hearne, the Irish High Commissioner, was more successful when he sought the intervention of the Canadian Prime Minister.[2]

Conscription was already an extremely controversial topic in Canada, where the French-speaking population was bitterly opposed to it. In fact, the Canadian government dared not draft men for service abroad until very late in the war because the whole issue provoked such intense feelings that talk of civil war had not been uncommon. Consequently, Mackenzie King was anxious that trouble over the issue should be avoided in Northern Ireland lest it should spill over on to the Canadian scene.

He warned Malcolm MacDonald, the British High Commissioner, that a conscription crisis could have severe consequences for the Allies. It would, he said, provoke intense resentment among Irish-American elements in the United States as well as among the Irish in Canada. On 25 May, therefore, the Prime Minister sent an urgent telegram to Churchill, explaining that he did not want the British cabinet to think that he was trying to interfere in its affairs by expressing his views on conscription :

I am sure, however, you will not misunderstand my motive if I suggest that, in case the step has not already been taken, it would be well to seek from the Ambassador at Washington an expression of his views as to the possible effect, especially at this very critical moment, upon Irish-American opinion and the attitude in the United States of a decision by the British government to enforce conscription in any part of Ireland. My colleagues and I would be grateful, if possible repercussion which such a step might have upon public opinion in Canada might also be considered. We are at the moment engaged in a recruiting campaign for further voluntary enlistments in Canada's armed forces for overseas service. The more it is possible to avoid the conscription issue becoming a matter of acute controversy, the less difficult, I feel sure, will be the task of maintaining Canadian unity.

Meanwhile the Americans were also working behind the scenes. In view of Gray's warnings, Roosevelt ordered that the American Ambassador in London should discuss the problem with Churchill. At the same time Gray tried to persuade de Valera to accept a compromise. When he showed him copies of his telegrams to Washington concerning the crisis, the Taoiseach seemed pleased. And when Gray suggested a plan whereby the Roman Catholic minority would be exempted from conscription, de Valera accepted the proposal, but he telephoned a few hours later to say that he had changed his mind and was not prepared to accept conscription in any form.

Gray became enraged and said that he would have nothing to do with the subject, if the Irish government was going to drag in the partition issue. He reportedly warned de Valera 'that in the interest of saving a tragic situation if he were not willing to accept a compromise without prejudice to his position he was taking a dangerous course and skating on thin ice'.[3]

William T. Cosgrave told Gray that he would accept an escape clause, but he added that the Taoiseach would not because he was looking for a political issue. While Gray was talking with Cosgrave, de Valera telephoned again, saying that since their previous conversation had been so unsatisfactory, he was explaining his position in a letter, which he was sending over. 'This', Gray wrote, 'was a very temperate reasonable document'.

Sir John Maffey agreed with the American Minister on the need to avoid conscription. He told Gray that the situation should be handled first, with a view to the American scene, next the protection of the Irish opposition, and finally, the military needs of Ulster. Following this conversation with the British representative, Gray warned Washington that although a clash with de Valera was 'probably inevitable', the conscription question was not the right issue on which to confront him.

On 26 May 1941 de Valera denounced conscription during a special sitting of the Dáil. 'The Six Counties are a part of

Ireland,' he said. 'They have always been a part of Ireland. No Act of Parliament can alter that fact.' He went on to assert that more than one-third of the population of Northern Ireland had been cut off from the rest of the country against their wishes. As a result, he warned that 'It would be an outrage to compel them to fight in the forces of another country which has done them, and continues to do them, grievous wrong.'

Both principal opposition leaders also spoke out. William Norton, leader of the Labour Party, declared that 'Conscription of our people in the Six Counties would be an outrage on every canon of liberty.' Cosgrave was more reserved, but no less forceful. Describing the whole question as 'exceedingly dangerous', he warned that if it were 'not properly handled it may involve not merely the future welfare, but the very existence of this State'.

That same day a very gloomy cabinet met in London. For in spite of the opposition of Gray, Maffey, Roosevelt, Mackenzie King, and Prime Minister Robert Menzies of Australia, Churchill wanted to go ahead with conscription. He argued that to back down would show irresolution, but he had very little support. Most of his cabinet colleagues were unimpressed. Sir Alexander Cadogan of the Foreign Office recorded in his diary that Churchill was in the habit of jumping to ill-considered decisions and then arguing that to recede from them would demonstrate weakness. But Cadogan himself saw it differently. 'It shows stupidity to jump to them,' he wrote.[4]

That evening Churchill told John Winant, the American Ambassador, that the cabinet had decided to forgo conscription. He explained that Northern Ireland's position had weakened during the past few days and it had become obvious that policing the border between the Six Counties and the rest of Ireland would probably absorb all the men drafted. Consequently the Prime Minister asked that Roosevelt be told that the proposal had been dropped and that the less made of the affair the better.

Churchill closed the matter on 28 May 1941 by telling parliament that after thorough consideration, the government had decided to drop the proposal. 'It would be more trouble than it was worth to enforce such a policy,' he said.

Sir John Andrews, who had taken over as Prime Minister of Northern Ireland after Craigavon's death the previous autumn, accepted the decision without protest. He said that London knew what was best for the war effort, but he added that he and his colleagues had always believed that conscription would be particularly good for the Six Counties. 'It places all classes and creeds on the same level', he said, 'and each man is told just where his duty is, whether it is in the fighting forces of the crown, in the workshop making indispensable implements of war or on the farms producing the necessities of life.'

Just as the draft in the United States had the effect of eventually breaking down some racial prejudice by forcing the races to associate, conscription in Northern Ireland could have helped ease some of the religious intolerance. This was what Andrews apparently hoped would happen, but de Valera was sure that the effect would be exactly opposite. He believed that the overwhelming majority of Roman Catholics would resist conscription, thereby creating further tensions.

The balance of Irish history would seem to support de Valera's position. The *Round Table*, the intellectually orientated journal serving the British Commonwealth, was surprised that the cabinet in London had even given a second thought to conscription. 'That such a project was ever seriously considered under present conditions', the journal's authority on Ireland wrote, 'makes one wonder whether the British cabinet has any competent adviser on Irish affairs.'

Upon hearing of Churchill's decision to let matters stand, de Valera telephoned the American Minister to thank him for his help. He was convinced that Gray had played a major role in averting trouble. Yet the Taoiseach was still not prepared to modify his adherence to neutrality.

Even after the Germans again bombed Dublin on the night of 30 May 1941, killing thirty-four people, injuring ninety, and damaging hundreds of homes, de Valera made no effort to excite public opinion against the Nazis. It was therefore obvious that he had not weakened in his determination to remain neutral.

'I don't think de Valera is going to change his line unless forced to do so', Gray wrote to Roosevelt on 9 June 1941. 'He has deliberately passed up the chance to excite anti-German feeling over the recent bombing. He has in fact clamped down on expression of anti-German feeling. He either has an understanding with the Germans on which he relies or what is more likely he is blindly taking the thousand to one chance that he can escape involvement.'

In view of Gray's recent co-operation, Joseph P. Walshe approached him about supporting further Irish efforts to secure American arms. But the American Minister made it clear that he would not help unless de Valera were prepared to guarantee that if Germany invaded, Ireland would get into the war 'without reservations' and would make Irish facilities available to both Britain and the United States.

Writing to Roosevelt on 9 June, Gray explained that de Valera would probably not put up anything but a token opposition to a German invasion. If the Germans attacked, he predicted that the Taoiseach would say that neither Britain nor the United States had been willing to arm Ireland properly, so he was not going to have the Irish slaughtered in a fight with Germany.

Gray's letter apparently had an effect on Roosevelt, who was under intense Irish-American pressure to arm Ireland. When asked at a press-conference on 27 June 1941 if he had made any concession to a delegation of Irish-Americans who had called on him recently, the President replied that he had told them that some rifles might be available, but no ammunition. He then went on to imply that a stumbling block had been the unwillingness of the Irish to give 'some fairly definite assurance that they will defend themselves against any German attack'.

One reporter then asked if the Irish government had ever given any assurance that it would resist a German invasion.

'No. No,' replied the President.

The Irish were indignant at Roosevelt's reply. De Valera complained that he had given Gray assurances on a number of occasions.[5] The latter agreed and said that he personally had passed on the information to the State Department, so he did not know the reason for the President's statement. What Gray did not explain, however, was that he had, in effect, advised Roosevelt not to believe the assurances.

The Irish Minister in Washington protested to the State Department that, in addition to the assurances given to Gray personally, the Taoiseach had stated in various public speeches and newspaper interviews that he would resist any invader. Moreover, Aiken had made the same point in conversations with Roosevelt, Vice-President Henry Wallace, Hull, Welles,

Acheson, and others. Brennan added that his government was therefore at a loss to understand why Roosevelt had made such a statement.

Some weeks later Sumner Welles closed the affair by explaining that the President had not meant to question the willingness of the Irish to defend themselves, but, rather, their ability to do so successfully. He added that Roosevelt was opposed to arming Ireland because Dublin had not made proper preparations to receive British help in the event of an attack. As a result any arms that the United States might supply would be likely to fall into enemy hands, if such an attack took place.

In the letter that apparently prompted Roosevelt's remarks concerning Ireland's failure to give adequate assurances to resist a German invasion, Gray also reiterated the importance of being able to use Fine Gael to divide the Irish people, if the United States should decide to seize Irish facilities. He suggested, for example, that Roosevelt should publicly offer Ireland some anti-aircraft guns in order 'to combat "German barbarism"'. Of course, it was obvious that Dublin would refuse any offer made in such a way, but the important thing was that it would make a favourable impression on the Irish people. 'Keep the people behind us and the Opposition,' Gray counselled. 'Then if you have to do anything you can split the country.'

In his next letter to the President on 26 June 1941, Gray suggested a scheme that could be used in order to secure the ports. In accordance with it, the British would cut off all supplies to Ireland and allow famine conditions to develop. Then the United States would adopt the attitude that since Americans had helped Ireland during the Great Famine of the previous century,[6] they would do so again. But they would now claim that naval and air facilities were necessary to protect ships carrying supplies to Ireland. Since it was 'certain' that de Valera would refuse these facilities, the United States would just seize them, declaring that the action had been taken in order to ensure the continued delivery of supplies, so that the Irish people would not 'suffer from the obstinate stupidity of their present government'.

Gray explained that Fine Gael would 'probably' accept a seizure in this manner with gratification, and he also noted that a majority of the Irish people would agree, even though they would be opposed to giving up the ports if consulted in advance. At the very essence of this scheme was Gray's belief that Dillon would be able to command enough support to split the Dáil. But it soon became apparent that the deputy leader of Fine Gael would not have had the kind of backing envisioned by the American Minister.

Dillon, who genuinely thought that Ireland's own long term interest lay in actively supporting the Allies, had already tried to persuade the Fine Gael shadow cabinet to seek a declaration of war in March 1941. He argued then that the Irish people had a moral responsibility to help the democracies. In addition he noted that the war offered an opportunity to end partition.

Contending that the United States would soon be in the war, Dillon explained that Gray had told him that if Ireland helped, Roosevelt would insist on ending partition at the post-war peace conference. Although some of the Fine Gael leaders were interested in the possibility of a bargain concerning the Ulster question, there was no real support for a declaration of war under existing circumstances because, as T. F. O'Higgins noted, the overwhelming majority of the electorate favoured neutrality.[7]

Nevertheless Dillon was a courageous politician who was not merely content to lead people in the direction they were going; he was anxious to direct them where he thought they should be headed. As a result he was prepared to go against the tide of public opinion.

On 18 July 1941 he spoke out publicly in the Dáil. Admitting that 'the government's policy of indifferent neutrality' had the support of not only a majority of Fianna Fáil, but also a majority of the Irish people and even most of the members of Fine Gael, Dillon nevertheless contended that the policy was wrong. Ireland, he argued, should provide whatever facilities the United States and Britain desired.

The Dáil was shocked. One Fianna Fáil deputy interrupted the proceedings, referred to Dillon as a 'cornerboy' and called for his expulsion from the house. 'If he doesn't shut his—mouth', the deputy added, 'we will shut it for him.'

Members of Fine Gael were no less surprised by the speech of their own deputy leader. Richard Mulcahy immediately disassociated himself from his colleague's views. And Cosgrave followed with a reasoned appeal. He argued that the best thing that members of the Dáil could do was to demonstrate 'that we are united in the view that neutrality is the best policy for the country at the moment' and also 'that we are united in the view that, if aggression comes, a united country will meet it'.

In contrast with Dillon's speech, which received no open support in the Dáil, Cosgrave's address was well received. As a result the American Minister had to reconsider his advice concerning the best means of securing the ports.

It was noteworthy that the next plan that Gray mentioned did not envision using either Dillon or Fine Gael. Writing to Roosevelt on 28 July 1941, the Minister outlined a scheme suggested to him by some Irishman, whom he at first identified but then cut the name out of the letter in order to preserve the proposer's anonymity. He explained that the suggestion was 'an idea in which there is merit if the British could understand it'.

The scheme, which was essentially in line with what the Irish feared the British were trying to do with the propaganda campaign in the summer of 1940, called for the British to give Ireland 'mediocre elderly rifles, a balloon barrage and such other out of date conspicuous equipment as could be spared by the Home Guard as they get equipped with modern stuff'. Britain would then publicise the gift by having someone object to it in parliament, and the government would respond by suggesting that it had handed over the equipment in accordance with a secret agreement reached with de Valera. Then by broadcasting this on radio a few times, either the IRA or the Germans might be provoked into taking action that would bring Ireland into the war. 'You have to fight fire with fire', Gray explained to the President, 'and glory be to God *you* understand this situation.'

It is important to stress here, however, that Gray did not actually advocate that this policy should be pursued, or that the ports should be seized. He was only suggesting ideas that could be of use in the event that either Washington or London decided that it needed Irish facilities. At the time he could not determine whether the ports were really needed or not.

Nevertheless in conversations with various people both inside and outside of government, the American Minister maintained that the facilities were important and he adopted the aggrieved attitude of one who had helped Ireland but received nothing except trouble in return. Every chance he got he stressed that Washington resented that Aiken had, by addressing Irish-American groups opposed to United States foreign policy, given what was tantamount to the Irish government's approval to Roosevelt's critics. Consequently, Gray emphasised that the United States would no longer be willing to make any sacrifices for Ireland. 'It is a great shock to them', he wrote, 'that we have a grievance and that we do not take kindly to their playing their politics in *our* yard.' It was not that Washington was questioning Ireland's right to remain neutral, he explained, but that 'majority opinion in America would not sanction our making sacrifices for people who will do nothing for us.'

It was probably inevitable that Gray and de Valera should clash, given their different political outlooks. For the American Minister, Irish independence was little better than sublime non-sense, because Ireland was too small to be really independent. The Irish relied on Britain for their economic stability and political freedom, seeing that without Britain to stave off the Nazis, there could be little doubt that Hitler would overrun Ireland. As a result Gray viewed Irish neutrality as ridiculous. He thought that Ireland should recognise her dependence on the British and should support them completely.

Gray explained the situation to Roosevelt on 11 August 1941 :

If Britain completely shuts off coal and gasoline this place would be a disorganised and howling wilderness in three months. There would be no transport except by water and horse and Dublin is a city of 600,000 people with distribution problems which you can picture for yourself. It probably would be a wise thing to do to explode this nationalistic dream of 'self-sufficiency' and this glorification of non-co-operation and opposition to federation with their neighbours. It's all pathetic.

Whether it was pathetic or not, the Irish government's opposition to a federation with Britain was certainly understandable in 1941. After all it was barely twenty years since de Valera and his colleagues were engaged in a life and death struggle to withdraw from a union with Britain.

Although Gray realised that he was making himself very unpopular in Dublin, he was not worried. For one thing, he was sure that Roosevelt approved of his actions, seeing that there had been no word of caution or reproach from the White House. In fact, two short letters which the President wrote to him during August 1941 could be considered an encouragement. On 2 August Roosevelt's only reference to Irish affairs was a cryptic exclamation, apparently referring to de Valera and Aiken : 'Praise the Lord', he wrote, 'you have got the number of certain persons in the Emerald Isle !' Three weeks later the President echoed Gray's own sentiments on the economic situation. 'It is a rather dreadful thing to say', he wrote, 'but I must admit that if factories close in Ireland and there is a great deal more suffering there, there will be less general sympathy in the United States than if it happened six months ago. People are, frankly, getting pretty fed up with my old friend Dev.'[8]

A second and more important reason why Gray was not worried about antagonising Irish authorities was because he was convinced that American policy was forcing Dublin to co-operate with Britain and that Anglo-Irish relations were on a better footing as a result. During September 1941 he told John Winant and Myron Taylor, the American representative to the Vatican, that the British had been having a certain amount of success by giving Ireland specific defence equipment. He explained that British policy was 'to conciliate the Irish army and to obtain its goodwill by procuring from time to time equipment, which it greatly needs, but of a nature which in the event of an Anglo-Irish crisis would not seriously threaten Britain'.[9]

It was a measure of the improved Anglo-Irish relations that, on 5 October 1941, de Valera publicly praised Britain during a speech in Mullingar. 'So far', he said, 'our rights have been in the main respected, and I think it is only fair in this connection to acknowledge that the belligerent nearest to us, Great Britain, in spite of temptation and the urgings of certain propagandists, has not succumbed to them and has not behaved unworthily.'

At the time some Irish-Americans believed that a member of the Irish parliament, Senator Frank MacDermot, was acting as an unfavourable propagandist in the United States. On the same day as de Valera's Mullingar speech, the American Friends of Irish Neutrality (AFIN) called on the Irish government to have MacDermot recalled to Ireland on the grounds that his presence in the United States was 'undesirable to many millions of American citizens'. The organisation had taken exception to a radio broadcast in which MacDermot asked for arms for Ireland and then added that Americans 'might reasonably do even more for us than send us arms'. This, the Kerry-born secretary of AFIN, Michael McGlynn, interpreted as 'an invitation to the United States to occupy Irish ports and bases'.[10]

Members of AFIN believed that MacDermot was being used by a newly formed group, the Committee for American Irish Defence (CAID), which consisted mainly of American writers of Irish extraction. On 11 September 1941 that group called on the Irish government to allow the United States to establish naval and air bases in Ireland. 'And, in return for the use of such bases,' the committee summoned 'the United States to grant Ireland substantial aid in arms and other materials under the Lend-Lease Bill.'

AFIN wanted to combat this propaganda, but it was seriously in need of money. It could not match the resources of CAID, which it suspected was being financed by the British. It was ironic that while Gray was annoyed at the Irish government for involving itself with Irish-American groups like AFIN, members of AFIN were bitterly critical that they had not been able to get any help from the Dublin government or its representatives in the United States. At an executive council meeting of the organisation in New York on 18 September 1941, for example, Sean Keating, a Cork-born member of the executive, was applauded when he condemned Brennan and his staff :

They have failed to co-operate with us in any way. I refuse to be a fall guy for either the Minister at Washington or the Consular Service here. We have been entirely too silent. The government needs strong men. We are trying to do a job for Ireland but can't get an ounce of co-operation. I may be speaking out of order, but I must have my say. In Washington this committee of writers organised to put forth British propaganda was formed under the very eyes of the Irish Legation. I think AFIN should resent that. We should send our government representatives to posts where initiative isn't needed and put somebody else in their places.

AFIN was up against a well-financed committee, which was really a front for activities that might conveniently be compared with some of the subsequent covert operations of the CIA. In fact, Col. William J. Donovan, who later organised the CIA, was intimately involved with CAID. This was exposed in early November 1941 by Senator Burton K. Wheeler of Montana who somehow got hold of the minutes of a meeting held in Donovan's Washington office on 8 October 1941. The meeting, which was attended mainly by representatives of United States government departments, discussed the launching of a CAID campaign to gather petitions to demonstrate Irish-American support for Roosevelt's foreign policy.

Wheeler, who was a bitter opponent of the President, denounced the government representatives for their part in the whole affair:

> They are thinking about what is good for the British Empire and they are not acting as either the friends of the Irish people or of the American people when representatives of three or four Government offices in Washington are being used by Colonel Donovan and his Co-ordination of Information Bureau to bring into existence the fraudulent Irish Defence Committee to fool the Irish in America, and to fool the Americans themselves, and to fool the Irish in Ireland in order to get both Ireland and the United States into this wicked war.

By this time Irish authorities actually distrusted the Americans more than the British. At least, this was the conclusion of John D. Kearney, who had become Canadian High Commissioner to Ireland in August 1941, following the death of his predecessor. De Valera complained to Kearney that the State Department did not understand Ireland's problems, but the real Irish ire was reserved for Gray, whose criticism of Irish neutrality was greatly resented.[11]

Joseph Walshe actually asked Kearney to try to get Gray recalled. He contended that a new minister would probably be able to secure Irish bases for the Americans, if the United States entered the war and could guarantee an end to partition.

Both Maffey and Gray told the Canadian representative, however, that Walshe was probably not reflecting de Valera's attitude. They were convinced that the Taoiseach would not give up the ports, and Kearney began to suspect that they were right. He therefore decided to ask the Taoiseach personally.

On 20 November 1941 de Valera confirmed what Maffey and Gray had predicted. The Dublin government would not give bases to anyone. 'I ascertained that even a promise of unity of Ireland would not alter his attitude,' reported Kearney, who concluded that 'Mr de Valera's attitude on neutrality seems to be based upon principle. He has for years held the view that in the event of a war between great nations, small countries like Ireland should remain neutral under any circumstances except direct attack.'[12]

Not only did the Taoiseach show no inclination of allowing the United States to use any bases in the Twenty-Six Counties, but he even demanded that his government should be consulted if the United States ever decided to assume control of any facilities in Northern Ireland. His demand was sparked by reports that the Americans were building bases in Northern Ireland.

During the summer Roosevelt had admitted that American technicians were constructing a base on Lough Foyle, but he said that they were working in the capacity of ordinary citizens and that they were being paid by the British. When de Valera learned about this, he told Gray that he expected to be consulted if the United States ever decided to use the bases. The Taoiseach explained that while he recognised the 'de facto occupation' of the Six Counties by Britain, he was not waiving Dublin's claim to sovereignty over the area.[13]

Somewhat indignant, Gray replied that the Dublin government would have to take the matter up with the State Department through the Irish Minister. Realising that the Americans were building the base for themselves in case the United States entered the war—which he confidently anticipated—Gray began telling people that the Americans were putting all their 'defences into Northern Ireland and that Ireland could in effect get its own supplies and arms'.

Other than his demand that he be consulted if the United States ever decided to seek facilities in the Six Counties, de Valera apparently ignored Gray's assertions about basing American defences in Northern Ireland. In early October 1941, however, the *Daily Mail* published an article on the progress being made by the American technicians and suggested that Americans should man the base. Disturbed by the article, the Taoiseach instructed Brennan to find out what Washington's intentions were in the Six Counties.[14]

At first Brennan tried informally. But when this failed, he sent a formal diplomatic note to the State Department.

On 18 November 1941 the Americans replied to the inquiry in blunt diplomatic language to the effect that the Irish should mind their own business. Hull later recalled that Roosevelt authorised the State Department to say that the 'inquiry related to territory recognised by this government as part of the United Kingdom, and to suggest that the Irish government address its inquiry to the United Kingdom government'.[15] The President's contemptuous treatment of de Valera's claim to sovereignty over Northern Ireland was an indication of the extent to which relations between Dublin and Washington had deteriorated, even before the United States became an overt belligerent.

8. The United States Enters the War

AMERICAN TROOPS IN NORTHERN IRELAND
December 1941—October 1942

AFTER learning of the attack on Pearl Harbour, Churchill cabled de Valera: 'Now is your chance. Now or never. "A Nation once again." Am very ready to meet you at any time.'[1]

De Valera understood the elliptical message as an invitation for him to go to London in order to discuss with Churchill how Ireland would help the Allies so that sufficient goodwill could be built up to dissipate Belfast's opposition to Irish unity. In other words it was another vague offer to end partition in return for an Irish alliance. Believing that there was no possibility of such talks bearing fruit, the Taoiseach refused to go to London but suggested instead that Lord Cranborne, the Dominions Secretary, should come to Dublin.

Churchill quickly approved of the suggested visit. He hoped that Dublin might be willing to conclude an alliance seeing that there had been many changes on the international scene since June 1940 when his government first tried to persuade the Taoiseach to abandon neutrality. For one thing the entry of the United States into the war made Irish neutrality at once both more difficult to defend and easier to abandon.

The policy was harder to defend, on the one hand, because Ireland could no longer rely on the support of Irish-American nationalists. They were Americans first and in time of war were likely to rally to the support of their government, notwithstanding the meagre sympathy that it had shown for Irish neutrality. This change in their attitude became very apparent with the disbanding of AFIN within days of the Pearl Harbour attack.

American involvement also made it easier for Dublin to adopt a new policy, because instead of having to ask the Irish people to support Britain, a traditional enemy, the government could call on them to aid the United States, a long-standing friend. In addition two other factors strengthened de Valera's hand.

First, the prospects for an Allied victory had become incalculably greater than when the British were fighting almost alone with victory looking virtually impossible. Then, the Taoiseach would have had to ask the Irish people to support a likely loser, but with the United States and the Soviet Union also fighting Hitler, he could call on them to join with a possible, if not probable, victor. The second major factor was the decline in the danger of civil war with the arrest of virtually the entire leadership of the IRA, following a bitter wrangle within the organisation.

Some members of the IRA had kidnapped Stephen Hayes, their Chief of Staff. They accused him of being an agent of the de Valera government, held him incommunicado for several weeks, convened a mock trial, and sentenced him to death as a traitor. They then tortured him, forcing him to write a confession of his supposed treachery.

While writing this confession Hayes managed to escape and turned himself over to the police for protection. Widespread arrests of IRA members quickly followed and the organisation was thrown into almost total disarray. But what was probably even more damaging was that the torture of Hayes provoked a general revulsion throughout the country, seriously undermining the public sympathy on which the IRA was so dependent. As a result the organised republican opposition that would have resisted any effort to ally with Britain had been greatly weakened and the Dublin government was in a stronger position to join with the Allies than at any time in the past.

De Valera quickly showed, however, that he did not have the slightest intention of abandoning neutrality. Speaking in Cork on 14 December 1941 he sympathised with the United States over the Japanese attack, but added that Ireland's policy was going to remain unchanged. 'We can only be a friendly neutral,' he said. From the moment the war began, neutrality was the only policy possible. 'Any other policy', he explained, 'would have divided our people, and for a divided people to fling itself into this war would be to commit suicide.' Yet the Taoiseach was under no illusions about the difficulties on the road ahead. 'We are fully aware', he said, 'that in a world at war each set of belligerents are ever ready to regard those who are not with them as against them, but the course we have followed is a just course.'

On meeting Lord Cranborne three days later de Valera was adamant about remaining neutral—not that the Dominions Secretary was offering much in the way of a bargain. He was not. He simply claimed that Stormont would probably agree to some form of unity after the war, if Dublin supported the Allies.

In reply de Valera reiterated essentially the same argument that he had put forward in Cork. As long as Ireland was partitioned, he said, it would not be possible to secure adequate unity within the Twenty-Six Counties for a declaration of war. He therefore asked for a promise that Britain would respect Irish neutrality.

Cranborne explained that he could not give a firm commitment for unforeseen circumstances. But, he added, the gesture in handing over arms could be taken as proof that London did not actually intend to invade Ireland. He later admitted that he was not dissatisfied with the interview, in spite of his failure to win over de Valera.

The following week Roosevelt also made an unsuccessful effort to influence the Taoiseach with a message warning that Ireland's freedom was at stake in the war. 'No longer can it be doubted', the President declared, 'that the policy of Hitler and his Axis associates is the conquest of the entire world and the enslavement of all mankind.'

The Canadians made no effort to influence de Valera because their representative was satisfied with the situation as it stood. 'It has been demonstrated', Kearney explained in a report to Ottawa, 'that the Irish government will do almost anything to help us short of involving themselves in the war.' With approval of the Dáil necessary for a declaration of war, Kearney thought that the Taoiseach had no choice but to remain neutral because the Irish people were clearly opposed to involvement in the conflict. 'So long as Ireland is partitioned', he wrote, 'the only thing that could unite them for war purposes is invasion—just as it required a declaration of war by Japan to unite the Americans.'[2]

The American Minister, however, was ignorant of the extent of the secret Anglo-Irish co-operation, so he was not content to simply accept the situation without exerting some pressure on Ireland. What he also did not realise was that the British had already been pursuing a policy of economic pressure. Since

Britain's exports to Ireland had only declined by approximately one-third during 1941, he did not suspect that the British were not being candid when they explained that trade cuts had been due to a need for shipping space.

Now that the United States was in the war, the British no longer needed to worry about their Irish policy antagonising American public opinion. Gray therefore believed that it was only logical that Britain should adopt really stringent economic measures against Ireland. In a letter to Roosevelt on 17 December 1941 he predicted that 'No one will need to go hungry but the economic life of the country is going to be squeezed and the protected industrialists who have been such strong neutrals are going to get theirs.' By forcing Irish factories to close and by generally disrupting the country's economic life, Gray hoped that the Irish people could be turned against neutrality and could thus be persuaded to give up the ports.

Writing some years later Robert Brennan contended that any student of Irish history would have known that an economic blockade would have produced results opposite to those desired.[3] The American Minister was actually no exception. He realised that the policy he was advocating would backfire unless its coercive design was carefully concealed from the Irish people. He therefore advocated in a letter to Roosevelt on 1 January 1942 that the economic pressure should be tempered with protestations of American friendship:

> The severer these pressures, the better, as it is the only way in which the Irish people can be made to realise the fatuity of their government's programme. But the severer they are, the more need for expressions of good-will and token offerings similar in spirit to the sterile friendliness of Mr de Valera. The Cosgraveites, except Dillon, have been as strong for neutrality as de Valera. But it may dawn on them sooner than on him that in this world we get what we give and that a policy which leaves Ireland without a friend is unprofitable.

Since Britain supplied ninety per cent of Ireland's imports, British support was necessary if the economic pressure was to be fruitful. Yet London showed no inclination of following Gray's lead. Churchill, for one, was stoutly opposed to giving de Valera even token arms at the time. Consequently, relations with

Ireland were on essentially the same footing on 26 January 1942 when Maffey informed the Taoiseach of the impending arrival of American troops in Northern Ireland.

Churchill and Roosevelt had decided to station three divisions of United States troops in the Six Counties, where they could complete their training, while British soldiers stationed in the areas could be used elsewhere. It was hoped that the replacement of the British troops by Americans might even help to further improve Anglo-Irish relations. But such was not to be the case.

Although Maffey had implored him not to protest against the landing, de Valera issued a public statement explaining that while the Irish people harboured no hostility towards the United States, it was his 'duty to make it clearly understood that no matter what troops occupy the Six Counties, the Irish people's claim for the union of the whole national territory and for supreme jurisdiction over it, will remain unabated'.

The American Minister believed that de Valera's action had been partly an expression of personal frustration and partly an attempt to satisfy republican elements within Fianna Fáil who were annoyed that the failure of United States officials to consult Dublin prior to the landing was tantamount to a public rejection of Irish claims to sovereignty over the Six Counties. Gray, for his part, was disturbed lest the statement should inflame passions in Northern Ireland against the American troops. He fully realised that there was a possibility that the Americans could get into trouble with the nationalist minority in the area. 'We might as well face the fact that the chance of American troops getting into trouble with the Irish civilian population is much greater than of British troops' he wrote, 'for the Irish are used to British troops and get on with them.'[4]

More determined than ever to bring the Irish government to heel by using economic pressure, Gray suggested that without waiting for Britain to act, the United States should put an embargo on petrol for Ireland and should prohibit Irish ships from travelling in American convoys. 'I think the British are boobs not to adopt the same policy,' he wrote to Roosevelt on 27 January 1942. 'Why should coal be rationed in Britain yet exported to Éire, or why should gasoline that we need be sent to Éire? It is not coercion; it is simple justice.'

That very day, however, there was an excellent example of just why the British were unwilling to pursue such a policy. An American pilot serving with the Eagle Squadron of the RAF landed in Dublin, but insead of interning him, as they did with all German pilots, Irish officials quietly refuelled his plane and allowed him to return to his base.

Gray viewed the incident as de Valera's way of indicating that Dublin was not really bitter over the arrival of American troops. As a result there was a certain amount of confusion over whether or not the Taoiseach intended that his statement should be viewed as a protest. Although most Irish newspapers and the international press generally featured the word 'protest', de Valera's own newspaper carried the caption, 'Statement by Mr de Valera'. So after discussing the affair amongst themselves, the Allied representatives in Dublin decided that Kearney should seek a clarification from the Taoiseach.

On 31 January de Valera explained that the statement should not actually be considered a protest. The Canadian representative reported:

> Mr de Valera made it clear that he felt obliged to make some statement in case silence might be interpreted as acquiescence in the status of partition. He also told me that he feared a worsening of relationship between Ireland and the United States by reason of the presence of the American troops in the North, because the American soldier would not understand the Irish the way the British soldier did, and if the nationalist minority . . . showed resentment at the arrival of the American troops, they might take offence—whereas the British soldier, under similar circumstances, would not.

Although the Taoiseach saw his pronouncement as a simple statement, it was taken as a protest in the United States where it was greatly resented, and there were reports of a rise in anti-Irish feelings among the American people.

The San Francisco *Leader* was disturbed by what it believed was an anti-Irish trend among the communications media, especially radio commentaries and films. It reported that villains on the screen were being given Irish names and advertising reminiscent of Know-Nothing days, with the 'No Irish Need Apply', was appearing in large cities in the eastern part of the country.

The *Leader* also noted that an unscrupulous campaign was being waged against Irish neutrality, involving the major wire services, Associated Press and United Press. At the same time numerous large daily newspapers were again calling on de Valera to allow the Allies to use Irish bases—among them the previously isolationist New York *Daily News*.[5]

The trend of American opinion appeared to lend credibility to German propaganda asserting that the United States was making industrious preparations for an invasion of Ireland. Seeing that Berlin had already used this type of propaganda to justify what were supposed to be pre-emptive invasions of various neutrals, there were grounds for renewed speculation about Hitler's intentions towards Ireland.

Gray, for one, was worried that the Germans might make a desperate effort to gain control of Ireland in order to knock Britain out of the war before the United States was properly mobilised. He thought, for instance, that Germany might be able to seize Irish airfields with an airborne invasion. Then with the aid of air cover, the Germans would 'undoubtedly' be able to land an invasion convoy on the south coast of Ireland and, if they gained control of the island, they would have little difficulty defeating Britain.

Mindful of the strategic importance of the island, the American Minister wanted to improve his government's popularity in Ireland, so in a letter to Roosevelt on 16 February 1942 he suggested that Washington should 'swallow de Valera's protest and make a token gift to sweeten the Irish people'. He actually proposed that the best gift would be some fighter planes, because the Allies could always render them useless, if necessary, by cutting off petrol supplies to Ireland. Concluding the letter, he suggested that the President should do something to counter the German propaganda concerning American intentions towards Ireland without much delay.

The response to the suggestion came, not in the form of an arms shipment, as Gray had hoped, but a personal assurance from the President. On 26 February Roosevelt sent de Valera a note explaining that there never had been 'the slightest thought or intention of invading Irish territory or threatening Irish security'. Instead of posing a danger to the Irish people, he claimed that the presence of American troops 'can only contribute to the security of Ireland and of the whole British Isles, as well as furthering our total war effort'.

Nothing ever came of the suggestion to furnish the Irish army with additional arms, because Britain was firmly opposed to the idea and Washington was prepared to defer to London on such matters concerning Ireland. The British were satisfied with the existing policy, as they realised that the Taoiseach had done great damage to himself by his statement concerning the arrival of American troops. Cranborne therefore believed that the best policy was 'to sit tight and let him make a few more mistakes'.[6]

At the same time London was tightening its economic pressure on Ireland, with the result that many factories were forced to close as they could not get either sufficient fuel or raw materials. The efficiency of the transportation system was seriously impaired when the cut back in coal supplies hit the railroads, and the decline in petrol forced the government to ban the private use of that fuel in 1942. The same year authorities were also forced to ration bread and clothing, in addition to the rationing introduced earlier on sugar, tea, and fuel. By 1943 the country's normal requirements of tea had been cut to 25 per cent, textiles to 22 per cent, petrol to 20 per cent, coal gas to 16 per cent, and paraffin to less than 15 per cent.[7]

An intensive turf-cutting campaign partly eased the energy shortage but, while the native peat was sufficient to keep homes warm, it proved to be a very poor industrial substitute. Still there was no real shortage of essential food in Ireland. Meat, eggs, and dairy produce were in plentiful supply, and the government pursued a compulsory programme to increase tillage. In October 1941 it ordered that 25 per cent of arable land holdings of ten or more statute acres had to be cultivated.[8] Later, as yields fell due to the fertiliser shortage, the area for minimum cultivation was increased to thirty-seven and a half per cent.[9] The country was thereby able to produce ample vegetables and about three-quarters of its normal wheat requirement. The food situation was actually good enough in March 1943 for the government to decide to send two cargoes of potatoes, sugar, and other supplies to Spanish refugees.[10]

A couple of basic factors prevented the overall economic situation from deteriorating to the extent that Gray believed possible. First of all the unemployment situation was never as grave as it might have been, because many of those who lost their jobs due to factory closures were absorbed by the army recruiting campaign. Others found employment in turf-cutting and in the agricultural sector, and many more emigrated to Britain. De Valera later revealed that 124,500 men and 58,000 women went to Britain and Northern Ireland between 1940 and 1945. The volume of emigration actually threatened to bring about a shortage in the labour force, so the government ordered in October 1941 that 'travel permits should not be granted to persons, whether men or women, who are employed or for whom employment is immediately available in this country.'[11] The second factor mitigating the severity of the economic dislocation was Britain's unwillingness to introduce a complete embargo on supplies to Ireland, because the London government was anxious to continue some of its Irish trade. The parliamentary secretary to the British Minister of transport explained that 'drastically reduced' exports of petroleum were being sent to Ireland in order 'to ensure the continued export to the United Kingdom of valuable agricultural products received from Éire'.[12]

In mid-March 1942 Gray actually learned to his dismay that the British had concluded a deal for Irish beer in return for 30,000 tons of wheat. Since the wheat fulfilled some of Ireland's most pressing needs, the American Minister complained to Maffey that the deal 'suspends the operation of augmenting economic pressures and postpones the only position which is favourable to our obtaining our greatest desideratum, "the ports"'. The American people, he added, would not understand why Britain had used shipping for the benefit of Ireland when the Irish government was unwilling to help the Allies. If beer had been essential, he suggested that 'the wheat should have been given as a highly publicised humane gesture'.[13]

What was especially exasperating was that some people in de Valera's own party were so ungrateful. Gray noted, for example, that Martin Corry, a Fianna Fáil deputy from Cork, had recently told the Dáil that the British people were so badly off that they were supposedly eating crows, and he added that he would not shed any tears if they were reduced to eating rats.

One explanation for Gray's inability to understand London's reluctance to adopt more stringent economic measures against Ireland was because he still did not know the true extent of the secret co-operation between the British and Irish military. But his condemnation of the beer-wheat deal apparently prompted the British to confide in him about the military liaison—the extent of which did genuinely surprise him. On 23 March 1942 he reported to the State Department 'that a mutual good feeling and confidence have been established between the Irish and British Military chiefs beyond what might reasonably have been believed possible. Unquestionably, the transfer of certain unimportant armament has been the prime factor in this success.'[14]

With the aid of Lieutenant Colonel John Reynolds, the United States military attaché, Gray prepared an extensive report on the military situation in Ireland. He allowed Irish authorities to study the document which put a great deal of emphasis not only on the danger of a German attack, but also on the importance of helping the Dublin government to maintain morale in the Irish army at as high a level as possible. 'The concession of such armament to the Irish Army as may be available', he wrote, 'is the most practical way of attaining this end.'[15]

The report was actually written partly 'for Irish consumption'. In covering letters to the President and the Secretary of State, Gray explained that he was still only looking for 'token' concessions.[16] He wrote to Hull, for instance, that the proposal was 'purely a political gesture for political ends'. While in a letter to Roosevelt he requested that in addition to handing over 'token arms', he should be instructed to tell Irish authorities that Washington found it 'undesirable to freeze any armament of importance where it could be used against the enemy only under certain circumstances and conditions'. In other words, the Irish should not expect significant help unless they were prepared to furnish some direct assistance against the Axis powers.

'I think if you gave them some "good-will" arms', the American Minister concluded, 'you could take back the two ships which you let them charter under pleas of emergency needs and gain by it.' It was apparent that the knowledge of the extent of the Anglo-Irish military liaison had not even temporarily weakened Gray's desire to eventually exert economic pressure on Ireland.

Of course de Valera, who had been shown the report suggesting that American arms be supplied to Ireland, could not have known what the American Minister was secretly advocating. He apparently took the report at face value and again began to hope that the arms help first promised in the summer of 1940 might yet be forthcoming. So when there was still no word about arms by 20 April 1942, he sent a letter to Roosevelt. It was ostensibly to thank the President for the assurance that American troops would not invade Ireland, but was obviously trying to bring attention to the armament situation. Stressing the need for arms, de Valera explained that the Irish government had 250,000 men prepared to defend the country, if he could only get weapons for them.

Roosevelt was unimpressed. He ordered that the letter should be ignored. In a memorandum to Welles he complained about the Taoiseach:

> If he would only come out of the clouds and quit talking about the quarter of a million Irishmen ready to fight if they had the weapons, we would all have a higher regard for him. Personally I do not believe there are more than one thousand trained soldiers in the whole of the Free State. Even they are probably efficient only in the use of rifles and shotguns.[17]

The policy that Gray had been advocating for the past four months had obviously come to nothing, because Britain was not willing to exert sufficient economic pressure and Washington was not prepared to supply weapons. Since the main reason for advocating economic pressure sweetened with the token arms gesture was to persuade the Irish people to allow the Allies to use Irish bases, it was therefore necessary to reassess the situation in May 1942.

Previously Gray had suggested that if the Allies should decide to seize bases they should announce their intention in advance so that James Dillon would have time to split the Dáil on the issue. At the annual Fine Gael convention in February 1942, however, Dillon failed to secure any support when he advocated that Ireland should join the Allies. In fact, he was actually repudiated and forced to resign from the party. Consequently it was obvious that he would not be able to cause a significant split within the Dáil, if the question of resisting Allied seizure were debated.

On 20 May 1942, therefore, Gray advised Roosevelt that under the circumstances the *'fait accompli* procedure would now be best, accompanied by simultaneous publication of our demands

F

and of their justification to the Irish people'. He suggested that a naval force should seize the ports while aeroplanes would drop leaflets explaining the reasons for the move. 'If Mr de Valera refused to accept the situation and ordered his troops to fire', he continued, 'I think a few well placed bombs on the Irish barracks at the Curragh and in the Dublin area would be the most merciful way of shutting off opposition.' The American Minister went on to explain that it would be best to keep de Valera on as Taoiseach, but if he refused, then the 'Cosgrave people' should be invited to form a government. If they refused, Major-General M. J. Costello of the Southern Command, who had received his military training in the United States, should be asked. And if he declined, Gray added, 'I would put an American general in Dublin in charge till an Irish government could be formed.'

Although Gray was really only outlining a contingency plan that could be used in the event that Washington decided to seize the ports, he did propose that some definite preparations should be made as soon as possible. He explained that it was important to set up some propaganda machinery which could go into action should the United States decide to invade Ireland. As it was, the Americans had been unable to get their propaganda into Irish newspapers because of censorship, and since any invading forces would not have time to conduct propaganda, Gray suggested that 'If we get a big propaganda shop going here it might very likely prepare things.'

The idea was accepted in Washington and some months of preparations followed before the Office of War Information (OWI) brought out the first issue of *Letter from America* on 30 October 1942. Each week thereafter the press attaché at the United States legation, who was attached to OWI, sent copies of the newsletter free of charge to people on a mailing list, which grew from about 18,000 names at first to about 30,000 by the time the last issue was published in April 1945.

As the United States never decided to invade Ireland, the newsletter did not fulfil its original sinister purpose. Instead it published frequent articles on Nazi tyranny, including gruesome pictures of the opening of the concentration camp at Lublin, Poland. In addition, it devoted considerable space to pro-war speeches of Irish-Americans like Alfred E. Smith, James A.

Farley, Cardinals O'Connell and Dougherty, and various other members of the Roman Catholic hierarchy. Also published were accounts of the heroism of both Irishmen and Irish-Americans serving with Allied forces.

Although *Letter from America* never provoked a protest from Irish authorities, other United States propaganda relating to Ireland did at times give rise to official concern, especially during the summer of 1942. Then, the Taoiseach seemed to fear that the Americans were deliberately trying to provoke a German attack on Northern Ireland. On 6 July, for example, Gray found him 'in a sour, discouraged mood, evidently labouring under some acute apprehension of hostile conspiracy'. According to the American Minister de Valera apparently thought that extensive publicity being given to the completion of the American base in Derry was designed to invite an attack on the Six Counties without regard to 'the lives of Irish non-combatants'.[18]

Gray's report of the conversation clearly showed that the suspicion between himself and de Valera was mutual. Because after giving an assurance that the United States was not trying to provoke a German attack, Gray turned the conversation to the subject of talks arranged between General E. P. Hartle, the Commander of United States forces in Northern Ireland, and Lieutenant-General Daniel McKenna, the Chief of Staff of the Irish army. He brought up the matter even though he knew that de Valera did not want to discuss it, or even let on that he knew about the talks. 'I did not wish', Gray wrote, 'ever to give Mr de Valera the opportunity to disavow all knowledge of the liaison and charge me, and possibly also Sir John Maffey, with tampering with his General Staff without his knowledge.' The distrust had reached such proportions that there was no confidence of goodwill even in co-operation.

Some weeks later the possibility of trouble in the Six Counties surfaced in a serious way when six IRA gunmen were sentenced to death for killing a Belfast policeman. Fearing that the executions would lead to unrest, Gray used his influence to help calm the situation. He warned the State Department that Maffey, Kearney, and himself were all of the opinion that the executions would cause trouble. 'Hanging six for one', he explained, 'would shock public opinion.'

As their troops were stationed in Northern Ireland, the possibility of internal strife there was very much a concern of the Americans. Winant therefore made representations in London about American interest in the matter. The death sentences of five of the six men were duly commuted, and the tension eased considerably.*

If Gray expected any gratitude from the northern minority, however, he must have been sorely disappointed, because on 27 September 1942 Cardinal MacRory denounced the United States, along with Britain, for occupying Northern Ireland: 'When I read day after day in the press that this war is being fought for the rights and liberties of small nations and then think of my own corner of our country overrun by British and United States soldiers against the will of the nation, I confess I sometimes find it exceedingly hard to be patient.'

Gray was infuriated at the outburst on the grounds that it played 'directly into the hands of the IRA and might reasonably be expected to incite the murder of American troops in Northern Ireland'.[19] He protested strongly in a letter to the cardinal. The Dublin government's stand concerning the landing of the American troops, he explained, 'came to the American people with a shocked and pained surprise. And now your utterance, which indicates that you regard us in effect as invaders, I feel will intensify the unhappy impression made by Mr de Valera's protest.' He went on to explain:

> Some Americans understand that Mr de Valera in protesting the arrival of American troops may have wished to emphasise his claim to sovereignty over the Six Counties, but they ask why he protested American troops coming as friends for the protection of Ireland, and did not protest German bombers coming to bomb Belfast and kill Irish nationals. They feel that his attitude has been more friendly to Germans, from whom he obtains nothing but bombs, than to Americans and their Allies from whom he receives what is needful to maintain Irish economy.

Elaborating on Allied generosity to Ireland, Gray complained that it was not being properly appreciated. As the American

---

*Joe Cahill, who later became a leader of the Provisional IRA during the late 1960s and early 1970s, was one of the men reprieved.

people continued to think about such ingratitude, he explained that 'there will be engendered resentments that will last for generations and be inscribed in history, unless we can find some means of arresting this tide of tragic misunderstanding.' Warning that some misguided members of the IRA might take the cardinal's words as encouragement 'to drive the invader' from Irish soil, the American Minister predicted that 'if murder follows, the consequences to Irish-American friendship will not be pleasant'.[20]

Seeing that the Tánaiste, Seán T. O'Kelly, had asked him in 1940 to talk to the cardinal about the necessity of not making trouble over partition during the war,[21] Gray knew that it was most improbable that Dublin had instigated the speech. But the government did provide what he believed amounted to official sanctioning by not censoring it in the press. Not only that, but Irish newspapers were also allowed to publish a resolution of Cork City Corporation congratulating the cardinal 'on his timely denunciation of partition and the occupation of the Six Northern Counties by the armed forces of foreign nations against the will of the Irish people'. Yet the censor had earlier suppressed a pastoral of the Bishop of Achonry condemning the German attitude towards the Roman Catholic Church.

While the instances cited were not really analogous, Gray was convinced that American interests had been jeopardised. He therefore sent a letter of protest to de Valera complaining that the actions of the censor 'in observing one policy towards publication of sentiments inimical to the Axis Powers and another toward publication of sentiments inimical to the United States, is scarcely observing the benevolent neutrality which Your Excellency proclaimed upon our entry into the war'.[22]

Gray also complained to Seán MacEntee about 'the Aiken group running the censorship and playing up anti-American sentiment'. When shown a copy of the letter to the cardinal, MacEntee asked for several copies of it so that he could pass it around among all but about three members of the government. Gray, of course, gladly complied with the request from which he derived the distinct impression that 'a majority of the cabinet are against Aiken but are unable to move Dev away from him and are glad when we do anything to indicate to Dev that he is on a dangerous course'.[23]

Although the American Minister never bothered to secure approval from the State Department for his various protests in connection with the cardinal's speech, he did report fully on his actions. He knew that he was on safe ground in acting on his own initiative because he had not received any rebuke for doing so in the past. In fact, in September 1942 he had received a very friendly letter from Roosevelt, explaining that many people had been reporting to the White House on 'what a perfectly magnificent job' Gray was doing in Ireland. 'I did not have to be told that because I knew it,' the President added, 'for the very simple fact that you have not given me the remote shadow of a headache all these years.'[24]

In the same letter Roosevelt explained that his policy towards de Valera was what he called 'the absent treatment'. In accordance with it he simply ignored Ireland and her problems. On one occasion, for example, when a person whom he described as 'a typical professional Irish-American' complained to him about economic conditions in Ireland, the President looked at the man inquisitively and asked, 'Where is Ireland?' Then again in the autumn of 1942, the President's wife stayed with Gray in Dublin, but Irish officials were not notified and apparently did not know that she had visited until she had gone.

'I do wish', Roosevelt wrote, 'the people as a whole over there could realise that Dev is unnecessarily storing up trouble because most people over here feel that Dublin, by maintaining German spies and by making all the little things difficult for the United Nations, is stirring up a thoroughly unsympathetic attitude toward Ireland as a whole when we win the war. That is a truly sad state of affairs.'

The President's remark about 'maintaining German spies', which apparently referred to the Axis consular and diplomatic representatives, gives rise to the serious question of just how informed he was about the Irish situation, because by September 1942 Irish authorities had taken steps to ensure that the Axis representatives were not spying and there was no evidence to the contrary. Later, in another letter to Gray on 18 December 1942 the President remarked that the Irish 'must be told that because of their geographical situation they will never be permitted to allow any other nation to use them in a military way or otherwise against the United States or Britain'.

The Irish had actually been told this repeatedly by de Valera himself, as this had been at the very heart of his foreign policy since long before the war. Indeed, it is possible to trace the idea back to his controversial *Westminster Gazette* interview of 1920, when he antagonised many Irish-Americans by indicating that the British had a right to an assurance that Ireland would not be used as a base for an attack on them. In August 1941 the Taoiseach demonstrated that he was prepared to carry the idea to the limit by insisting that the German legation desist from using its radio transmitter.

Irish authorities began keeping a close watch on the German legation with radio detection equipment supplied by the British, and for some months there were no transmissions. Suddenly in December 1941 there were three more messages. The Irish Department of External Affairs protested, but in February 1942 there were further messages which gave rise to much disquiet in Dublin, because the Department of External Affairs was afraid that the messages might have been weather reports which could possibly have helped the two German battleships, *Scharnhorst* and *Gneisenau*, in their dramatic dash through the English Channel.[25]

Under instructions from de Valera, Joseph Walshe issued a stern warning to the German Minister that the transmitter would be confiscated if the legation used it again. Although Hempel protested that he was legally entitled to use the equipment, the Irish were adamant that Ireland was not going to be used as a base to hurt the Allies. This was fundamental to de Valera's brand of neutrality, so the Germans had little choice but to accept the decision.

In spite of Dublin's vigilance, however, some wild rumours still persisted in the United States. In late October 1942 Robert Brennan called on Sumner Welles at the State Department to protest about statements in the *Pocket Guide to Northern Ireland*, a pamphlet published by the United States War Department and issued to each American soldier going to Northern Ireland. It declared:

Éire's neutrality is a real danger to the Allied cause. There, just across the Irish Channel from embattled England, and not too far from your own billets in Ulster, the Axis nations main-

tain large legations and staffs. These Axis agents send out
weather reports, find out by espionage what is going on in
Ulster . . .

Brennan complained that the material was erroneous, because
the Axis missions were under constant surveillance and Irish
authorities were sure that no radio messages were being sent.
According to the Irish Minister, the only means which the Axis
representatives had of making reports was by using the cable
passing through Britain.

Welles was obviously poorly informed about the situation,
because he asked if it were not true that the Axis legations were
greatly oversized. Brennan denied this, as he had on numerous
other occasions, and he pointed out that even *The Times* of
London had refuted such rumours. Although Welles later took
up the question with the War Department, it refused to retract
the statements.

Probably the most ridiculous of all the rumours was a report
by one agency in Washington a few weeks later to the effect
that there were hundreds of Japanese tourists in Ireland. Brennan
was virtually dumbfounded when a State Department official
telephoned asking him to get a report on the matter from the
Department of External Affairs in Dublin. It was ludicrous,
but the Irish Minister complied with the request.

When Dublin replied, Brennan called on Welles and expressed
exasperation that such an inquiry had ever been made. There
were, he explained, only four Japanese people in the whole of
the Twenty-Six Counties, the *Chargé d'Affaires*, his wife, the
consul, and one stranded seaman. According to Welles, the Irish
Minister said that his government 'was deeply irritated by the
inquiry' which showed that the United States government was
determined to believe that the Irish were 'permitting every kind
of Axis subversive activity to be going on in Ireland notwithstanding the frequent and official denials on the part of the
Irish government'.

Potentially one of the most nettlesome problems between the
United States and Ireland concerned the possible internment
of American airmen who came down in the Twenty-Six Counties.
Forty-six Allied airmen had already been interned. Nevertheless many others were released in instances where publicity could

be avoided, and even those interned were confined under very liberal conditions at a camp near the Curragh military barracks.

Each day the internees were allowed to sign-out on parole on condition that they would not use their freedom to escape, but once they signed back in, they were under no obligation not to try to escape. British authorities co-operated by promising to return anyone who escaped by violating his parole.

The only American in the camp, Pilot Officer R. N. Wolfe of Nebraska, who had been interned while serving with the Eagle Squadron of the RAF, was actually returned after he had escaped to Belfast. He had signed-out on parole, but came back on the pretext that he had forgotten his gloves. He then went out again without signing-out, but since he had not signed-in the first time, Irish authorities claimed that he was under obligation not to attempt to escape. The British agreed and Wolfe was returned to the Curragh.

In October 1942 Gray reported that Irish authorities had secretly allowed a rescue party from the Six Counties to pick up two American pilots who came down in Ireland. Since sixteen American bombers had recently been lost over the country for some time before finding their bearings, the American Minister warned Washington that 'this luck cannot last'. Sooner or later the Irish would probably decide to intern someone serving with the United States armed services, and he was convinced that the internment should not be accepted without a rigorous protest. In fact, Gray advocated that the Irish should be asked to agree to some kind of formula under which American pilots would not be interned. If the Irish refused to comply, he suggested that all supplies of coal, petrol, steel, wheat, and chemical products to Ireland should be cut off. 'I know inside me that this is simple justice,' he wrote to Roosevelt, 'but I haven't the ability to frame the formula that you can, which will cover the case.'[26]

Some weeks of discussions followed between Allied representatives in Dublin, London, and Washington, before a formula was agreed upon in accordance with which the United States would informally request the Irish government not to intern any Americans. There was to be no exchange of notes; Gray was simply given instructions to talk to the Irish Department of External Affairs and to claim that Americans should not be interned because there was a vast difference between their flights and those of the Germans.

'American planes which may come down in Ireland', the State Department contended, 'will ordinarily be on training or transit flights and not at the time engaged in any hostile activity nor any hostile mission.' But such could not be said of German flights. 'In view of distances from Germany and German occupied areas,' the instructions to Gray continued, 'it cannot even remotely be supposed that such German planes have lost their way on peaceful flights.'

On 1 December 1942 Gray put his government's case to Walshe by contending that American flights were 'non-operational'. Walshe had no objection, so Gray was able to assure the State Department that American pilots would not be interned if they declared that they had been on training flights or just testing equipment.

The Irish also applied the same formula to British and Canadian airmen. According to Winston Churchill's son, Randolph, the whole 'non-operational' argument was 'convenient fiction'. It was a way for Ireland to help the Allies, while still preserving the appearance of strict neutrality.

Some months later the Canadian representative reported that Irish authorities were not even bothering to check the 'non-operational' claims of pilots forced to land in Ireland. 'Under the circumstances', Kearney wrote, 'the meaning of the words "non-operational flight" has, sometimes been stretched almost beyond recognition. Since the above attitude has been adopted by the Irish government, many American air crews have made forced landings but none of them has been interned.'[27] In fact, Gray reported to the State Department in April 1943 that five of the first six air crews that landed in Ireland failed to claim that they had been on 'non-operational flights', but they were released anyway, thus demonstrating the true benevolence of Irish neutrality towards the Allies.[28]

During the following months Kearney tried to persuade Irish authorities to release those already interned. In September 1943 de Valera agreed to free most of the men on the grounds that they had supposedly been engaged in 'non-operational flights' at the time they came down in Ireland. Before releasing the men, however, it was first necessary to move them to a new camp being prepared at Gormanstown, County Meath, away from the German internees being held at a separate compound at the Curragh.[29] All but eight of the Allied airmen were eventually freed the following month, and in June 1944 the remainder were let go.[30]

Yet none of the Germans were released. Even more than one hundred and fifty men picked up in the Bay of Biscay in January 1944 by the Irish ship *Kerlogue* were detained, and there was no question of them having violated Irish territory. Of course, it was likely that many of those men actually welcomed their internment because they were allowed the same liberal conditions of parole as the Allied internees, and they were spared the trauma of the final days of the war in Germany, where food and other supplies were already running short. Indeed many of the internees admitted that they had never been so well fed in their lives as at the Curragh.

9. To Seek or Not to Seek the Irish Ports?

IRISH THREATS TO THE ANGLO-AMERICAN ALLIANCE
October 1942—December 1943

As de Valera's constitutional mandate was due to run out in mid-1943, the attitude of the Fine Gael opposition towards neutrality began to take on added significance in late 1942. Sir John Maffey was anxious to determine if the Allies could expect any change in policy if Fine Gael should replace the Fianna Fáil government. Of course, he realised that no party could expect to get much support unless it fought the upcoming election on a neutrality ticket, but once in power he hoped that Cosgrave might be prepared to give bases to the Americans, especially if the latter made it clear that they would otherwise seize such facilities.

The British representative soon found that Cosgrave was already afraid of the Americans.[1] A couple of months earlier two prominent members of the British Labour Party, Aneurin Bevan and Richard Stokes, had visited Dublin and warned Fine Gael leaders that the Americans were 'bloody minded' and would not be stopped from getting their hands on Irish ports. Bevan, who had been acting as a kind of one man opposition to the Churchill government, realised that something would have to be done about the Ulster question, if there was to be any chance of the Irish throwing in with the Allies. He therefore proposed that the Six Counties should be run by a joint Anglo-American commission with the Americans taking charge and the British acting as 'mere window dressing'.[2] Yet nothing ever came of the Bevan-Stokes initiative, except possibly that the Irish were left more uneasy than ever about the attitude of the Americans.

On 18 October 1942 Cosgrave told Maffey that he was afraid of the Americans but he emphasised that it would be hopeless for any Irish government to attempt to abandon neutrality because popular support for the policy had been increasing, rather than diminishing, since the war began.

Maffey admitted that 'there was obviously good reason for a measure of apprehension' concerning the attitude of the United States, but he went on to note that he could not understand how Dublin could refuse a request for bases, if 'it took the form of an appeal to Irishmen' from the twenty million Irish-Americans.

'That', said Cosgrave, 'would be the only possible line of approach.'

The British representative was able to take some comfort from the Fine Gael leader's response. 'This shows at any rate that he does not close his mind to such a development,' Maffey reported, 'but at the same time the conversation revealed the present firm and unyielding adherence of all parties to the policy of neutrality.'

'I think my conversation with Mr Cosgrave brings the whole question down to bedrock', the British representative continued. 'If a move for Irish facilities for the prosecution of the war is to be made it must be an American approach and no basis would be complete unless it included some formula dealing—though possibly at long range—with the partition question, as without that no Éire government could rally the support it would need in putting through a tough proposition.'

As far as the American Minister was concerned, however, there was no possibility of any agreement on the Ulster question as long as de Valera was in power. In fact, from talking with one of de Valera's friends, Conor Maguire, the president of the Irish high court, Gray concluded that de Valera really did not want a solution, because if eight hundred thousand Northern Irish Protestants were represented in an all-Ireland parliament, they would possess a balance of power and would hold an inordinate influence over Irish affairs. Instead of desiring to settle the question, therefore, Gray thought that de Valera only wanted to use the grievance of partition to stir up a nationalistic fervour which Fianna Fáil would be able to exploit.[3]

Although the Americans were not a party to the Ulster dispute, Gray nevertheless believed that the question could have ominous repercussions in the United States if it became an international issue in the post-war period. As the American Minister saw it, de Valera planned to raise the issue even though he had no intention of compromising. Since Belfast was unlikely to capitulate and the British were not likely to abandon the loyalists of

Northern Ireland who had provided bases, the American President would have to support the British position on partition, if he wished to avoid Anglo-American difficulties. But this, in turn, would probably provoke the ire of many Irish-Americans, so the possibility had to be taken into account that the latter might combine with other discontented elements to undermine the White House and destroy the fruits of the peace settlement in much the same way as the Versailles Treaty of 1919 had been undermined in the United States.

In view of his White House connections, Gray was able to voice his apprehension in the highest Allied circles. In November 1942, for instance, when he went to London for consultations with Winant, he was invited to dine at 10 Downing Street with Churchill and General Charles de Gaulle, the Free French leader. The following evening he had dinner with Clement Attlee, the Deputy Prime Minister; Herbert Morrison, the Home Secretary; Lord Cranborne, and Maffey.

During both dinners Gray stressed the need to prevent the Irish question from poisoning Anglo-American relations.[4] He already had a vague idea about how to do this. In his account of the discussion at the second dinner, he wrote that he had stated that 'the attitude of the de Valera government in protesting the advent of our troops to Northern Ireland and the anti-American agitation stemming from this attitude were, if suitably exploited in America, likely to make it easier for the American government to maintain a friendly and co-operative policy toward Britain. The problem was what to do or not to do that might further this desirable consummation.'

No one made any suggestion, and several weeks followed before Gray figured out how to implement his idea. It was actually Maffey and Kearney who provided the inspiration.

They had been discussing the best means of approaching de Valera for bases, after the Germans intensified their submarine campaign in the Atlantic in January 1943. The Canadian High Commissioner believed that there was a real possibility that de Valera would hand over facilities, if Roosevelt asked for them. They therefore decided to discuss the proposition with Gray.

Kearney argued that the danger of German air-raids had originally compelled de Valera to hold on to Irish bases, but the Allies had since gained almost total air-supremacy and the

Germans had suffered serious reversals in both the North African and Russian campaigns. And as the German position deteriorated, the Irish government had 'given additional tangible evidence of a disposition to be of some assistance to the Allied cause'. Moreover, news of the most recent Allied successes had been received in Ireland with 'a satisfaction approaching enthusiasm', and many people were beginning to worry about the country's postwar position. Consequently, Kearney believed that there was a real chance of securing co-operation if Roosevelt made a public request for facilities and exploited de Valera's desire to preserve internal political harmony on the neutrality issue. He explained :

> At least some support either from the electorate at large or the opposition parties would be forthcoming should a request for facilities be made in the near future. Mr de Valera has repeatedly stressed the importance of unity in regard to Ireland's attitude towards the war, and I believe he would stretch a point to maintain such unity, and in case he is doubtful as to what course to pursue he might be influenced in favour of acceding to the request if such a course found favour in other quarters.[5]

Maffey went over to London and explained the plan to Attlee, but the latter displayed little interest in it. Neither military nor naval leaders had shown any desire for Irish facilities for some time, so Attlee suggested that the proposal should be shelved. In a letter to Anthony Eden, the Foreign Secretary, on 5 March 1943, he explained that he was opposed to taking the chance that de Valera would comply with the request because Britain would then become obliged to defend Ireland, which would 'probably' be more trouble than the facilities were worth.[6] Paradoxically, Attlee had belittled the value of Irish bases at the very time that the Allies were in the midst of their gravest crisis in the Atlantic. The Admiralty later recorded that 'the Germans never came so near to disrupting communication between the New World and the Old as in the first twenty days of March, 1943.'[7]

When Maffey reported what had transpired in London, Kearney was satisfied to drop the proposal.[8] But Gray was not.

Although confident that such a request would be rejected, Gray was anxious to pursue the matter for the propaganda value that it would have in educating the American people, who were pitifully uninformed about Irish neutrality. In fact, a Gallup poll published in January 1943 revealed that half of them did not even know that Ireland was neutral. Unless such a request were therefore made, many people might never know that Ireland was not an ally. In addition, de Valera would be able to cause confusion even amongst those who knew, if he were to assert that Irish neutrality had been favourable to the Americans and that he had never refused any assistance to them. It was to avoid this happening that Gray suggested to Roosevelt that de Valera's refusal to help would be worth securing because it 'would at least put him on record for the purposes of post-war adjustments and would prevent him from saying that he had been with us all along which is probably what he will say if he is not put on record'.[9]

During the following weeks the genesis of what appeared to be an anti-partition campaign began to appear publicly, as Cardinal MacRory, Robert Brennan and de Valera all made pronouncements concerning the Northern Irish question. On 4 April 1943 the cardinal delivered a speech contending that the Atlantic Charter contained a promise of Irish unity. Describing the charter as 'a sign of repentance', he said that it gave 'a solemn undertaking which, in case the Allies win the war should be certain to bring the partition of Ireland to a speedy end'. The cardinal was referring to a clause asserting that all people had a right to choose their own form of government and that sovereign rights should be 'restored to those who have been forcibly deprived of them'. Seeing that a majority of the people in the thirty-two counties of Ireland desired a united Irish government, MacRory seemed to believe that the Allies were committed to the ending of partition.

That same day, in response to an attack on Irish neutrality by Henry A. Commager, an eminent American historian, the *New York Times* published a letter from Robert Brennan defending the Irish government's policy by placing particular emphasis on the ills of partition. De Valera also stressed the same theme some weeks later. In a public speech on 8 May 1943 he said that partition had been the one problem that had prevented Irish co-operation with Britain.

Yet there was obviously little chance of any settlement in the near future. Next day, 9 May 1943, British newspapers published a letter that Churchill had recently sent to Sir John Andrews upon the latter's retirement as Prime Minister of Northern Ireland. In it the British leader expressed gratitude for the use of Northern Irish facilities which, he noted, had made Britain's survival possible during 1940 and 1941. As a result, Churchill added, the bond between Britain and the Six Counties was unbreakable.

Seeing that the State Department had already reported that some Irish-Americans had initiated a campaign against partition, Gray was very uneasy. And even an assurance from Hull that the Atlantic Charter did not relate to the Irish case did not allay his apprehension.[10] He was becoming obsessed with the fear that the Irish question might undermine Anglo-American relations. There seemed to be a danger of a repetition of events that followed the First World War when Irish-Americans contended that the Allied victory guaranteed Ireland's rights as a small nation. Then, when the Paris Peace Conference refused to recognise Irish independence, de Valera brought his case to the United States and helped wreck Woodrow Wilson's peace plans.

On 14 May 1943 Gray sent the State Department a long memorandum evaluating the significance of Irish political affairs and outlining the various alternatives open to Washington. He explained that there were at least three points on which Anglo-American interests were 'gravely prejudiced by the policy of the Irish government'. First, the Allies had been denied facilities to protect their Atlantic shipping. Second, the Axis missions in Ireland were an espionage threat. Third, de Valera was apparently planning to use the partition issue to create a post-war disagreement between the United States and Britain.

'Whatever the rights and wrongs of partition,' Gray wrote, 'it should be clearly understood that a solution on any basis of reason and compromise is not the primary object of the de Valera leadership at this time.' Instead, the Taoiseach was simply using the issue in order to preserve his power, with the result that the grievance of partition was politically of more importance than a solution.

With de Valera apparently unwilling to accept anything less than Irish unity—a proposition repugnant to Northern Ireland leaders—there could be no solution to the problem within the foreseeable future. While this in itself should have been of no concern to an American Minister, Gray explained that the Taoiseach would involve the United States in the affair by appealing for Irish-American support in order to force Washington to put pressure on the British to abandon the Six Counties. Consequently, if the United States wished to avoid distracting difficulties with Britain, it would be necessary to resist the Irish-American pressure, because the British were determined to sustain the Belfast government, which had furnished the Allies with much needed bases. What was more, Gray was convinced that the United States was morally obliged to support Stormont on the same grounds.

Yet, as things stood de Valera could confuse the issue by arguing that the Twenty-Six Counties had also been helpful. He could, for instance, contend that Dublin had co-operated fully with the Americans, who had never formally requested either facilities or the withrawal of Axis representatives. In addition he could cite the thousands of Irishmen who served with Allied forces. Gray had reported in December 1941 that the number of volunteers could be put at 150,000 men, which, in relation to the country's population, would have been equivalent to more than six million Americans.* The Taoiseach could also point to intelligence co-operation, the secret release of Allied airmen, and to the Irish government's help both by handing over the seven oil tankers and by allowing Britain to keep some tug boats in Irish waters for air-sea rescue purposes.

Using such arguments, Gray warned that de Valera would be able to confuse people about Irish neutrality and would thus be in a strong position to open a rift in the Anglo-American alliance by feeding some of Roosevelt's opponents with formidable anti-British and anti-partition propaganda. 'It has become increasingly apparent', Gray added, 'that he intends to use the

---

* There is a great deal of confusion about the actual number of Irish volunteers. In March 1944 the Manchester *Guardian* estimated that there were 300,000, but that figure was apparently inflated. The following August General Gough found that 165,000 people in the services had given Irish addresses for their next of kin. This figure, no doubt, included many people who had emigrated to Britain before the war. The only official figures available are that 38,554 men from the Twenty-Six Counties volunteered in Belfast for British services.

alleged wrong of partition to open this rift and to enlist the sympathies and support of the Irish-American groups to this end.'

The disruptive potential of the Irish-Americans should not be underestimated.* Many of those who had been prominent in isolationist circles right up to Pearl Harbour, were facing the political oblivion to which Hitler's appeasers were condemned. There was, as a result, a danger that they might use the partition issue to stir up popular support in order to salvage their waning political influence.

It was certainly necessary to reckon with men like Father Charles Coughlin and Father Edward Curran, or with such men as Senator David I. Walsh, John Cudahy, or even James A. Farley. As state chairman of the Democratic Party in New York, Farley demonstrated in the summer of 1942 that he still wielded a great deal of political power by securing the party's gubernatorial nomination for his own hand-picked candidate, in the face of opposition from both President Roosevelt and Governor Herbert Lehman. Such political muscle could not be ignored, and the Irish-American threat was not something to be taken lightly.

Gray therefore suggested a number of possible courses that the United States could follow in order to clarify Irish policy for the American people. The alternatives were to ask the Taoiseach for bases, to request the recall of Axis representatives from Ireland, or to demand that Dublin clarify whether or not Ireland was a member of the British Commonwealth. A fourth alternative did not involve any approach to de Valera; it simply consisted of enacting conscription in Northern Ireland.

Each of the suggestions was primarily designed to create a climate conducive to a propaganda campaign in which the Fianna Fáil government could be discredited. As Gray himself explained, 'The important thing from the viewpoint of Anglo-American co-operation is to bring to the notice of the American people the unfair and destructive policy of the de Valera politicians at the time when British and American interests are essentially the same and to obtain a verdict of American disapproval

* De Valera himself had told Maffey on 14 September 1939 that 'the Irish element' in the United States 'had ruined and would ruin any possibility of Anglo-American understanding', see p. 18.

which will remove the pressure of the Irish question from Anglo-American relations.'

If de Valera refused to co-operate, Gray contended that the Allies could undermine Fianna Fáil by placing an embargo on supplies to Ireland and thereby persuade the Irish people that the Taoiseach's policies had brought on economic hardships. 'It would seem', Gray wrote, 'that the obvious means of putting pressure upon Éire and discrediting the leadership of the de Valera group, from which trouble is to be expected in the post-war period, is by withholding supplies.'

In early June 1943 Gray returned to the United States for consultations. Just two days before he was due to leave Dublin he received what he believed was further confirmation that the Taoiseach intended to raise the Ulster question after the war. In the course of a private discussion, de Valera explained to the American Minister that a solution to partition within the appreciable future was not beyond the capability of good statesmanship, 'especially since the precedent for the exchange of populations has been established'. Believing that this was a reference to the Lausanne Treaty of 1923, Gray took the remark as an indication that the Taoiseach intended to demand that the international post-war settlement include an imposed solution whereby Northern Ireland Protestants would be moved to Britain and replaced by Roman Catholics of Irish extraction who would be transferred from Britain to the Six Counties.[11]

The American Minister never seriously considered this scheme a workable solution. Of course, it could hardly have been surprising that any American would adopt such an attitude, seeing that the Protestants of the Six Counties could trace their ancestors in Northern Ireland back to the early seventeenth century, which was a great deal earlier than the vast majority of Americans had their ancestral roots in the United States.

In the following weeks Gray had meetings with various American officials and spent some time with Roosevelt at both the White House and the President's home in Hyde Park, New York. At these meetings he emphasised the need to undermine de Valera's political appeal in the United States and he suggested that the best method would be to get the Taoiseach on record as formally refusing to allow the United States to use Irish ports.

Roosevelt liked the idea. 'I think Mr Gray is right in his desire to put de Valera on record,' he wrote to Hull on 15 June 1943. 'We shall undoubtedly be turned down.'

The Secretary of State, however, was not nearly so enthusiastic. He was afraid that the United States might become embroiled in a purely Anglo-Irish dispute. Seeing that Britain and Ireland distrusted one another as a result of centuries of feuding, he advised Roosevelt to be sure that it would be 'impossible for any-one to maintain that we took sides with the British against the Irish and "pulled British chestnuts out of the fire" '. Only if the military really needed facilities should Washington ask for them, he suggested. Consequently, the views of military leaders were sought.

While their reply was being awaited, Gray visited selected Irish-American centres in order to sound out community leaders on the possible consequences that an anti-partition campaign would have on the American political scene. During July he had talks with a number of people, especially members of the Roman Catholic hierarchy known to be sympathetic to Roosevelt's foreign policy.

In Chicago he talked with Archbishop Samuel Stritch, who believed that the danger was being exaggerated. The archbishop contended that the strength of Irish-American political bosses had declined. On the other hand, in Detroit—a stronghold of Father Charles Coughlin—Archbishop Edward Mooney was even more concerned than the American Minister, who next went to Buffalo, New York, where the local Roman Catholic bishop was indisposed. Gray therefore took the opportunity to consult one of the local political leaders who noted that although Irish-Americans in the area were dissatisfied with Irish neutrality, they were still suspicious of England and would go anti-British if the Anglo-Irish question were revived. Bishop Joseph Hurley of St Augustine, Florida, and Joseph P. Kennedy both agreed with that assessment. But Gray was not able to have a very involved discussion with Kennedy who was under a great strain, having just been informed that his son John, the future president, was missing following the sinking of his boat in the Pacific. In Portland, Maine, Bishop Joseph McCarthy explained that the Irish-American community in his area was too small to really influence the political situation. Gray also talked with a former United States Minister to Ireland, Frederick Sterling, who agreed with his assessment of the situation.

While in the United States Gray found that more Americans were unhappy with Roosevelt's policy than he had imagined. Upon his arrival in Washington, for instance, there was a letter waiting for him from John Cudahy contending that there was 'growing bewilderment among our people concerning the real issues of this war'. The former Minister to Ireland explained that many Americans were puzzled about being asked to fight for the principles of the Atlantic Charter when it was obvious that one of the Allies, the Soviet Union, had no intention of upholding those principles, especially in regard to Poland. Cudahy was actually so critical of Roosevelt's leadership that he suggested that Gray should try to persuade the President not to seek a fourth term in 1944 because there was a danger of 'something almost approaching a civil war'.[12]

Replying to Cudahy some weeks later, following his trip to the Irish-American centres, Gray wrote that he did not believe that there could 'be more bitterness against F.D.R. than there now is'. In another letter to an American intelligence officer, he explained 'that Pearl Harbour had not scotched the venomous minority groups, whether Irish, German, Italian, or purely lunatic Americans'. As a result Gray was more convinced than ever about the need to weaken the potential American support that an anti-partition campaign might receive.[13]

On 14 August 1943 he discussed the problem with Roosevelt and Churchill over dinner at the President's Hyde Park home. The only record of the meeting is an inconclusive memorandum written by W. Averell Harriman, who noted that Gray argued his case on the Irish situation, but Churchill 'seemed unimpressed'.[14]

Harriman attended the dinner only to discuss his own forthcoming assignment as Ambassador to the Soviet Union, so he paid little attention to the conversation involving Ireland.[15] From a letter that Gray later wrote to Roosevelt, however, it is apparent that the point of disagreement with Churchill concerned, not whether an approach should be made, but the tone of the note to be sent. The American Minister thought that it was 'very important to keep a friendly ending to the Irish communication', but Churchill objected to telling de Valera that if he went his separate way, the Allies would wish him well. In the end it was decided that Gray would draft the kind of letter he wanted Roosevelt to send to de Valera. Then the President and Churchill would consider it.[16]

On 16 August Gray submitted the draft letter, which was designed for eventual publication in order to inform the American people about what he believed had been unfavourable aspects of Irish neutrality. Written in the form of an invitation to Ireland to join the Allies in the fight against fascism, it began by outlining American aid to Ireland, such as the chartering of the two cargo ships, the gift of $500,000 worth of Red Cross supplies, the rights to purchase American products such as wheat, cotton, and steel, and the 20,000 American rifles, which had actually been handed over by the British. 'Thanks to this policy of friendship and supply,' the note declared, 'normal standards of living have been less impaired in Éire as the result of war than in any country in Europe.'

A magnanimous American policy having thus been outlined, Gray went on to assert that Ireland's policy towards the United States had been less than generous. The Irish government had protested against American use of Northern Ireland bases and had permitted the Irish press to publish protests against the American presence in the Six Counties, while it censored items critical of Germany for bombing Ireland. Moreover, the Irish government had allowed Axis diplomats to remain in Ireland, thereby affording them a tremendous opportunity to spy on Allied war efforts, but Dublin had been unwilling to allow the Allies to use Irish bases and had thus made 'no contribution to the safety and maintenance of a supply line by which in so important measure your national economy is maintained'.

Explaining that Washington would not have been justified in asking the Irish to change their policy earlier, because it could not adequately assist in defending Ireland against German attacks, the note continued:

Now, however, the outcome of the war is no longer in doubt. Our victory is assured though it is not yet won, and it appears to the American government to be a friendly act to offer the Irish people a share in that victory as we have given them a share of our supply.

Proceeding in terms that seemed deliberately designed to prompt de Valera's refusal, the draft document pointed out that the American 'offer cannot be construed as a plea for aid or as an effort to purchase co-operation'. It was simply supposed to be a generous offer to share the glory of victory. The outcome of the war was not going to be altered by Ireland's participation, but the country could 'play a notable and honourable part in contributing to the shortening of its duration by leasing us bases for the protection of the Atlantic supply lines and by the elimination of Axis spy centres on Éire territory'.

The Irish government should have no difficulty accepting the request, the note added, seeing that the Germans had bombed Ireland, causing a million dollars worth of damage and killing seventy-eight civilians, in addition to sinking a dozen Irish ships. Finally the document concluded with a statement to the effect 'that the American government's obligation to the American people will require the publication of this note and your reply thereto'.

When he forwarded the draft letter to the President, Gray also enclosed a memorandum outlining his reasons for advocating the proposed approach. There were, he wrote, benefits that the United States could derive, regardless of whether or not the Irish accepted the offer. First, if Ireland accepted, the United States would obtain both Irish bases and the removal of Axis diplomats. In addition, he believed that if Ireland became one of them, the Allies would be able to control Irish representatives at the post-war peace conference.

Yet this was all pretty much academic to Gray, because he thought that it was 'probable' that the American approach would be rejected. He knew, for instance, that de Valera had told Maffey some months earlier that Ireland could not join the Allies.

'They would mock me,' the Taoiseach declared, 'if I changed after it appeared certain that you were going to win.'

According to Gray, 'It is this egotistical vanity which apparently in the past inspired his refusal to accept the Treaty of [1921] ... and thus precipitated a wholly needless civil war.'[17]

The American Minister was confident that de Valera would remain consistent and would reject the American offer. If this happened, he noted that the United States would benefit in two distinct ways. Firstly, de Valera would be put on record as refusing a generous offer and this would afford the United States government an opportunity 'of meeting the Irish issue and its repercussions on American sentiment while the war is in progress instead of after hostilities have ceased as Mr de Valera would wish'. Secondly, the note would 'disseminate important facts not generally known either by the Irish or the American peoples'. He went on to explain that 'The note is composed primarily for the American public and designed to reveal to them how generously Éire has been treated and how little the government of Éire has done in return for the people of America.' In other words the approach would be essentially a kind of propaganda exercise.

While his suggestions were being considered in Washington, Gray returned to Ireland where he showed the proposed note to both Maffey and Kearney. He said that he hoped that the offer would be accepted because it would be best that Ireland should join the Allies so that the Taoiseach would 'be placed in a position where he would be controlled by conference conditions'. Yet, he added that he did not believe that there was much chance of acceptance and that it was therefore 'most desirable' that the 'note should be drawn to make the record for the American public'. In his report to Hull, Gray wrote:

> I explained that the object of my recommendation was to prevent the Irish partition issue being injected into post-war American politics by de Valera and exploited by the subversive elements in America which tried to block preparedness and lend-lease in order to oppose your plans for co-operation with the British Commonwealth and other nations. We know these forces are still active and organised.

Kearney, who was on the verge of securing the release of most of the interned Allied pilots, was stunned by these arguments. He had had different reasons for suggesting an American note in the first place. 'I had in the forefront of my mind the winning of the war', he told Maffey, 'and not post-war relations between Great Britain and the United States of America, and not at all the part certain Irish elements in the United States of America might play in post-war relationships.'[18]

Kearney believed that the Taoiseach was certain to reject the note. 'Although it contained some honeyed phrases', he explained to his own Department of External Affairs, 'it was almost tantamount to an indictment.' Indeed, in spite of Gray's claims to the contrary, the Canadian High Commissioner concluded that the document 'seemed to be drafted in such a way as to provoke a refusal'. He added that he was therefore opposed to it, because 'If a refusal were received, which was the only answer one could anticipate, I foresaw that resentment would replace any benevolence which Ireland had heretofore exhibited, and the elimination, or curtailment of acts of goodwill could not be of any advantage in so far as the Allied war-effort was concerned.'

Maffey agreed with his Canadian colleague's assessment of the situation and told him that the Foreign Office in London also felt the same way. What was more, State Department and military representatives in Washington were opposed to the note.

Having been asked by the White House for their views on the strategic value of Irish ports, the Chiefs of Staff replied that they could not see any advantage to securing such facilities. In fact, they actually perceived certain drawbacks.

Writing on their behalf General George C. Marshall, the Army Chief of Staff noted—what the Irish had been arguing for almost three years—that bases in the Twenty-Six Counties would not be of much use as long as the French coast was under German control. He explained that ships travelling by the south of Ireland would be easy targets for German submarines based in the Bay of Biscay. If de Valera acceded to a request and handed over ports, Marshall added that American forces would possibly be handicapped because they would be morally obliged to divert personnel and equipment to protect defenceless Irish cities. Instead of actually requesting use of the ports, therefore, the Chiefs of Staff advised that Washington should only ask the Irish government to guarantee that bases would be made available, if the United States ever needed them. As a result the State Department drafted a new note merely asking Dublin to give a secret commitment to make facilities available, should they be needed.

On 13 September 1943 Hull forwarded the new draft to Roosevelt with the explanation that the Joint Chiefs of Staff had 'recommended that an approach should be made to the Irish government for permission to use Irish bases in the event such bases should be needed but that we should not make any commitments to establish such bases'.

The new note was similar to Gray's in some respects. Both outlined the history of American assistance to Ireland during the war, and both contrasted it with the German air and submarine attacks, but the new approach, which omitted all mention of American grievances against the Irish, was written in the form of a request rather than an offer. It explained that it would be helpful to those planning American strategy if they could count on being able to use Irish facilities should the occasion arise in which the use of such facilities would 'help to save American lives and the lives of nationals of those countries associated with us in the war'. The Irish government was to be asked 'to grant to the United States, for the duration of the war and six months thereafter, permission to use existing air and naval facilities in Ireland at any time these facilities should be required and also permission to establish and use such other naval and air facilities as may be needed by American forces'. Nevertheless the document emphasised that it was 'entirely possible' that the United States would not need any bases, but 'it would be of real assistance to us *now* in planning our war strategy to be able to count upon the use of such bases if they should be needed'.

Roosevelt approved the new approach, which was then forwarded to London for consideration.

When Gray saw it he was disturbed by some of its aspects. First, he thought the note's 'extremely mild phrasing' tended to play down Washington's resentment over de Valera's protest against American troops in Northern Ireland at the time that the Irish were permitting the Axis representatives to remain in Dublin. Secondly, he warned that the Taoiseach would simply reply that he could not be expected to make so fundamental a change in policy without knowing the circumstances. In other words, the United States should ask for bases when they were needed, at which time Dublin would consider the request. If the Irish adopted such a stance, Gray explained that the United States would have neither the promise of facilities, nor the record of a refusal.

Hull replied, however, that the new note had certain advantages. He pointed out that the Chiefs of Staff did not want to take any chance of de Valera agreeing to come into the war, but they did wish to know if they could 'count on the use of bases in Ireland whenever they may be needed'. It was in the planning stage that the United States needed to find out if such help could be depended on, he explained, with the result that an evasive response on the lines that Gray anticipated from de Valera would actually be tantamount to a refusal. The Secretary of State also noted that the amicable tone of the request actually made the document more potent for future publication, in the event that the Irish rejected it, because it would mean that they would have refused a limited request made in the 'friendliest terms'. If de Valera accepted, on the other hand, Hull concluded that the United States 'would then be in a much stronger position to ask as a next step the removal of Axis representatives as a necessary security measure'.

On realising that the new note was only one step in a series of moves that could be used in preparing a political position to counter any Irish attempts to wreck the Anglo-American alliance, Gray 'heartily' approved of it. 'But believe me,' he wrote to Roosevelt, 'you will have to face this situation and handle it without gloves later on. Dev's political survival depends on his injecting the vitality of hate into this issue of partition.'[19]

The Taoiseach had himself provided concrete confirmation that he planned to make an international issue of partition. In late September 1943 he told the annual Fianna Fáil convention that 'We will try to do everything we can in order that the wrongs of this partition of our country would be brought to the notice of all those who would have any power to remedy it.'

Gray was becoming uneasy about the delay in presenting a note to de Valera, because he realised that some of the more radical Protestant elements in Northern Ireland could do incalculable harm to his plans. During September, for instance, he had to caution Maffey about the actions of the *Ulster Protestant*, which suggested that Pope Pius XII should be put on the list of war criminals. 'Since my visit to America', Gray explained, alluding to the newspaper's suggestion, 'I am more than ever convinced that it is so loaded with political dynamite as to make one suspect the activity of German agents.' He therefore asked the British representative to try to stop such charges, because they could make Washington's determination to support Northern Ireland vulnerable to attack that could ultimately damage Anglo-American relations.

The ideal moment to present the new note to de Valera seemed to be at hand on 12 October 1943 when Churchill announced that Antonio Salazar, the dictator of neutral Portugal, had given Britain bases in the Azores. As a result Gray urged that the American request be delivered as soon as possible, but the State Department did not want to move without London's approval, and the British procrastinated for almost three months before responding, in spite of repeated urgings from Washington.

Winant learned from Lord Cranborne that the delay was a result of the British cabinet's determination 'to make certain of the security of the British Isles and insure protection for those who had stood with the British in North Ireland'. Maffey, however, went into a little more detail with Gray. He told him that the delay had been caused by some members of Churchill's government who seemed to believe that de Valera's existing policy was discrediting him sufficiently in the United States already, and they were afraid that the Taoiseach would comply with the request and would thus be in a stronger position to demand an end to partition.

Hull thought the British were possibly suspicious that the American proposal was intended as a first step towards ending partition, so he gave Winant permission to assure them that the Ulster question was an Anglo-Irish problem in which the United States had no intention of becoming involved. The proposed note, Hull explained, was intended to 'serve an extremely useful purpose not only with regard to our domestic situation and our relations with Ireland but particularly with reference to certain vicious influences which may otherwise be brought to bear on Anglo-American relations after the war'. He added that he did not want British approval in the sense of assuming responsibility. 'We merely wish to know', Hull wrote, 'whether they are opposed to this independent approach wholly on our own responsibility.'

It was not until the Cairo conference in early December 1943 that Churchill finally told Roosevelt that the British wanted the whole matter dropped. Their official explanation was that they were afraid that de Valera would not give a direct answer to the request but would try to confuse the issue by making a pronouncement on the grievance of partition.

Even though the American approach for the ports had been killed, the State Department did have an opportunity to give vent to its frustrations before the end of the year, after the Irish sought permission to purchase another ship as a replacement for the two ships chartered in 1941, which had since been lost while carrying wheat to Ireland.

When Hull informed Gray that Washington intended to reject the Irish request, the latter heartily agreed with the decision, pointing out that the Irish government had not even protested when the first two ships were sunk, even though there was evidence to suggest that the Germans had torpedoed at least one of them. Gray also noted that the gesture in handing over the previous two ships had 'had negligible propaganda value in Ireland as the government continuously ignored any obligation to the United States for them'. What was more, he concluded, the Irish still had enough ships to take care of their 'imperative requirements'.

The State Department then forwarded a note for delivery to de Valera, rejecting the request. In the note, which Roosevelt personally approved, Hull explained that the United States could not comply with the request because the Irish government had allowed the two ships it had chartered earlier 'to be sunk by Nazi submarines without offering the slightest word of protest to the German government'. Since the Germans had clearly demonstrated that they were 'in fact making war upon Ireland,' the Secretary of State contended, any further ships transferred to Ireland were likely to meet the same fate as the other two.

The American reply was a foretaste of what the State Department had in store for Ireland.

10. Axis Representatives in Dublin

THE 'AMERICAN NOTE' AND DE VALERA'S REFUSAL TO EXPEL THEM
December 1943—June 1944

In August 1943 when Gray drafted the note inviting Ireland to join the Allied war effort, he did so fully confident that the Irish government would refuse. But this really did not matter, because he was obviously only looking for evidence of that refusal.

However, State Department and military leaders in Washington opposed this approach and drafted a second note. They simply did not want to take any chance that de Valera would accept the offer, as they were afraid that the United States might become responsible for defending Ireland. One important difference between the two notes was that the second one made no mention of the Axis representatives in Dublin. Although Gray wanted concrete evidence of de Valera refusing to expel them, he enthusiastically accepted the new approach, once he realised that the United States could ask for their expulsion at a later date.

Gray wrote to Roosevelt on 4 November 1943 that 'It would be a logical development for the record when and if Dev turns down the request for the ports to follow with a request that he at the least get the Axis spy missions out of the country.' Their continued presence in Ireland, the American Minister believed, was disadvantageous to the United States seeing that they were in a good position to learn about American troop movements in Northern Ireland. In fact, he observed that it was so easy to get information in Dublin about such troop movements in the Six Counties that 'for Axis observation purposes' the American forces 'might just as well be in Vichy France'.

Yet when Gray discussed the problem with the Canadian High Commissioner, the following week, the latter surprised him by expressing complete satisfaction with Irish security arrangements. Kearney noted that Irish authorities had been co-operating with the Allies on intelligence matters and had been using electronic equipment to make sure that the German legation was not using its radio transmitter.[1]

Nevertheless Gray was dissatisfied. As long as there was a possibility—even the remotest possibility—that the Axis representatives might pass on important information, he was determined to make an issue of their presence. He therefore suggested that the State Department should formally ask de Valera to have the Axis representatives recalled.

Gray sent the Secretary of State his arguments on the subject on 13 December 1943. He also enclosed a suggested draft for a formal note contending that Irish neutrality favoured the Axis powers because Ireland's geographic location afforded their representatives an opportunity for highly organised espionage, while it denied any such advantage to the Allies. Since it was common knowledge that Allied troops in Northern Ireland and Britain were preparing for the invasion of Europe, Gray argued that the success of the operation and the lives of thousands of men were being endangered by the possibility that the invasion plans could be betrayed from Ireland. As a result the note suggested that the Irish government should make its policy 'truly neutral' by taking appropriate steps for the recall of German and Japanese representatives in Ireland.

In a covering telegram, Gray explained that he had discussed the note with Maffey and that both of them believed that de Valera would reject the request and thus provide the United States with 'an important political advantage' by placing himself 'on record in such a manner as would strengthen our defence against pressure group attempts to involve [the] United States in the partition question'.

Although the American Minister was primarily motivated by political considerations, he warned the State Department that the German Minister might indeed get hold of some vital information that could be forwarded to Berlin in an emergency by using the legation's radio transmitter. While Gray admitted that the transmitter had not been used for more than a year, he nevertheless noted that 'it remains ready to use for the immediate transmission of any message deemed important enough to risk complications with the Irish government.'[2]

Before Washington could act on the question, however, the

British persuaded Irish authorities to demand that the Germans surrender their transmitter. Hempel's position had been seriously undermined in mid-December 1943 when two German spies were captured in the west of Ireland only hours after being dropped by parachute. He therefore agreed to deposit the transmitter in the vault of a Dublin bank, from where he could only get it with the approval of the Irish Department of External Affairs.

Of course, the depositing of the transmitter did not affect the political considerations of the Americans. Gray still pressed for action, and since the joint Chiefs of Staff had no objection, Hull instructed him to relay the proposal to Winant, who could sound out the British.

When forwarding the proposed note on 7 January 1944, Gray enclosed a long letter summarising events since he first proposed the need to discredit de Valera. The latest document, he explained, was essentially the third draft of the note originally prepared by himself in August, which had been killed in Washington by the State Department and Chiefs of Staff for fear that de Valera would comply with it. Their anxiety was understandable, according to Gray, who noted that 'It was in fact extremely difficult for reasonable men to believe that the head of a small and powerless State could assume the lunatic arrogance which at times is characteristic of Mr de Valera.' They, therefore, drew up a second draft, which the British vetoed for fear the Taoiseach would comply with it in order to strengthen his hand for an anti-partition campaign after the war.

It was in order to meet this British objection, Gray explained, that he prepared the third and latest draft. It did not ask Ireland for help; it merely requested that the Irish be 'truly neutral'. Thus, if de Valera acceded to the request and expelled the Axis representatives, the note was so worded that he would not really be able to claim that he had given any assistance. Yet this was superfluous because, Gray added, it was 'certain' that the Taoiseach would reject the request, with the result that the Allies would have the documentary material with which to discredit him.

Realising that the British were reluctant to get involved in a dispute with Ireland at the time, the American Minister warned that they were going to have to face the question sooner or later, and he was convinced that from the American viewpoint, the

G

sooner the better. 'The only choice open to us', he wrote, 'appears to be whether we shall meet this situation while the war continues, while Anglo-American solidarity is strong, while American obligation to Northern Ireland for facilities is remembered, or wait upon a time and circumstance favourable to Mr de Valera.'

The request for removal of the Axis representatives was therefore designed as a means of providing Washington with material with which it could provoke American resentment against de Valera, if he later tried to cause trouble over partition. Authorities in Washington would be able to call on the American people to support Stormont on the grounds that it had helped the United States by providing bases, in contrast with the Twenty-Six Counties, which would have endangered the lives of Americans by allowing potential spies to remain in Ireland during the crucial months immediately prior to the Allied invasion of Europe. This propaganda line would be especially effective for, as Gray explained to Winant, 'A threat to the lives of American soldiers will unfailingly excite American resentment.'[3]

The British gave tentative approval to the proposed approach, so the State Department drew up a note, essentially on the lines suggested by Gray. It was then submitted to the Foreign Office in London for final approval.

On 9 February 1944 Foreign Secretary Eden formally approved of the note but stipulated that Washington should not publish it, nor make any public pronouncements on the affair without first conferring with London. Eden added that British authorities would send a separate note to de Valera, announcing that they had been consulted by the United States and that they warmly welcomed the American initiative and supported the request.

Everything having been prepared, Gray was instructed to deliver the note to de Valera personally. A meeting was therefore arranged with the Taoiseach for the afternoon of 21 February 1944.

Anxious to obtain de Valera's immediate reaction to the note, Gray decided to wait around until after the Taoiseach had finished reading the document.[4] In some respect it was an ideal day for the meeting, because the daily newspapers were carrying Cardinal MacRory's latest pastoral letter, which condemned partition. The American Minister, therefore, opened the meeting by criticising the cardinal's statement that the Allies should be thankful that Ireland was not actively supporting the Axis powers.

De Valera said that he could understand Gray's attitude, but added that the latter should try to appreciate the cardinal's position. Eighty per cent of the Irish people, the Taoiseach said, were being forced to live with the injustice of partition.

Gray was unconvinced. From a practical standpoint he thought the cardinal's statement was ill-advised. 'It is certainly not going to make it easier for you to make the response which I hope you can make to this note,' he said as he handed over the State Department's request.

Although de Valera showed no anger, he looked 'very sour and grim' as he read the note slowly, often pausing to re-read certain passages carefully. The document read:

Your Excellency will recall that in your speech at Cork delivered on the fourteenth of December, 1941 you expressed sentiments of special friendship for the American people on the occasion of their entry into the present war and closed by saying, 'The policy of the state remains unchanged. We can only be a friendly neutral.' As you will also recall, extracts of this speech were transmitted to the President by your Minister in Washington. The President, while conveying his appreciation for this expression of friendship, stated his confidence that the Irish government and the Irish people, whose freedom is at stake no less than ours, would know how to meet their responsibilities in this situation.

It has become increasingly apparent that despite the declared desire of the Irish government that its neutrality should not operate in favour of either of the belligerents, it has in fact operated and continues to operate in favour of the Axis powers and against the United Nations on whom your security and the maintenance of your national economy depend. One of the gravest and most inequitable results of this situation is the opportunity for highly organised espionage which the geographical position of Ireland affords the Axis and denies the United Nations. Situated as you are in close proximity to Britain, divided only by an intangible boundary from Northern

Ireland, where are situated important American bases, with continuous traffic to and from both countries, Axis agents enjoy almost unrestricted opportunity for bringing military information of vital importance from Great Britain and Northern Ireland into Ireland and from there transmitting it by various routes and methods to Germany. No opportunity corresponding to this is open to the United Nations, for the Axis has no military disposition which may be observed from Ireland.

We do not question the good faith of the Irish government in its efforts to suppress Axis espionage. Whether or to what extent it has succeeded in preventing acts of espionage against American shipping and American forces in Great Britain and Northern Ireland is, of course, impossible to determine with certainty. Nevertheless, it is a fact that German and Japanese diplomatic and consular representatives still continue to reside in Dublin and enjoy the special privileges and immunities customarily accorded to such officials. That Axis representatives in neutral countries use these special privileges and immunities as a cloak for espionage activities against the United Nations has been demonstrated over and over again. It would be naïve to assume that Axis agencies have not exploited conditions to the full in Ireland as they have in other countries. It is our understanding that the German Legation in Dublin, until recently at least, has had in its possession a radio sending set. This is evidence of the intention of the German government to use this means of communication. Supporting evidence is furnished by the two parachutists equipped with radio sending sets recently dropped on your territory by German planes.

As you know from common report, United Nations military operations are in preparation in both Britain and Northern Ireland. It is vital that information from which may be deduced their nature and direction should not reach the enemy. Not only the success of the operations but the lives of thousands of United Nations' soldiers are at stake.

We request therefore, that the Irish government take appropriate steps for the recall of German and Japanese representatives in Ireland. We should be lacking in candour if we did not state our hope that this action will take the form of severance of all diplomatic relations between Ireland and these two countries. You will, of course, readily understand the compelling reasons why we ask as an absolute minimum the removal of these Axis representatives whose presence in Ireland must inevitably be regarded as constituting a danger to the lives of American soldiers and to the success of Allied military operations.

It is hardly necessary to point out that time is of extreme importance and that we trust Your Excellency will favour us with your reply at your early convenience.

De Valera rejected the request without hesitation. 'Of course our answer will be no', he said before he had even finished reading the note; 'as long as I am here it will be no.' When he reached the phrase calling for the removal of the Axis diplomats 'as an absolute minimum', he asked if it was an ultimatum.

'I have no reason to believe that it is more than a request to a friendly state; as far as I can see there is no "or else" implication in this communication,' replied the American Minister.

The Taoiseach then finished reading the note and repeated his earlier rejection. 'As long as I am here', he declared, 'Éire will not grant this request; we have done everything to prevent Axis espionage, going beyond what we might reasonably be expected to do and I am satisfied that there are no leaks from this country; for a year and a half you have been advertising the invasion of Europe and what has got out about it has not been from Éire; the German Minister, I am satisfied, has behaved very correctly and decently and as a neutral we will not send him away.'

Gray explained that he could not say definitely that Axis representatives in Dublin were conducting espionage activities, but he assumed that they were in view of the conduct of their diplomats in other neutral countries. The United States government would, as a result, be lax in its duties, if it did not try to do something about the matter.

Immediately after the meeting, Gray went over to Maffey's office and told him what had transpired. They discussed the best time to deliver the British note, and both agreed that it should be handed over as soon as possible.

Maffey delivered it the following afternoon. The document was a short note explaining that British authorities had been consulted by Washington and therefore wished to make it clear that they 'warmly welcome the initiative which has been taken by the United States government and that they fully support the request for the removal from Éire of German and Japanese diplomatic and consular representatives'.

Although de Valera had remained calm with Gray, he became quite angry with Maffey, whom he accused of conspiring against a weak neutral. The Taoiseach seemed especially upset that the British representative with whom he had been on cordial terms, should support what he described as an American ultimatum.

Maffey argued that it was a reasonable request, not an ultimatum, but de Valera was not placated. He was annoyed that in spite of the working relationship that had existed, the Allies had delivered formal notes without making any informal representations beforehand. The Taoiseach contended that the move was an effort to push him into the war and thus deprive Ireland of the symbols of her independence. 'It was obvious', Maffey reported, 'that he attached immense importance to this symbolic factor.'[5]

In addition to some more important ramifications, de Valera had obviously supported neutrality as a means of proving that Ireland could determine her own policy and was thus independent, in spite of her ties with the British Commonwealth. Viewing the notes as a threat to this newly manifested freedom, it was natural that the Taoiseach should turn to Canada for help.

The Canadians had long shared the Irish leader's desire to demonstrate dominion independence. Indeed, they had been so concerned about it at the outbreak of hostilities that they waited for several days before declaring war, thereby proving that as a dominion Canada had a right to remain neutral. As a result Ottawa would be loath to support any British effort to compel Ireland to abandon neutrality for fear of setting a precedent that would undermine dominion rights and negate Canada's own symbolic gesture at the start of the war.

On the morning of 23 February 1944, therefore, de Valera discussed the affair with Kearney, who was taken completely by surprise.[6] Neither Gray nor Maffey had told him about the notes, but he nevertheless adopted the attitude that they must have been moved by a genuine concern about the espionage danger.

The Taoiseach explained that there was no evidence to justify ordering the removal of the Axis representatives, even if he were so inclined. And he stressed that he was relying on information supplied by the Irish secret service, which had been working closely with British intelligence. According to the Canadian representative, de Valera 'thought the delivery to him of formal notes instead of more or less informal verbal representations which have hitherto been made by the American Minister and British representative was alarming and significant'. In fact, the Taoiseach contended that the formal notes were designed for propaganda purposes in order to prepare public opinion for an Allied attack on Ireland. He therefore asked that the Canadian government use its influence to have the notes withdrawn. 'He made it clear, however,' Kearney explained in a telegram to Ottawa, 'that even if verbal representation were substituted for formal notes he would not do away with Axis missions but would give assurances that he would take any measures which might be suggested to eliminate any possible espionage.'

In Ottawa Prime Minister Mackenzie King's initial reaction was certainly sympathetic to de Valera's suggestion calling for the withdrawal of the notes. He attached to the High Commissioner's telegram a short memorandum for Norman A. Robertson, the Under Secretary at the Department of External Affairs. 'I view favourably the suggestion made in this telegram,' the Prime Minister wrote, 'but would like you to think it over and let me know your reaction.'

Before Robertson could reply there was some hectic diplomatic manoeuvring. On learning from Kearney that Canada had been asked to intervene, Maffey got in touch with London and suggested that Churchill himself should contact Mackenzie King. The Dominions Office quickly despatched a message to Ottawa explaining that Churchill hoped that the Canadian government would not only reject de Valera's request but would actually associate itself with the British and American notes.

This was a little too much for the Canadians, and they told a British emissary so. Robertson reported to Mackenzie King:

We pointed out that the Canadian government had not been consulted about this new approach to the Irish government, and had only been informed of it after it had taken place. In the circumstances, I thought it extremely unlikely that the Canadian government would be prepared to consider associating itself, formally and belatedly, in the way Mr Churchill had suggested. We would be very glad to see the Irish government compel the withdrawal of Axis diplomatic representatives from Dublin, but the measures taken did not seem very well designed to achieve the end in view.[7]

Nevertheless the Canadians really had little choice but to reject the Irish request. They were fighting alongside both Britain and the United States and could hardly strain their alliance by supporting a neutral government against the wishes of their own allies.

'In the circumstances,' Robertson advised Mackenzie King, 'I think it was a mistake in judgment for the United Kingdom and United States government to present formal notes on this subject to the Irish government at this time, but I do not think we could act as Mr de Valera's intermediary in attempting to bring about their withdrawal.'[8]

A telegram instructing Kearney to tell the Taoiseach that Canada could not intervene was already prepared when a second telegram was received from the High Commissioner in Dublin. Having tendered no advice in his first telegram, he now suggested that Canada should turn down de Valera's request but should show good faith by suggesting that all notes on the subject be kept secret. In this way Dublin could be reassured that there were no sinister propaganda motives involved.

Mackenzie King accepted the secrecy suggestion, so Kearney was instructed to act essentially on the lines of his own advice.[9] On the evening of 26 February he told de Valera that Canada had 'a good deal of sympathy' with Irish objections to the timing and formal nature of the American and British notes but nevertheless felt 'that the Irish government would be well advised to comply'.[10] Quoting from his instructions the High Commissioner explained:

We have welcomed each indication of Irish sympathy and support and we keep alive the hope that sooner or later Ireland will feel able to make some more direct contribution to the winning of this war. In this spirit we would naturally be very glad to see Axis Missions removed from Dublin and are thus in full sympathy with the object of the approach which the United States and United Kingdom have made.

He concluded by advocating that each of the parties involved should come to some arrangement to avoid publicity.

Gray was just as anxious to keep the affair secret as were the Canadians, because he realised that there was a danger that de Valera might try to make 'political capital' out of the note 'by charging that it was not the reasonable request that it is but the first step in a conspiracy to crucify Éire with hostile propaganda as a prelude to armed invasion'. The American Minister wanted the Allies to play the role of aggrieved friends who had helped the Irish but received nothing in return. He even suggested that the State Department should be prepared to announce with great fanfare the release of strategic material for the Irish Sugar Company, so that the United States could demonstrate that there were no hostile intentions towards Ireland.

Meanwhile de Valera continued to attribute the most sinister motives to the whole affair. On the night that the United States note was delivered, for instance, he put the army on alert and the Defence Conference met for several hours making preparations for an American attack. While the conference was in session the British military attaché, who did not know about the note, telephoned inquiring where Irish authorities wished to take delivery of some motorcycles that he had procured for them. Even though such a call could easily have been taken as a reassuring sign, it was not in this case. Instead, the Taoiseach went ahead and interpreted the American approach as an ultimatum in spite of Gray's explanation to the contrary. Subsequently he also disregarded similar arguments by Maffey and Kearney.

With the army on alert, there was a great deal of public uneasiness, especially when de Valera told a gathering in Cavan on 27 February that it was 'a time of extreme danger' in which defence forces should be prepared. 'No words which I can use', he said, 'would be strong enough to express my conviction of the necessity of maintaining these forces at their maximum strength and efficiency.'

Wild rumours abounded. There were reports, for instance, that the Allies had invaded from the Six Counties and that there were battleships off the Dublin coast. There were also rumours that Richard Mulcahy had been arrested and James Dillon shot.

On 29 February Gray passed on to de Valera an assurance that had been given to the Irish Minister in Washington three days earlier by John D. Hickerson of the European affairs division of the State Department. Brennan had been told then that the note was not an ultimatum, that no military action was contemplated against Ireland, and that the principal sanction that American authorities had in mind 'was the wrath of American mothers whose sons' lives would be placed in jeopardy', if Axis representatives were permitted to remain in Ireland.

Having failed to get the notes withdrawn, de Valera had Brennan deliver his formal rejection on 7 March 1944. The reply declared that the Irish people wanted to remain neutral and since the demand for removal of diplomatic representatives 'is universally recognised as the first step towards war', the Dublin government could not comply with the request. The Taoiseach went on to explain that his government had taken great care to ensure against espionage and was holding twelve suspected spies, most of whom had been captured shortly after arriving in Ireland. 'These are the facts', he asserted, 'and it is doubtful if any other country can show such a record of care and successful vigilance.' Indeed, it later became clear that this was no idle claim.

In spite of the apparent desire of all parties concerned to keep the whole affair secret, the press somehow got hold of the story.* Consequently, on 10 March 1944, the State Department decided to make public the exchange of notes.

Since there was little important news next day, the Irish refusal received banner headlines on front pages of newspapers throughout the United States. And for the next two weeks the American press portrayed Ireland as being infested with Axis spies.

'Call for St Patrick!' exclaimed a *Dallas Morning News* editorial. 'The snakes are back in Ireland.' The same day the *Fort Worth Star-Telegram* claimed that 'The German and Jap embassies in Éire are nothing less than spy bases from which helpful information can be furnished Hitler and Tojo.' It added that 'A Nation either is a friend of the Axis or the United Nations. But not meeting co-operatively with the latter it becomes a friend of the former.' The *Atlanta Constitution* was almost

---

* Gray believed that one of the opposition representatives on the Defence Conference was responsible for the leak.

hysterical as it declared that Ireland had been 'notoriously loose' in dealing with the Axis legations and that 'thousands and thousands of American soldiers will die because of the Irish position'. Although the *New York Times* was not quite so definite, it warned that despite Irish vigilance, Axis agents might possibly pass on information which could 'be sufficient to endanger the lives of many thousands of allied soldiers, including many of Irish descent'.

In such an emotional atmosphere American newspapers gave currency to wild and ridiculous rumours, many of which had already been discredited. In spite of repeated explanations that the German legation consisted of only about half a dozen people, the influential *New York Herald Tribune* reported that the German Minister had a staff of seventeen who were 'free to operate with all diplomatic privileges'. The old charge that there had been U-boat bases on the Galway coast reappeared in *PM*, which published a particularly inflammatory series of articles by Michael Sayers and Barnett Bildersee, carrying one headline that took up most of the front page: 'HOW IRELAND HAR-BOURS NAZI SPIES.' Instead of commending the Irish government for its work in preventing espionage, these writers merely justified the American note by citing the capture of German agents as proof that there had been spies in Ireland. They added that many more had possibly gone undetected, and concluded their articles by stating that Axis nations thrived on Irish neutrality.

The *Fort Worth Star-Telegram* carried an especially bitter and distorted editorial in its evening edition on St Patrick's Day. It provoked strong criticism from de Valera's *Irish Press*, which accused the Forth Worth publisher of exposing himself to 'every cheapjack lie spoken about Ireland'.

The Texas newspaper had accused the Irish government of permitting the Axis powers to retain excessively large staffs with nothing to do 'other than spying upon the Allied forces in England and North Ireland'. Dublin's attitude had supposedly 'opened a dangerous threat to the Allied invasion of Europe and to the safety of the American troops moved up to participate in that invasion'. In fact, the Irish were accused of actually 'fighting America and Americans' in a covert manner by providing beacons to enable 'Nazi raiders to get their bearings and easily locate targets, such as Coventry, Liverpool and Belfast. The point may be well made that Éire's "neutrality" has served only the Germans and to a lesser extent the Japs.' As a result, the editorial continued, the American note was 'a logical and reasonable demand' and the most extreme measures, even military invasion, would be justified to secure the removal of the Axis representatives. The editorial's author was actually so poorly informed that he claimed that Ireland had gained her independence through a 'bloodless revolution' with the aid of financial help from the United States. Now, he added, America's sympathy had worn out. 'The case demands action,' the editorial concluded. 'Either Éire throws out the Jap and German spies or stands the consequences. Whether blockade or more extreme measures will be necessary to bring Prime Minister de Valera to face realities is for him to decide.'

The attacks on Irish neutrality were not confined to uninformed editorial writers on small city newspapers. Sumner Welles, who had resigned from the State Department some months earlier, denounced the Taoiseach in a front-page article in the *New York Herald Tribune*.[11] Claiming that 'Éamon de Valera has never been noted for possessing an elastic mind', he criticised an editorial in a Dublin newspaper which claimed that the people of Ireland were so fond of peace that they would fight to preserve it. 'The Irish are not going to be doing any fighting,' Welles contended. 'It will be the men of the United Nations, whom they will not even lift a finger to help, who will be doing the fighting and dying to make it possible for the Irish to enjoy the peace of which they are "so fond".' He added, nevertheless, that the Irish would suffer later because they would not have much influence in the post-war world. 'Those who will not lend a hand in the supreme effort to make it possible for a real peace once more to exist', he concluded, 'have no right to expect to be heard by the victors when the war is won.'

In his analysis of the Irish stand, James Reston, the Washington correspondent of the *New York Times*, wrote that as a result of the Irish refusal, de Valera would not again 'have quite the same political support from the United States that he has always counted on in his ancient battles with the British'.

In mid-March 1944 one public opinion survey conducted on the refusal to expel the representatives found that seventy-one per cent of the American people were aware of the affair and two out of three of those who knew about it thought that the United States should take further action. Of those, thirty-eight per cent recommended the use of trade sanctions, while thirty-five per cent thought that a degree of force should be used to compel the Dublin government to be more co-operative. There were even some people who advocated declaring war on Ireland. Indeed, if the survey was accurate, there were more than a million Americans in favour of such action.

Gray had certainly succeeded in discrediting the Irish government, but he realised that if any pressure were to be exerted on Dublin, the Irish people would rally around de Valera. The American Minister therefore became primarily concerned with the need to avoid the appearance of trying to coerce Ireland. He suggested that the State Department should authorise him to announce that the United States was releasing the material for the Sugar Company, and he also proposed that Churchill should be warned to forestall any possible denunciation of Ireland.

The Secretary of State did not think, however, that the United States should reassure the Irish that further measures would not be taken against them. Rather, he informed Winant that Washington should follow Britain's lead in the matter. And Churchill had no intention of reassuring Dublin. In fact, on 13 March 1944 he gave the distinct impression that Britain was about to retaliate by isolating Ireland 'from the outside world during the critical period which is approaching'.

The announcement gave rise to immediate fears in Dublin that the Allies were going to introduce economic sanctions. Kearney happened to arrive at the Irish Department of External Affairs shortly after the speech, and he found Joseph Walshe in an extremely agitated state. The High Commissioner tried to convince him that the speech did not portend economic pressure, that Churchill must have had 'his tongue in his cheek', and that the announcement was possibly intended only 'as a sop to British sentiment' which had been disturbed by Ireland's refusal to expel the Axis representatives.[12]

The British Prime Minister had apparently caught even his own people by surprise. Immediately after leaving Walshe, Kearney hurried over to Maffey's office, where he found the

British representative 'obviously worried over the Churchill pronouncement'.

Gray, who also found Maffey troubled and anxious lest Churchill should 'jump the reservation and gum things up', telegraphed Washington suggesting that Churchill should be advised to simply play the role of an aggrieved party. Roosevelt agreed. So a message was quickly despatched to the British Ambassador in Washington advocating that no economic sanctions should be applied against Ireland.

The measures that Churchill had announced were actually designed mainly to avoid leakage of any information from Ireland, but the Prime Minister was in no hurry to give Dublin any reassurance on this point. On 19 March 1944 he informed Roosevelt that although Britain was cutting off all shipping from Ireland, British ships would continue to supply the Irish. He added, however, that it was still too early to placate de Valera's fears.

'Gray's lead in Ireland has been followed by us and it is too soon to begin reassuring de Valera,' wrote Churchill. 'A doctor telling his patient that the medicine prescribed for his nerve trouble is only coloured water is senseless. To keep them guessing for a while would be much better in my opinion.' He added that the Allies 'should let fear work its healthy process rather than to allay alarm in de Valera's circles. In that way we shall get a continued stiffening up of the Irish measures behind the scenes. At the moment these are not so bad to prevent leakage.'

Public opinion in Dublin was greatly excited and Gray was in an uncomfortable position, as he was being openly blamed for having inspired the crisis by misrepresenting Irish neutrality in his reports. Had he informed the State Department about the true state of affairs, Irish officials were convinced that the Americans would never have sent their note. Matters were only made worse by reports filed by two American press correspondents, each of whom claimed that Gray had been the source of his story.

The first report, which was written by Frank King of the Press Association and carried in the *New York Times*, attributed the American Minister with having said that the Irish government did not have the legal power to stop the leakage of military information from Dublin to Berlin, 'so long as the German and

Japanese diplomatic missions remained in Dublin, and so long as they had the diplomatic privilege' of sending couriers back and forth from Ireland with diplomatic pouches.

Irish officials were understandably furious because the Germans no longer had a diplomatic bag and the Japanese did not have diplomatic status. Nevertheless Gray was able to avoid responsibility for the report by denying the statements attributed to him.

Two weeks later, however, there was further embarrassment when an AP correspondent, Roger Green, reported that he had been told by Gray that the Irish had deliberately slighted the United States government by not inviting an American representative to a Red Cross function at which the German Minister and Japanese Consul were guests.

The charge was inaccurate. The Irish Red Cross had not sent specific invitations to any foreign representatives but had circularised each mission with a notice about the function. The German and Japanese representatives had purchased tickets, so the United States legation—which admitted that a notice had probably been received—announced that the charge of 'discourtesy was without basis'.

For his part, Gray denied that he had been the source of the story, and the affair might have rested there, except that the Irish got hold of an unpublished portion of Green's report which went on to quote a verbal exchange between Gray and de Valera during their meeting of 21 February when the American note was handed over.

Since de Valera had not given an interview to Green and was not therefore the source of the details of the February meeting, the *Irish Press* claimed that either Green had falsified the whole report, or else the American Minister was guilty of undiplomatic conduct in revealing a secret discussion.[13]

As Gray had already denied the story, T. F. O'Higgins raised the question in the Dáil with a blistering attack on the government for using its own semi-official organ to attack a foreign diplomat. He also denounced the censor for permitting the editorial to be published, but Frank Aiken replied that it had not been censored because it was considered as questioning the veracity of the reporter rather than the American Minister. Next, the AP got into the act by defending Green with an announcement that he had received his information directly from Gray on 18 March during an interview at the United States legation.

The AP was right. Gray explained to Roosevelt that he had 'talked off the record' to Green, who then let him down and thus provoked 'a teapot tempest'.[14]

Other than his denial of the affair, Gray declined to say anything further publicly and refused to give out any statement or provide any interviews. 'Now', he explained to the President, 'the opposition has a chance without welshing on neutrality to attack Dev in the Dáil for affronting the representative of a friendly power and has taken it in a big way. The way to handle this ugly group of bad hats is to tell them to go sit on a tack.'

Under intense public criticism, Gray was showing signs of frustration. Yet he still possessed a genuine affection for the Irish people in general. His ire was directed against 'the little group of political racketeers who have captured the country'.

The Canadian High Commissioner felt sorry for his American colleague. 'I have a great deal of sympathy for Mr Gray,' he reported, 'because I have never found him otherwise than most agreeable and co-operative. He is a very forthright type of person who always speaks his mind.'[15]

Much of the criticism being directed against the American Minister contended that he was responsible for misinforming Washington about the true security situation in Ireland. Brennan argued in the United States, for instance, that Ireland had established effective measures to prevent espionage. He noted that the German legation consisted of only three men and two women, all of whom were without means of communicating with the outside world, except by using the cable passing through London. 'Therefore', he concluded, 'they can transmit no message that the British are not willing to forward.' He also pointed out that Irish authorities had little difficulty apprehending Axis agents sent to Ireland. 'They are picked up within a few hours of their arrival,' he said. 'Ireland is a small country where every one knows every one else. A stranger immediately attracts notice.'[16]

While the Allied representatives in Dublin were not able to refute these arguments, Kearney thought that the Irish government was 'dangerously over-confident with regard to its own effectiveness in counteracting Axis espionage'. Obviously intelligence people were not in a position to say publicly what they knew, so it would be 'Only when the war is over, and when what those in the Secret Service alone know may be told, will the entire situation be revealed.'

More than thirty years after the conclusion of the war Allied intelligence files are still closed to researchers, but captured Axis documents have been studied and various American intelligence people have been willing to talk. Together these sources corroborate Brennan's arguments.

According to Enno Stephan's *Spies in Ireland*, the most authoritative work on German espionage in Ireland, the Germans sent ten spies to Ireland, all of whom were captured, seven within hours of their arrival, and two within a matter of weeks. Only Hermann Goertz, who was free for eighteen months, remained at large for any appreciable length of time, but Irish authorities were aware of his presence and so harassed his lines of communication that he was of no use to his country's war effort.

Irish authorities were, of course, confident all along that they had the situation under control. As a result they were greatly annoyed at the bad press they were receiving in the United States, especially since a representative of the Office of Strategic Services (OSS)—the precursor of the CIA—had acknowledged in November 1943 that Irish security arrangements to prevent Axis espionage were satisfactory. And the OSS had never indicated that anything was amiss since then.

In fact nothing was amiss. Colonel David K. Bruce, the OSS Chief for Europe, believed that Irish security was satisfactory at the time.[17] So also did Ervin R. Marlin, who was officially supposed to be an assistant to Gray but was in fact an OSS agent.[18] He later wrote that subsequent disclosures have demonstrated conclusively that Axis representatives 'were impotent and performed no useful services to their governments during the critical months before the invasion'. J. Russell Forgan, who was deputy chief of the OSS for Europe at the time, explained that the Irish had provided 'very useful' co-operation to the Allies on intelligence matters. 'In general', he concluded, 'despite the American news media, the Irish worked with us on intelligence matters almost as if they were our allies. They have never received the credit due them.'[19]

Just how or to what extent the Irish co-operated, however, is not clear, although it is known that they turned over all information derived from captured German agents. In his best-selling book on espionage, *The Game of the Foxes*, Ladislas Farago claimed that Ernst Weber-Drohl, one of the German spies captured in Ireland, was eventually used as a double agent by the Allies. But the most dramatic instance of co-operation was related by a former employee of the CIA, J. Harris Smith, who claimed in his book *The O.S.S.* that the Irish diplomatic service assisted United States intelligence by transporting information on bombing sites in Japan.

According to Smith, the affair—known as the 'Vassel Project' —originated when a member of the Vatican secretariat, Monsignor Giovani Montini (later Pope Paul VI), offered to forward information from a source in Japan on strategic bombing sites in that country. With de Valera's consent, Michael MacWhite, the Irish Minister to Italy, forwarded the information to Dublin, from where it was turned over to the Americans.

In early April 1944 Joseph Walshe called on American intelligence in London and protested vigorously to Forgan about the treatment being afforded to Ireland in the American press. In order to make sure that Axis missions would not be able to spy on the Allies, he even offered to allow the United States to station agents in Ireland, but the OSS was reluctant to accept the offer for fear that this would exonerate the Irish government, if the Axis representatives did somehow manage to expose the invasion plans.

Gray was opposed to the suggested co-operation on the grounds that such a gesture could be used 'as a political means of wiping off the record' the stigma of de Valera's refusal to dismiss the Axis missions. The American Minister perceived that any talk of Ireland being helpful posed a real threat to all that had been accomplished. He did not want to take any chance of de Valera getting favourable publicity, because he realised that as long as the Taoiseach remained discredited with the American people, there was little chance that he could cause problems for the Anglo-American alliance by stirring up trouble over partition. Gray's determination to ensure that nothing should upset this plan was actually such that he wrote to Col. Bruce suggesting that Marlin—who he believed had told Irish authorities that their security was completely satisfactory—should be transferred to North Africa in order to keep him out of Irish-American circles.[20]

At the same time, however, Gray did not want Washington

to press the issue of the presence of Axis representatives any further, and he was uneasy when he learned that Hull was unwilling to drop the matter. The Secretary of State was arguing that a second note should be sent to de Valera making it clear 'that the continued presence of Axis representatives in Ireland must be regarded as a danger to American lives and military operations for which the Irish government cannot escape responsibility'.[21]

Allied representatives in Dublin were unanimously opposed to sending a further note. And when the State Department forwarded a draft document to London for approval, Churchill himself asked that the matter be dropped.

Hull reluctantly concurred. On 17 May 1944 he notified Roosevelt of the decision, explaining that things had become particularly complicated because de Valera had called a general election for the end of the month. 'This development', he wrote, 'would appear to make the sending of a further note definitely undesirable.'

Having governed for almost a year with a minority government, de Valera had dissolved the Dáil and called a general election after he lost a vote on a minor transportation bill in early May. The time seemed right to capitalise on his defence of Irish neutrality. And it was. At the polls Fianna Fáil gained seventeen seats to give the party a comfortable majority.

At least one popular American news magazine believed that the Taoiseach had the United States government to thank for his victory. *Time* declared that American pressure had simply made the Irish people 'more devoted to their own belligerent neutrality than ever'. According to Robert Smyllie, editor of the *Irish Times*, the incident provided de Valera with 'a God-given opportunity once more to demonstrate Éire's absolute independence of everybody, including on this occasion the United States and to figure in the eyes of his own followers as one of the greatest statesmen since Abraham Lincoln'.*[22]

Gray realised this even before the election, seeing that he had

---

* Another factor that probably helped de Valera's popularity was the well publicised stand he had taken in an effort to have Rome declared an open city, on account of its importance to Roman Catholics throughout the world. It is not possible to say whether the Taoiseach's stand actually played any role in the German decision not to defend the city, but many Italians were convinced that it had, and they sent him a message of thanks.

explained to a State Department official that the affair surrounding the American note had 'put the great mass of the people behind de Valera as the man who told America where to get off'.[23] As a result the American Minister was not surprised by the outcome of the election, nor was he disappointed for that matter. In a letter to Roosevelt on 2 June 1944 he explained that it was 'a good thing' that the Taoiseach had been returned with a clear majority :

> He is in now for five more years and if his mistakes are what we think they are, he will have to liquidate them. There was a danger that he would duck responsibility for a while and let the opposition pay the bills and clean the slate and then come back when they bungled. No engagement or refusal to enter into an engagement without his sanction, in the postwar period would be worth the paper it was written on.

11. The Bitter End

June 1944—June 1947

DURING the final months of the war Irish neutrality faded into the background as the Allies concentrated on the liberation of Europe. Although relations between the United States and Ireland remained strained, de Valera was still willing to co-operate on some matters, such as releasing the few remaining Allied internees, including Wolfe, the American. He also agreed to accept responsibility for the care of 500 Jewish children from France in August 1944, at the request of the United States government.

The Taoiseach took a rather equivocal stand, however, when asked for a commitment that the Irish government would not grant political asylum to Nazi war criminals. 'The Irish government', he explained, 'can give no assurance which would preclude them from exercising that right should justice, charity or honour or the interest of the nation so require.' But then confusing the issue somewhat, he added that his government had no intention of altering its long observed practice of denying 'admission to all aliens whose presence would be at variance with the policy of neutrality, or detrimental to the Irish people, or inconsistent with the desire of the Irish people to avoid injury to the interests of friendly states'. In other words the Irish government would not guarantee that it would not grant political asylum to war criminals, even though it had no plans to do so.

On 12 April 1945, less than a month before the war finally ended in Europe, President Roosevelt died. Even though Irish neutrality had lost one of its severest critics, there was no rejoicing in Dublin. Gray was surprised; members of the Irish government were actually grieved. He wrote to the late President's wife next day:

This is indeed a strange country. All this forenoon members of the government, their wives and leaders of the opposition have been coming in a stream to pay their respects. Mr de Valera made a very moving tribute to the President in the Dáil this morning and moved adjournment till tomorrow. I thought I knew this country and its people but this was something new. There was a great deal of genuine feeling.

Although the Irish gesture went virtually unnoticed in the American press, the same did not happen a little over two weeks later when de Valera paid an official call on Edouard Hempel to express sympathy over the death of Hitler. The Taoiseach's action set off a firestorm of criticism in the Allied press. That he had merely followed the strict protocol of a neutral state did not matter. 'Considering the character and record of the man for whose death he was expressing grief', a *New York Times* editorial declared, 'there is obviously something wrong with the protocol, the neutrality, or Mr de Valera.'

Even the Canadian press, which had previously been very restrained in its comments on Irish neutrality, was outraged. According to a report sent to Kearney, Canadian editorials were unanimously critical, with comments ranging from 'neutrality gone mad' to expression of sympathy for the embarrassed Irish people in view of what was described as de Valera's 'bad taste'.[1]

Although the censored Irish newspapers did not reflect it, there was a great deal of criticism of the affair in Ireland. According to Kearney, 'nothing which Mr de Valera has done during the years which I have been in Dublin has evoked such widespread criticism, and much of it comes from persons who are normally supporters of his own party.'[2]

Why did de Valera go to such lengths to express sympathy for the death of a man he really despised? John Gunther, the noted American journalist and author, thought that the Taoiseach was probably only trying to tweak the tail of the British Lion,[3] but it seems that a more correct analogy would have been that he was ruffling the feathers of the American Eagle.

While Gray believed that de Valera had reluctantly made the visit at the insistence of Aiken, Maffey thought that the gesture had been in reaction to recent American efforts to get the Irish government to allow the Allies to seize the German legation before Hempel could destroy his secret files. The British representative was certainly nearer to the truth.

De Valera explained his reasons in a personal letter to Brennan in Washington. 'During the whole of the war', he wrote, 'Dr Hempel's conduct was irreproachable. He was always and invariably correct—in marked contrast with Gray. I certainly was not going to add to his humiliation in the hour of defeat.'4 The Taoiseach was maintaining neutrality to the bitter end. And the end was indeed bitter in Dublin.

On 7 May 1945 when it was announced that Germany would formally surrender the following day, some students at Trinity College, Dublin (which was then still identified with the Ascendancy class), began flying the Allied flags from the flagpole on the roof of the entrance to the college. A group of rival students from the National University gathered in the streets below and took exception to the flying of the Irish tricolour beneath the Allied flags. Some of the students on the roof then tried to burn the Irish flag and threw it smouldering from the roof.

What had initially been a good humoured incident turned ugly and the police had to make a number of baton charges to disperse the crowd. Later that evening some students from the National University started a demonstration in protest at the burning of the Irish flag. They gathered a crowd and marched to Trinity College, where the police again forcefully broke up the demonstration. But this time some demonstrators went directly to the offices of the United States Consul-General and the residence of the British representative and stoned both buildings. While the attack on the residence of a British representative in Ireland was not unusual, the attack on the American building was unprecedented. It symbolised the extent to which the normally cordial relations between the United States and Ireland had deteriorated during the war.

The Canadian representative in London thought that de Valera's actions following the death of Hitler provoked Churchill to unleash a strong attack on Irish neutrality and on the Taoiseach himself during a victory address on 13 May 1945. The Prime Minister claimed that the refusal to allow Britain to use Irish ports had been 'a deadly blow and if it had not been for the loyalty and friendship of Northern Ireland we should have been forced to come to close quarters with Mr de Valera or perish forever from the earth'. Of course, the British never did attack Ireland. Instead, Churchill explained, 'we left the de Valera government to frolic with the German and later with the Japanese representatives to their heart's content.'

There was a great air of anticipation in Ireland as people waited for the Taoiseach to respond to Churchill's address. It was generally assumed that he was going to deliver a tirade, but such was not to be the case. On 16 May 1945 de Valera went on Radio Éireann to deliver what was probably the finest speech of his long career. Beginning by thanking God for sparing Ireland from the conflagration that had left much of Europe in ruins, he proceeded to express gratitude to various people and groups who had contributed to the success of neutrality. Then he turned to Churchill's speech. The Taoiseach explained that he knew what many people were expecting him to say and what he would have said twenty-five years earlier. But he added, the occasion demanded something else because the British Prime Minister could be excused for being carried away in the excitement of victory, while no such excuse could be made for himself. Speaking calmly he said :

> Mr Churchill makes it clear that, in certain circumstances, he would have violated our neutrality and that he would justify his action by Britain's necessity. It seems strange to me that Mr Churchill does not see that this, if it be accepted, would mean that Britain's necessity would become a moral code and that, when this necessity became sufficiently great, other people's rights were not to count. It is quite true that other great powers believe in this same code—in their own regard—and have behaved in accordance with it. This is precisely why we have the disastrous succession of wars—World War No. 1 and World War No. 2—and shall it be World War No. 3?

He then turned to praise Churchill for resisting the temptation to violate Irish neutrality :

> It is, indeed, hard for the strong to be just to the weak. But acting justly always has its rewards. By resisting his temptation in this instance, Mr Churchill, instead of adding another horrid chapter to the already bloodstained record of the relations between England and this country, has advanced the cause of international morality an important step. . . .

The public reaction to this address was overwhelming. 'With little exception', the Canadian representative reported, 'Mr de Valera's broadcast is regarded in Ireland as a masterpiece, and it is looked upon as probably his best effort. It has served to almost still the criticism which his visit to the German Minister provoked, and, in so far as I can judge, on balance, Mr de Valera now stands in higher favour in Ireland than he did before his visit to the German Minister.'[5]

Maffey admitted to Kearney that Churchill's remarks concerning Irish neutrality had been a great mistake. It was not the British Prime Minister's speech, he said, but de Valera's reply 'which bore the stamp of the elder statesman'. As the Canadian representative saw it, 'Churchill gave Mr de Valera an opportunity to debate Ireland's neutrality with the number one man of the United Nations, and, as Sir John puts it—"to win on points".'

Although the war was over, there were still questions to be cleared up with the Irish. On 11 June 1945 the State Department instructed Gray to ask the Irish government to intern, or keep under house arrest, all German diplomatic personnel and agents captured during the war.

Fearing that de Valera would reject the request, Gray opposed it and suggested instead that the Allies should do nothing until the Irish government approached them about taking German internees off its hands. Then the Allies could demand that the diplomats and spies be turned over as well. He explained that the best chance that the Allies had of getting all the Germans that they wanted was to get them all together, seeing that the Taoiseach was particularly anxious to get rid of the 250 internees being held. But if the Allies took them off his hands first, Gray warned that de Valera would then be in a position to snub a request for the others, and would be able to make political capital out of portraying his government as an upholder of the right of asylum. The one trump card that the Allies had in order to avoid this was to exploit the 'nuisance value of those disorderly and expensive internees'.

While Gray was arguing over the timing and form of the approach, the British went ahead on their own and asked for the expatriation of the internees and the ten spies. Although de Valera flatly refused to give up the latter, contending that their offences were against the Irish government, he did agree to hand over the internees on condition that the British guaranteed that none of them would be executed nor sent into the Soviet zone.

Gray was bitterly opposed to the latter stipulation, believing that Dublin was trying to split the Allies by having them discriminate against one another. He tried to persuade the State Department to put pressure on the British to reject the request, but Washington refused. Instead, he was instructed to co-operate with Maffey, who by that time had already given the assurances sought by de Valera.

The American Minister, however, was insistent that any further approach for the spies or diplomats should be a joint project on the part of the Allies. Otherwise, he predicted that de Valera would continue to deal with the British alone and possibly drive a wedge into the relations between the United States and Britain.

A formula was eventually agreed upon under which the Allied Control Commission asked the various neutral governments to hand over all 'obnoxious' Germans, who were defined as anyone who played a part, no matter how minor, in the German war effort. Gray forwarded this note to de Valera on 5 December 1945, along with a letter explaining that the Germans in question might have a harmful influence on the Irish people, particularly on those who had attacked the American offices following the riot at Trinity College. Referring to those rioters, the American Minister wrote that 'The mentality of such people is favourable soil for the seed of National Socialist [Nazi] resurgence.'

Although he thought it probable that the Taoiseach would reject the request, Gray was opposed to the idea of imposing economic sanctions on Ireland in retaliation. He believed that such pressure would only serve to strengthen the Fianna Fáil government politically. 'Any suggestion of outside pressure', he explained to the State Department 'serves to unite the Irish people behind Mr de Valera and renew his mandate for isolation and separatism.' Gray therefore suggested that the best recourse for the United States was 'to give full publicity to our request and to his reply and place him on record before the world as choosing to be the apologist for the criminal Nazi regime and protector of its representatives'.[6]

Fearing that de Valera might try to confuse the issue by launching the long postponed anti-partition campaign, Gray wrote to various Irish-American leaders. On 5 January 1946 he explained to Senator James A. Murray of Montana that the Taoiseach might attempt to stir up a controversy over partition in order to distract public attention from his 'probable refusal to co-operate with us in expatriating the classes of Germans which the Allied Control Commission in Germany wishes to have returned for security reasons'. He added that it was 'unfair and improper of his groups to inject their issues into our politics after the support of their independence which we have given in the past'.

In succeeding days Gray also wrote to other prominent Irish-Americans, among them James A. Farley, John McCormack, and Joseph P. Kennedy. In each letter he enclosed an unsigned memorandum, 'The United States and Irish Partition', which was, in the words of a State Department official, 'a scathing indictment of the Irish government's attitude towards us during the war'.

The tone of the correspondence can best be understood by examining the letter to Farley, who was a sincere admirer of de Valera. Gray wrote that although the Taoiseach had originally condemned the invasion of Belgium by Germany, 'he abruptly abandoned that point of view after the fall of France and, very probably due to the influence of Mr Frank Aiken, pursued a policy with his newspaper and with the government censorship which favoured Hitler at every turn.'[7]

The censorship did basically favour the Germans in that it placed the murderous Nazi regime on the same moral plane as the Allies, but it certainly was not designed to help the German war effort, nor damage the reputation of the Allies, as could so easily have been inferred from Gray's letter. The real aim was to prevent people from trying to drag Ireland into the war on one side or the other.

The editor of the *Irish Times*, Robert M. Smyllie, later wrote that everybody realised 'that some form of censorship was necessary in order to preserve neutrality and the security of the state; but nobody except Mr Aiken and his staff ever expected that such depths of absurdity would be plumbed'.[8] For example, the censor ordered the *Irish Times* to alter an announcement concerning services at the Kingstown Presbyterian Church because Kingstown had been renamed Dun Laoghaire some years earlier. The fact that the church itself still retained its old name was no justification in the eyes of the censor. Such interference certainly ignored the real purpose of censorship as outlined by de Valera in the Dáil. But, as has already been pointed out earlier, Smyllie wrote in May 1941 that de Valera himself was 'more than anxious to be fair'.[9]

Censorship was really a domestic Irish concern because, notwithstanding the anomalies in its application, it did not prevent the Allies from getting their side of the story across to the Irish people, seeing that no effort was made to jam Allied radio broadcasts. In addition there was no attempt to censor British newspapers, which were openly available in Ireland, nor were any restrictions placed on the official American publication, *Letter from America*. The public reaction to de Valera's expression on condolence to the German Minister following the death of Hitler was proof that censorship had not prevented the Irish people from learning of the moral bankruptcy of the Nazis.

The State Department became disturbed at the manner in which Gray was freely criticising the Irish government. Even though the Minister explained that he had been acting in an unofficial capacity so that Washington could repudiate him, if necessary, John D. Hickerson of the State Department warned him that it would be virtually impossible to distinguish between his actions as a private citizen and those in his official capacity. Hickerson also mentioned that Gray was apparently exaggerating the possible impact of an anti-partition campaign in the United States, because Edward R. Stettinius had, as Secretary of State, made it clear that 'The American government could only take the position that the altering of political boundaries between the Irish Free State and Northern Ireland was not a matter in which it might properly intervene.'

On 12 February 1946 James A. Farley arrived in Ireland along with Archbishops Francis Spellman of New York and Edward Mooney of Detroit, who were on their way to Rome where each was to be elevated to the college of cardinals. De Valera and Joseph Walshe were at the airport to provide an official welcome.

Farley found them extremely bitter towards Gray, who was

also present, although he had not been invited, nor was he invited to join the official party when it departed for a state dinner in Killarney. This was, for de Valera, a diplomatic way of slighting Gray. It was a pointed insult that the American Minister should not be invited to a state dinner in honour of American guests.

That night at the dinner de Valera mentioned that he had gone to the United States during Ireland's struggle for independence in order to secure the help of Americans. 'I still want their powerful aid and influence to see that it is not merely the Twenty-Six Counties of this country, which will be free,' he said, 'but the whole Thirty-Two Counties.'

While this appeal was made privately to only a few Americans, de Valera went a step further by making a similar appeal to the American people in general in his St Patrick's Day address to the United States a few weeks later. In view of the public stand taken by the State Department against American involvement in the partition issue, it was obvious that the Taoiseach's speech was an effort to appeal to the American people over the head of their government. Gray believed that de Valera had two ends in view:

> One is to strengthen his domestic political situation by keeping the partition issue before the people. The second is to appeal to American sympathy in anticipation of unfavourable reaction when his refusal to co-operate in the matter of German property and personnel in Éire becomes known.

De Valera's efforts fell flat however. Secretary of State James F. Byrnes noted that only the largest newspapers in the United States as much as mentioned the St Patrick's Day speech and even those did not devote much space to it, nor make any editorial comment. By early August 1946 it was apparent to Gray that Irish efforts to inject the issue into American politics were being dropped.

Moreover, in December 1946, much to the astonishment of the State Department, de Valera indicated that he might be willing to hand over the captured German spies to the British. Surprised, Edward T. Wailes, chief of the Commonwealth affairs division at the State Department, wrote to Gray that 'none of us had really expected any co-operation from Dev.'

It was some months, however, before the German agents were handed over. The difficulty arose over a difference of opinion between de Valera and his Justice Minister, Gerald Boland, who was reluctant to agree to repatriation. Since the Germans had already been given to believe that they would be allowed to remain in Ireland, Boland threatened to resign if they should be deported. In fact, at one point he actually sent a letter of resignation to de Valera, but the latter prevailed upon him to withdraw it.[10]

Gray discussed the question with Boland, whom he described as 'a man of high character, great courage, and iron nerve combined with what in our view is a somewhat sentimental tenderness toward appeals on compassionate grounds'.[11] The Minister for Justice explained that he was particularly opposed to sanctioning the deportation of the spy Herman Goertz, because the latter was so afraid of the Allies that he might commit suicide.

Although Gray argued that Goertz could hardly come to any harm because he had been out of Germany and unconnected with the Nazis when most of the atrocities had been committed, Boland remained sceptical. On one occasion when Gray pressed the issue, Boland became so agitated that he ordered the American Minister out of his home.[12]

The matter had not yet been settled when, in April 1947, Gray returned to the United States. But the Americans did have their way a few weeks later. On 23 May 1947 Goertz was taken into custody and told that he was being deported. Then Boland's fears were realised. Goertz killed himself by taking cyanide.

Thus, when Gray formally resigned his post at the end of the following month, all the loose ends had been cleared up. Irish neutrality was but a part of history.

12. Conclusion

UPSTAGING THE PLAYBOY OF THE WESTERN WORLD

FOLLOWING his resignation as Minister to Ireland, David Gray retired to his home in Sarasota, Florida, where he began writing a history of Irish neutrality that he never finished. In it he characterised neutrality as immoral, and he compared de Valera's wartime actions to Nero fiddling while Rome burned.

Some years later in an introduction to William A. Carson's *Ulster and the Irish Republic*, Gray wrote that there had been two basic reasons why de Valera 'maintained a neutrality which served only Hitler's objectives'. The first reason, he argued, was to demonstrate that in spite of Ireland's association with the British Commonwealth, the Twenty-Six Counties were truly independent. The Taoiseach accomplished this by not following Britain into the war. But if demonstrating Irish independence had been his only aim, he could have done it by merely following the example of the Canadians, who waited for some days after Britain's declaration of war before declaring war themselves.

The second consideration behind neutrality, which Gray put forward, amounted to a serious charge. He wrote that 'accumulating evidence supports the view that even before the fall of France in 1940, de Valera believed that Hitler would win the war, and that in payment for keeping the Allies out of the Éire ports he would obtain Northern Ireland on his own terms.' Just what this 'accumulating evidence' was, Gray did not specify, nor has anybody produced any of it.

Indeed German diplomatic documents demonstrate conclusively that the German Minister in Dublin harboured no illusions that de Valera wanted Germany to win the war in order to end partition. In fact, on 13 November 1939 Hempel reported that some people in Ireland had expressed such a hope, but he doubted that de Valera shared their views. Then on 18 June of the following year the Taoiseach actually told Hempel that he could only adhere to a peaceful solution to the Ulster question. In other words he did not want Germany to force an end to partition. Even months after the fall of France, the German Minister had still received no indication that Dublin was looking towards Hitler to secure Irish unity. On 7 December 1940, for example, Hempel reported that 'Neither de Valera nor any official of the Irish Foreign Ministry has ever mentioned to me the possibility of recovering Northern Ireland with German help.'

Actually Gray had himself indicated in August 1940 that de Valera was pursuing so stringent a policy against would-be Nazi collaborators in the IRA that he could at best only expect to be liquidated painlessly if the Germans ever got control of Ireland. The Taoiseach never did ease up on his pressure. In the course of the war, six members of the IRA were executed, three were allowed to die on hunger strike, about six hundred were jailed for various offences, and a further five hundred were interned without trial. The adoption of such drastic measures was certainly not a way of helping Hitler.

There were really a number of reasons why de Valera decided to remain neutral, but the principal reason, in the last analysis, was his belief that a small country like Ireland would only be hurt in a conflict involving major powers. 'We tried to keep out of involvement in the last war because we believed', de Valera explained in 1957, 'that war would be made in spite of us and without consulting us and that war would be ended without consulting us and that the terms on which the war would be ended would not be the terms we would have wished for but the terms which would suit the interests of the large powers engaged in the war.'

Another potent argument in favour of neutrality concerned the defenceless state of the country. This, of course, was more a result than a cause of the original decision to remain neutral, seeing that de Valera had made little effort to secure arms even though he foresaw the coming of war. Yet once hostilities began, the lack of adequate defences made it almost suicidal to abandon neutrality.

A further argument used in defence of Irish policy was that partition made it impossible for Dublin to join the British without provoking civil strife in Ireland. But the Taoiseach's subsequent insistence that he would not bargain with neutrality even in return for an end to partition indicated that he considered the preservation of neutrality even more important than Irish unity. And there was little in his conduct during the war to indicate that he would ever have been willing to make such a bargain.

Gray's postwar portrayal of Irish neutrality was really seriously distorted, conceivably because his judgement had been influenced by bitterness over Irish involvement in American politics at a very crucial stage of the war. In late 1940 and early 1941 when the British were virtually alone in opposing the Nazis, Roosevelt was trying to increase American aid, but he was running into strong domestic opposition, with the arguments of opponents ranging from contentions that it was too late to assist Britain, to claims that Britain was not worth helping. Confronted with such opposition, the Roosevelt administration was very resentful when Irish authorities raised issues that were critical of Britain in addresses directed at the American people.

In November 1940, for instance, de Valera asked Irish-Americans to put Ireland's case concerning partition to the American people. In the context of the Dublin government's attitude towards the problem at the time, this was tantamount to asking for a propaganda campaign in the United States against Britain's occupation of Northern Ireland. Washington resented the outside effort to drag Americans into a dispute in which the United States was not involved, especially when that dispute cast Britain in an unfavourable light at a very crucial period. Yet the Taoiseach regularly harped on the Ulster question in broadcasts to the United States. No doubt he felt strongly about what he considered the grievance of partition, but there was an inconsistency in his attitude towards the problem during the war. In the spring of 1941 when the Germans bombed Belfast, for example, he made no protest that they had violated Irish sovereignty, but he did complain when the Americans sent troops to Northern Ireland some months later. In view of the circumstances, Gray was understandably annoyed.

The Americans were also infuriated that in broadcasts to the United States at Christmas 1940 and again the following St Patrick's Day, de Valera, in effect, went so far as to charge that

H

Britain was blockading Ireland. Subsequently Aiken frequently reiterated the charge in the course of his American tour, during which he associated with many of Roosevelt's bitterest critics, some of whom were actually being used by the Germans in an attempt to undermine American foreign policy.

Here the British really forced the Irish government's hand. Churchill wanted Irish ports, but he was afraid to seize them because of the effect that such a move might have on American public opinion. He therefore sparked what appeared to be a systematic campaign to convince Americans of Britain's need for Irish facilities, and he also began to exert economic pressure on Ireland in an attempt to weaken the Irish people's support for neutrality.

Although London claimed that the trade cuts were necessitated by a need for shipping space, de Valera correctly perceived that there were ulterior motives. He realised that the British were exerting economic pressure, and he became particularly uneasy when they continually refused to guarantee that they would respect the 1938 agreement renouncing their rights to Irish ports.

In an excellent study of the wartime co-operation between countries of the British Commonwealth, Professor Nicholas Mansergh, the eminent historian, concluded that

> Churchill's bitterness, coupled with his idiosyncratic assessment of political forces in Ireland, led him to embark upon a course of recrimination which, if anything, hardened Irish resolve to withhold the ports and lost to Britain some of the advantages that might otherwise have accrued from unqualified recognition, in time of extreme peril of an agreement freely negotiated some few years earlier.[1]

By repeatedly ignoring Maffey's advice that Dublin be reassured about British intentions towards Ireland, Churchill really left Irish authorities with little choice but to use their one trump card—Irish-American opinion—to make sure that Britain stayed in line. In using it de Valera and Aiken overstepped the bounds of normal diplomatic propriety by appealing directly to the American people over the head of President Roosevelt and his administration.

While Aiken's close associations with Roosevelt's opponents

were of questionable diplomatic taste, they were not without precedent. Gray had been associating with de Valera's critics in Dublin.

Although the American Minister never did try to appeal directly to the Irish people over the head of the Dublin government, this was partly because Irish censorship made such a move very difficult. He certainly would never have been able to secure anything like the freedom that Aiken had while in the United States. Yet, if it ever suited his purposes, the American Minister would have gone over de Valera's head. He went to the extent of establishing a propaganda newsletter at the United States legation, for example, to ensure that he would have the means of appealing directly to the Irish people in case the United States ever decided to invade Ireland.

Irish authorities were most annoyed at Gray because they believed that his reports were not accurately representing the true benevolence of Irish neutrality towards the Allies. Washington was obviously poorly informed, and this became most apparent when the State Department confronted Brennan with the ludicrous request for an explanation about the rumoured presence of hundreds of Japanese tourists in Ireland.

Initially Gray's failure to portray Anglo-Irish relations accurately was because neither British nor Irish authorities had taken him fully into their confidence about the extent of the secret co-operation. But even when he did find out and the Irish agreed to extend the same co-operation to the Americans after they entered the war, the American Minister did not appreciate the help.

Although the Canadian High Commissioner was satisfied that Irish authorities were willing to 'do almost anything to help [the Allied war effort] short of involving themselves in the war', and the British representative was prepared to give de Valera credit (for an always difficult and often generous interpretation of neutrality', the American Minister was not willing to give any such credit. Speaking some years later Maffey explained that

David Gray in that crisis of human affairs felt that 'those who are not with us are against us.' That was his stern unshakeable principle. In his diplomacy there was no room for compromises. . . .[2]

On coming to Ireland Gray had one overriding goal. He wanted to help Britain as much as possible in the struggle against Nazi Germany, not because he was an anglophile, which he was not, but because he believed it was in the best interest of the United States. He was therefore outspoken in his support of the British cause. While President Roosevelt was publicly advocating that the United States should give Britain all out aid short of war, Gray was calling on the Dublin government to go that final step and join the British war effort. He even took it upon himself to say things that he thought the British would like to say, but which prudence prevented.

In a wartime report to the Dominions Office Maffey explained that Gray 'recognised the need of extreme patience on our side of the table and continued to say exactly what he thought in the ideal setting of the American Legation'. United States Ministers to Ireland had been expected to say comfortable things, according to Maffey, but Gray 'had the temerity to make it plain to Irish Nationalists that they were no longer the darling Playboy of the Western World, and to point out that the audience were bored'.[3]

The American Minister was actually prepared to go further than just speaking his mind. His letters to the White House clearly demonstrated that he was an unabashed supporter of power politics. He had little hesitation in suggesting that the United States should invade Ireland, if some advantage could be gained thereby. He was, in effect, counselling that the United States should stoop to the same tactics employed by the Nazis on their way to overrunning most of Europe. His only real guide was his country's interest in the fight against Hitler. He somehow believed that an American incursion would be justified, because de Valera was avoiding moral responsibility by not providing more aid in the struggle against the murderous Nazi regime.

But how could de Valera have been of more assistance?

In 1943 Gray argued that Ireland should abandon neutrality because Irish policy hurt the Allies in two ways: one, by denying them bases; and two, by permitting Axis representatives to remain in Ireland in spite of the fact that they were an espionage threat to the Allies.

Even if one were to assume that the Irish government had a moral responsibility to join the Allies, notwithstanding the wishes of the vast majority of the Irish people to remain neutral, de Valera could not have helped by surrendering bases. Both London and Washington came to realise that they did not need such facilities because, even at the height of the German U-boat campaign, Northern Ireland facilities were sufficient to fulfil Anglo-American needs. Once the Allies realised this, they did not want Ireland to become involved in the war. Maffey later explained that Ireland's 'accession to the Allied cause, so far from affording help, would have created a dangerous liability'.[4]

Although permitting the Axis missions to remain in Ireland did undoubtedly entail at least a slight possibility that they might somehow be able to spy on the Allies, expelling them would have meant exposing Ireland to Nazi ire with the consequent possibility of German bombing attacks—the destructive potential of which on poorly defended Irish cities was brutally demonstrated in April 1941 when in one raid more than 700 people were killed in Belfast. De Valera chose to permit the Axis representatives to remain, and subsequent evidence has demonstrated that they provided no useful espionage to their governments.

Thus Gray's evaluation of the unfavourableness of Irish neutrality was inaccurate, but he was nevertheless on solid ground when he advocated the need to discredit de Valera. To understand that need one must look to the broader ramifications of the Irish leader's attitude towards the Ulster question and his intention of injecting the issue into postwar American politics.

De Valera had been instrumental in the enactment of a constitution that claimed sovereignty over the thirty-two counties of Ireland. Yet that constitution and laws enacted in Dublin were in some instances blatantly discriminatory against Protestant attitudes on such matters as divorce, birth control, and censorship.[5] In effect, Protestants of the Six Counties were being told that they should live by Roman Catholic standards of conduct and morality. While it was ridiculous to expect them to simply agree to such a proposition, it was possible—though most unlikely—that discriminatory aspects were deliberately included in the legal system in order to bring about a situation in which the only solution to partition would be the transfer of populations that de Valera had publicly spoke about before the war and to which he had privately alluded in a conversation with Gray in 1943.

As far as the American Minister was concerned, however, the idea of such a transfer was so absurd that he did not believe that de Valera was honestly putting it forward as a possible solution. Rather, he attributed the most sinister implications to the Taoiseach's behaviour. Crediting him with formidable political acumen, the American Minister could not conceive that de Valera could adopt such an attitude towards the Ulster question unless he really did not want an end to partition but only intended to keep the issue as an open political sore that he could exploit at will for his own ends.

Gray's assessment was probably inaccurate. The policy that he believed was the product of a sinister, calculating political mind, was more likely the result of de Valera's sheer culpable ignorance concerning the Northern Ireland question. After all, if Northern Irish Protestants would accept Irish unity, the Taoiseach had repeatedly expressed a willingness to grant them the local autonomy necessary to ensure against Roman Catholic discrimination. Yet he apparently failed to see that his own government's actions in discriminating against Protestant values actually belied his conciliatory words in the eyes of the Northern majority.

As long as the Twenty-Six Counties had a constitution and laws that were discriminatory, the majority in the Six Counties was hardly likely to agree to unity, nor could they be expected to simply accept being uprooted. What was more Washington could hardly push for the latter solution, any more than it could ask the vast majority of Americans to leave the United States and give America back to the Indians. Under the circumstances, therefore, Gray realised that there was no immediate possibility of a peaceful solution to partition, but he was afraid that if the problem became a political issue in the United States it could possibly lead to disastrous consequences.

One of the major reasons that the peace after the First World War had been destroyed was because the Allies had been unable to come up with a satisfactory peace agreement. In the United States concern over the Irish question contributed to the dissatisfaction that eventually led to the rejection of the Versailles Treaty. By 1943 there were signs that the same thing could happen again, seeing that isolationist Republicans were likely to cause problems for the President and there was a distinct possibility that they would be supported by normally Democratic ethnic groups, such as German, Italian, Irish, and Polish-Americans.

Being an astute observer of the American political scene, Gray fully appreciated the danger that such defections would entail. He therefore sought to ensure that de Valera would not be able to turn Americans against the postwar agreement on the grounds that it did not end partition. His aim was to discredit de Valera in the United States by getting him to refuse to help the Allies so that the refusal could, if necessary, be contrasted with Northern Ireland's help. Americans could then be made to feel that it would be ungrateful to support Dublin in a dispute with Belfast.

The American Minister accomplished his aim by getting de Valera to refuse to expel the Axis representatives, who were depicted as a danger to Allied plans for the invasion of Europe. When the American press learned of the refusal, there was a great smear campaign against Irish neutrality. Americans were told that the Irish were pro-Nazi and that Ireland was endangering the lives of American boys. Much of what the press reported was utter nonsense. The whole affair had little to do with Irish neutrality; it was simply a manoeuvre to make sure that de Valera would not be able to undermine the postwar peace settlement. As Gray himself admitted in late 1944, American policy towards Ireland was 'conducted primarily with reference to political conditions in America and to the end of protecting the Administration from pressure group attacks on our foreign policy'.[6]

Although no agreement comparable with the Versailles Treaty was signed after the Second World War, some of the recrimination against Roosevelt's foreign policy that Gray had feared was nevertheless heard in the United States. In fact, that recrimination, which led to one of the shoddiest chapters in American history, was scurrilously exploited by an Irish-American, Senator Joseph R. McCarthy of Wisconsin. The strong support that McCarthy received, especially among Irish-Americans, certainly justified some of the pessimistic predictions that Gray made in 1943.

Of course, the Irish question was of little significance in the postwar recrimination in the United States, but this was not because de Valera did not try to drum up American support for an anti-partition campaign. He did try. But his efforts never gathered much momentum, no doubt partly because Gray had done such an effective job of discrediting the Taoiseach by stirring up the controversy over the Axis representatives. Yet the very same controversy seemed to provide the Irish people with a dramatic example of de Valera's stout defence of Irish independence. He would henceforth be credited with keeping Ireland out of the war in spite of Allied pressure and German bombings. He had achieved what Gray had earlier believed was virtually impossible.

Gray once accused de Valera of 'lunatic arrogance', but the latter would have been guilty of that arrogance if he had deliberately involved Ireland in the war. The vast majority of the Irish people were in favour of neutrality and were likely to remain so unless attacked. According to the Canadian High Commissioner, 'the only thing that could unite them for war purposes is invasion —just as it required a declaration of war by Japan to unite the Americans.' It would therefore have been the epitome of arrogance for the Taoiseach to think that Ireland, a tiny, divided, and defenceless country, could have played a really significant role in the defeat of the Nazis. Future Irish generations may have been robbed of a footnote in history books that would have proclaimed that Ireland had been one of the Allies, but de Valera's duty was to serve the living generation, not some prophetic future. He was confronted with an enormous challenge.

During the early stage of the war he had the exquisite audacity to threaten Hitler with Churchill, and Churchill with Hitler. He even managed to threaten both of them with American public opinion, notwithstanding the contempt in which the Roosevelt administration held him. De Valera not only had to out-manoeuvre Hitler, Churchill, and Roosevelt, but also the IRA, which would have gladly dragged Ireland into the war on the side of Hitler, or British sympathisers such as James Dillon, who wanted to join the Allies.

Dillon demonstrated immense political courage in advocating a policy that he knew to be unpopular, but his actions were based largely on the faulty premise that Ireland could provide important help to the Allies. This miscalculation, coupled with his conduct in telling the American Minister that he would oppose resisting British seizure of Irish ports, could easily have resulted in disaster, because on the strength of the statement Gray encouraged the British to believe that they would have substantial support in Ireland if they seized Irish facilities. The danger was removed, however, when Dillon spoke out publicly and was not only repudiated by his party's leader, W. T. Cosgrave, but was also forced to resign from the party.

The loyal support given to neutrality by Cosgrave and also by Richard Mulcahy, who succeeded to the leadership of Fine Gael in 1944, undoubtedly helped to make de Valera's task somewhat easier, as did the able work of both Gerald Boland in handling the threat from the IRA, and Seán Lemass in dealing with the economic situation, not to mention the loyal support given by other members of the cabinet. Yet this should not detract from the Taoiseach's accomplishments.

When the war was over he could honestly say that Ireland had actually helped the Allies by co-operating on some military and intelligence matters, and by secretly releasing Allied airmen, while their German counterparts were interned for the duration of the conflict. In addition thousands of Irishmen served with Allied forces and many thousands more of their fellow-countrymen and women provided significant help by working in British factories and hospitals. Nevertheless in spite of the help and Ireland's proximity to the theatres of war, de Valera could still say that the country had come through the trying years of the Second World War relatively unmarked.

It was truly Éamon de Valera's finest Hour.

NOTES

These notes are intended primarily as a reference to sources not readily identifiable from the text, and also to some conclusions derived from published sources which might be considered controversial.

The research was extensively based on the Roosevelt-Gray correspondence at the Franklin D. Roosevelt Library (PSF file), Hyde Park, New York; Gray's personal papers at the Western Institute of Research, Laramie, Wyoming; State Department papers published in *Foreign Relations of the United States (FRUS)*; unpublished State Department papers at the National Archives, Washington, D.C.; and Canadian diplomatic papers at the Canadian Department of External Affairs and the Canadian National Archives in Ottawa, Canada. The papers of the American Friends of Irish Neutrality deposited at St John's University, New York, have also been used, as has the microfilm of British cabinet conclusions and papers presented to the British cabinet for the early years of the study, supplemented by Winston Churchill's *The Second World War* and Joseph T. Carroll's excellent study, *Ireland in the War Years*. Most of the material relating to German relations with Ireland is based on documents published in *Documents on German Foreign Policy*, Series D, though some other selected documents on microfilm at the National Archives in Washington, D.C. were also used. Irish government and cabinet minutes were also used at the State Paper Office in Dublin, but these contained few references to foreign policy. The notes and other pertinent material concerning the Defence Conference among Richard Mulcahy's papers at University College, Dublin, were particularly useful, especially for the views of Fine Gael leaders.

Personal correspondence with the following participants in events covered in the book also provided some useful information: Dean Acheson, Earl of Avon, Tom Barry, F. H. Boland, Kevin Boland, Earl of Brookeborough, David K. Bruce, Dan Bryan, Helmut E.

Clissmann, James Dillon, James A. Farley, J. Russell Forgan, W. Averell Harriman, John D. Kearney, E. R. Marlin, John W. McCormack, Frank MacDermot, Seán MacEntee, Mike McGlynn, Paul O'Dwyer, Eoin Ryan, and Robert Stewart.

Since much of the published material, especially volumes in both the *FRUS* and *Documents on German Foreign Policy* series, is well known to people interested in the field, reference is made to this material in the notes only in instances where confusion might otherwise arise.

CHAPTER 1 (pp. 1–23)

1. The most useful study of de Valera is an authorised biography by Lord Longford and Thomas O'Neill, *Eamon de Valera*, Dublin 1970.

2. Longford and O'Neill, *De Valera*, 93.

3. Speech, 25 January 1921, Dáil Éireann, *Minutes of Proceedings of the First Parliament of the Republic of Ireland, 1919–1921, Official Record*, Dublin 1921, 250.

4 See Patrick A. McCartan, *With de Valera to America*, Dublin 1932 and Charles C. Tansill, *America and the Fight for Irish Freedom, 1866–1922*, New York 1959.

5. T. Ryle Dwyer, 'The Anglo-Irish Treaty and Why They Signed', *Capuchin Annual, 1971*, Dublin 1971, 333–72.

6. Desmond Ryan, *Unique Dictator*, Dublin 1932.

7. De Valera to FDR, 25 January 1938.

8. FDR to Cudahy, 26 February 1938.

9. De Valera to FDR, 25 April 1938.

10. Speech, 5 March 1938.

11. Malcolm MacDonald, *Titans and Others*, London 1972, 82.

12. The best study of the IRA is J. Bowyer Bell's *The Secret Army*, London 1970.

13. Cudahy to FDR, 6 April 1939.

14. Speech, 2 July 1936.

15. The following material on Anglo-Irish relations is based on British cabinet records on microfilm at the FDR Library, Hyde Park, New York, supplemented by Winston S. Churchill, *The Gathering Storm*, Cambridge, Massachusetts 1948, 729; and Nicholas Bethell, *The War Hitler Won*, London 1972.

16. Irish cabinet minutes, 18 January 1940.

17. Speech, 29 September 1939.

18. Speech, 9 November 1939.

19. Irish cabinet minutes, 2 December 1939.

20. Cudahy to FDR, 7 December 1939.

CHAPTER 2 (pp. 24–46)
This chapter is largely based on W. L. Langer and S. E. Gleason, *The Challenge to Isolation*, New York 1952, and *The Undeclared War*, New York 1953; James McGregor Burns, *Roosevelt: The Soldier of Freedom, 1940–1945*, New York 1970; and Leonard Baker, *Roosevelt and Pearl Harbor*, New York 1970.

1. Poll material found in Headley Cantril, ed., *Public Opinion, 1935–1946*, Princeton 1951, and George H. Gallup, *The Gallup Poll: Public Opinion 1935–1971*, New York 1972.

2. Cudahy to FDR, 25 September 1939.

3. Walsh to FDR, 19 August 1940.

4. FDR to Walsh, 22 August 1940.

5. Gray to FDR, 4 September 1940.

6. Cudahy to FDR, 28 October 1939.

7. Edgar E. Robinson, *They Voted for Roosevelt*, New York 1970.

8. Transcripts of FDR's press conferences published in *Complete Presidential Press Conferences of Franklin D. Roosevelt*, New York 1972.

9. O'Connor to FDR, 6 May 1941.

10. Quoted in Ludovic Kennedy, *Pursuit*, London 1975, 207.

11. Gray to FDR, 2 October 1940.

CHAPTER 3 (pp. 47–65)

1. Cudahy to FDR, 22 January 1938.

2. *Irish Press*, 20 May 1940.

3. Related in Gray to FDR, 15 April 1940.

4. Gray to FDR, 21 March 1940.

5. Gray to FDR, 8 April 1940.

6. Gray to FDR, 15 April 1940.

7. Gray to FDR, 16 May 1940.

8. Gray to FDR, 31 May 1940.

9. Gray to Cooper, 30 May 1940.

10. Gray to FDR, 6–12 June 1940.

11. Except where noted, the following is based on Gray to FDR, 19–25 June 1940.

12. Gray to Abercorn, 14 June 1940.

13. Gray to Welles, 23 June 1940.

14. Gray to Maffey in unfinished letter and memo., 24 June 1940.

15. Following is based on material in Canadian Diplomatic Papers, File No. 822–39c.

16. Following is based on British cabinet conclusions and papers presented to the war cabinet, Cab 65 and Cab 66.

17. Gray to FDR, 28 June–4 July 1940.
18. Gray to FDR, 23 July 1940.
19. Mulcahy, memo., 5 July 1940.
20. Gray to FDR, 28 June–4 July 1940.
21. W. S. Churchill, *Secret Session Speeches*, London 1946, 30.

CHAPTER 4 (pp. 66–84)
1. Liddell Hart, *History of the Second World War*, London 1970, 55–64.
2. Gray to FDR, 8 April 1940.
3. Gray to FDR, 19 April 1940.
4. *Daily Express*, 4 July 1940.
5. Walter Warlimont, *Inside Hitler's Headquarters, 1939–1945*, New York 1964, 106.
6. Quoted in U.S. *Congressional Record*, 1940, 4928.
7. Joseph T. Carroll, *Ireland in the War Years*, London 1975, 68.
8. Gray, des. No. 37, 30 July 1940.
9. Gray, des. No. 40, 6 August 1940.
10. Gray to FDR, 25 August 1940.
11. Irish government minutes, 4 September 1940.
12. Gray to FDR, 8–9 September 1940.
13. Gray to FDR, 25 September 1940.
14. Gray, draft of letter to FDR, October 1940.
15. Gray to FDR, 2 October 1940.

CHAPTER 5 (pp. 85–106)
1. *FRUS.*
2. Walshe to Gray, 9 August 1940.
3. *New York Times*, 10 November 1940.
4. W. T. Cosgrave, memo., 11 November 1940. This and other material relating to Fine Gael is in Richard Mulcahy's Papers, University College, Dublin.
5. O'Higgins to Cosgrave, 11 November 1940.
6. Dillon, memo., 19 November 1940.
7. Mulcahy, memo., 21 November 1940.
8. Calton Younger, *A State of Disunion*, London 1972, 320.
9. Letter from Paul O'Dwyer, 30 September 1974 and MS of his unpublished memoirs.
10. *Congressional Record*, 1940, Vol. 86, A6590–91.
11. Kelly, des. No. 33, 15 November 1940.
12. Maffey to Churchill, 25 November 1940.
13. Longford and O'Neill, *De Valera*, 375–6.
14. Gray to FDR, 30 November 1940.

15. Longford and O'Neill, *De Valera*, 376.

16. The correspondence between Churchill and Roosevelt is published in F. L. Loewenheim, H. D. Langley, Manfred Jonas, eds., *Roosevelt and Churchill: Their Secret Wartime Correspondence*, London 1975.

17. Gray to FDR, 22 January 1941.

18. *FRUS.*

19. Mulcahy, memo., 8 January 1941.

20. Gray to FDR, 4 February 1941.

21. FDR to Gray, 6 March 1941.

22. The account of Willkie–de Valera meeting is based on Harold Nicolson, *Diaries and Letters: The War Years 1939–1945*, New York 1967, Vol. 2, 142–43; Harold Ickes, *Secret Diaries*, New York 1953, Vol. 3, 439–40; Ellsworth Barnard, *Wendell Willkie*, Marquette 1966, 563; and Gray to FDR, 4 February 1941.

23. *PM*, 18 April 1941.

CHAPTER 6 (pp. 107–121)

1. Carroll, *Ireland in the War Years*, 82.

2. Mulcahy, memo. of interview with de Valera, 30 January 1941.

3. Gray to FDR, 4 February 1941.

4. Gray to FDR, 28 June–4 July 1940; 31 December 1940.

5. Carroll, *Ireland in the War Years*, 101.

6. Longford and O'Neill, *De Valera*, 377.

7. Robert Brennan, 'My War-Time Mission in Washington', *Irish Press*, 7 May 1958.

8. Cordell Hull, *The Memoirs of Cordell Hull*, New York 1948, 1352–53.

9. Brennan, 'War-Time Mission', *Irish Press*, 8 May 1958.

10. New York *Daily News*, 24 April 1941; *New York Times*, 24 April 1941.

11. *PM*, 24 April 1941; *Time*, 5 May 1941.

12. Charles A. Lindbergh, *The Wartime Journals of Charles A. Lindbergh*, New York 1970, 477.

13. Langer and Gleason, *The Undeclared War*, 460.

14. *Irish World*, 3 May 1941.

15. San Francisco *Leader*, 17 May 1941.

16. *Irish Press*, 9 May 1941.

17. *New York Times*, 26 May 1941.

18. Lindbergh, *Wartime Journals*, 495.

19. Hempel, des. No. 284, 2 April 1941; tel. No. 56, 20 May 1941.

20. Mulcahy, memo., 20 May 1941.
21. Smyllie to Mulcahy, 21 May 1941.

CHAPTER 7 (pp. 122–138)
1. Gray to Duff Cooper, 4 April 1941.
2. Mackenzie King, memo. of conversation with Hearne, 23 May 1941.
3. Gray to FDR, 28 May 1941.
4. Alexander Cadogan, *The Diaries of Sir Alexander Cadogan, 1938–1945*, ed., David Dilks, London 1971, 381.
5. Gray to FDR, 28 July 1941.
6. T. Ryle Dwyer, 'Americans and the Great Irish Famine', *Capuchin Annual, 1974*, Dublin 1974, 270–78.
7. Minutes of Fine Gael front bench meeting, 4 March 1941.
8. FDR to Gray, 21 August 1941.
9. Gray, memo. of conversation, 27 September 1941.
10. McGlynn to Brennan, 4 October 1941. The following is based on AFIN Papers.
11. Kearney to N. A. Robertson, 17 October 1941.
12. Kearney to Robertson, 20 February 1942.
13. Gray to FDR, 28 July 1941.
14. Longford and O'Neill, *De Valera*, 390.
15. Hull, *Memoirs*, 1354.

CHAPTER 8 (pp. 139–159)
1. Longford and O'Neill, *De Valera*, 393.
2. Kearney to Robertson, 20 February 1942.
3. Brennan, 'War-Time Mission', *Irish Press*, 15 May 1958.
4. Gray to FDR, 27 January 1942.
5. San Francisco *Leader*, 31 January 1942; 4 April 1942.
6. Carroll, *Ireland in the War Years*, 115.
7. James F. Meenan, 'The Irish Economy during the War', in *Ireland in the war years and after 1939–51*, eds., Kevin B. Nowlan and T. Desmond Williams, Dublin 1969, 28–38.
8. Irish cabinet minutes, 17 October 1941.
9. *Ibid.*, 15 October 1943.
10. *Ibid.*, 26 March 1943.
11. *Ibid.*, 3 October 1941.
12. Quoted in letter Dulanty wrote to the *Spectator*, 31 March 1944
13. Gray to Maffey, 16 March 1942.
14. Gray, des. No. 320, 23 March 1942.
15. Gray, des. No. 317, 21 March 1942.

16. Gray to Hull, 21 March 1942; Gray to FDR, 24 March 1942.
17. FDR to Welles, 21 April 1942.
18. *FRUS.*
19. Gray to FDR, 8 October 1942.
20. Gray to MacRory, 7 October 1942.
21. Gray to FDR, 25 September 1940.
22. Gray to de Valera, 29 October 1942.
23. Gray to FDR, 6 November 1942.
24 FDR to Gray, 16 September 1942.
25. Letter from F. H. Boland, 22 February 1971.
26. Gray to FDR, 19 October 1942.
27. Kearney, des. No. 110, 12 August 1943.
28. Gray, tel. No. 52, 19 April 1943.
29. Kearney, des. No. 122, 14 September 1943.
30. Kearney, tel. No. 52, 15 June 1944.

CHAPTER 9 (pp. 160–178)

1. Maffey, memo. of conversation with Cosgrave, 19 October 1942.
2. Mulcahy, memo. of conversation with Bevan and Stokes, 17 August 1942.
3. Gray to FDR, 6–9 November 1942.
4. Gray to FDR, 29 November 1942.
5. Kearney to Robertson, 15 February 1943.
6. Carroll, *Ireland in the War Years*, 124–25.
7. Liddell Hart, *History of the Second World War*, 405.
8. Kearney to Robertson, 29 March 1943.
9. Gray to FDR, 13 February 1943.
10. Hull to Gray, 7 April 1943.
11. Gray, memo. on Irish situation, 16 August 1943. In this memo. he also gave an account of his trip to the Irish-American centres and again justified the need for an approach to de Valera.
12. Cudahy to Gray, 25 May 1943.
13. Gray to Cudahy, 25 August 1943; Gray to Col. T. A. McInerny, 14 September 1943.
14. *FRUS.*
15. Letter from Harriman, 1 July 1971.
16. Gray to FDR, 26 August 1943.
17. Gray to Hull, 21 April 1943.
18. Kearney to Robertson, 15 October 1943.
19. Gray to FDR, 20 October 1943.

CHAPTER 10 (pp. 179–200)

1. Gray, memo. of conversation with Kearney, 12 November 1943.

2. Gray, des. No. 756, 13 December 1943.

3. Gray to Winant, 7 January 1944.

4. Gray to FDR, 21 February 1944; also telegram of same date in *FRUS*.

5. Carroll, *Ireland in the War Years*, 143.

6. Kearney, tel. No. 12, 24 February 1944; tel. No. 13, 25 February 1944.

7. Robertson, memo. for Mackenzie King, 25 February 1944.

8. *Ibid*.

9. Secretary of State for External Affairs to Kearney, tels. Nos. 4 and 5, both 25 February 1944.

10. Kearney, tel. No. 24, 11 March 1944.

11. *New York Herald Tribune*, 22 March 1944.

12. Kearney, des. No. 45, 28 March 1944.

13. *Irish Press*, 23 March 1944.

14. Gray to FDR, 24 March 1944.

15. Kearney, des. No. 45, 28 March 1944.

16. Press conference in Washington, D.C., 17 March 1944.

17. Letter from Bruce, 16 November 1970.

18. Letter from Marlin, 5 January 1971.

19. Letter from Forgan, 6 November 1970.

20. Gray to Bruce, 17 June 1944.

21. Hull to FDR, 24 March 1944.

22. Robert M. Smyllie, 'Unneutral Neutral Éire', *Foreign Affairs*, January 1946, Vol. 24, 324.

23. Gray to Hickerson, undated, received 19 May 1940.

CHAPTER 11 (pp. 201–210)

1. Secretary of State for External Affairs to Kearney, tel. No. 16, 18 May 1945.

2. Kearney, des. No. 55, 14 May 1945.

3. John Gunther, *Procession*, New York 1965, 107.

4. Longford and O'Neill, *De Valera*, 411.

5. Kearney to Robertson, 22 May 1945.

6. Gray to Hickerson, 17 January 1946.

7. Gray to Farley, 10 January 1946.

8. Smyllie, 'Unneutral Neutral Éire', 323.

9. Smyllie to Richard Mulcahy, 21 May 1941.

10. Letter from Kevin Boland, 21 October 1975, enclosing a

copy of some handwritten notes on the subject by his late father, Gerald Boland.

11. Gray to Wailes, undated.

12. Michael McInerney, 'Gerry Boland's Story', *Irish Times*, 18 October 1968.

CHAPTER 12 (pp. 211–221)

1. Nicholas Mansergh, *Survey of British Commonwealth Affairs: Problems of Wartime Co-operation and Post-War Change, 1939–1952*, London 1958, 65.

2. T. de Vere White, 'Lord Rugby Remembers', *Irish Times*, 4 July 1962.

3. Maffey to Eric Machtig, 25 February 1943.

4. White, 'Lord Rugby Remembers', *Irish Times*, 4 July 1962.

5. Garret FitzGerald, *Towards A New Ireland*, Dublin 1973, 21–38.

6. Gray to FDR, 2 October 1944.

GLOSSARY

Dean Acheson (1893–1971) was appointed Assistant Secretary of State in 1941, Undersecretary in 1945, and became most famous in 1949–1953 as President Harry Truman's Secretary of State during the Korean War.

Frank Aiken (b. 1898) was born in what is now Northern Ireland. He was Chief of Staff of the IRA, 1923–1925. A founding member of Fianna Fáil, he served as Minister for Defence, 1932–1939; Minister for Co-ordination of Defensive measures, 1939–1945; Minister for Finance, 1945–1948; Minister for External Affairs, 1951–1954 and 1957–1969. From 1965 to 1969 he was also Tánaiste (Deputy Prime Minister).

Sir John Andrews (1871–1956) was Prime Minister of Northern Ireland, 1940–1943.

Frederick H. Boland (b. 1904) was Assistant Secretary of the Irish Department of External Affairs, 1938–1946; Secretary, 1946–1950; Ambassador to Britain, 1950–1956; and Irish representative at the United Nations, 1956–1964. In 1960 he was elected President of the 15th Assembly of the UN and was involved in a celebrated incident in which he broke his gavel while trying to restore order in the General Assembly during Nikita Khrushchev's famous shoepounding episode.

Sir Basil Brooke (later Lord Brookeborough) (1888–1973) was Northern Ireland's longest serving Prime Minister, 1943–1963.

David K. Bruce (b. 1898) was in charge of the OSS in Europe during the Second War and later had a distinguished career in the diplomatic service as US Ambassador to France, to West Germany, and to Britain, as well as chief US negotiator at the Vietnam peace talks in Paris, 1970–1971, and after that as his country's first representative to Red China.

James F. Byrnes (1879–1972) was born of Irish ancestry in South Carolina, served in the US House of Representatives, 1911–1925;

and in the US Senate, 1933–1941. He resigned from the Senate in 1941 to become an associate justice of the US Supreme Court. He later served as Secretary of State, 1945–1947; and as Governor of South Carolina, 1951–1955.

W. T. Cosgrave (1880–1965) took part in the Easter Rising of 1916, served as Prime Minister of the Irish Free State, 1922–1932, and was leader of Fine Gael from 1934 until his retirement in 1944. His son Liam was elected Taoiseach in 1973.

Lord Craigavon (formerly Sir James Craig) (1871–1940) was Prime Minister of Northern Ireland from the formation of its parliament in 1921 until his death in 1940.

Father Charles E. Coughlin (b. 1891) was born in Canada of Irish ancestry. As pastor of the Shrine of the Little Flower in Royal Oak, a suburb of Detroit, Michigan, he rose to national prominence with the broadcasting on radio of his sermons, which were heavily laced with political content. An early backer of FDR's New Deal he became very critical of the President prior to the 1936 election. Considered by many as fascist, he founded the National Union for Social Justice and used its magazine, *Social Justice*, and his own radio broadcasts to expound on strongly anti-communist and anti-Semitic ideas. Following Pearl Harbour he faded from the political scene when the government withdrew mailing privileges from the magazine and his bishop ordered him not to speak publicly on political matters.

John Cudahy (1887–1943), born of Irish ancestry, was a member of the famous Mulwaukee meatpacking family. He served in the ill-fated Allied Expedition to Archangel following the First World War and wrote an anonymous book about his experiences that was bitterly critical of Britain's role in the affair. He supported Roosevelt for election in 1932 and was rewarded with the post of Ambassador to Poland, 1933–1937; later at his own request he became Minister to Ireland, 1937–1940; and Ambassador to Belgium, 1940. Following the collapse of Belgium he became a leading isolationist. He died following a riding accident near his home in Wisconsin in 1943.

James M. Dillon (b. 1902), a member of an established Irish political family, was elected as an independent member of the Dáil in 1932, voted with de Valera at first but then helped to found the Fine Gael Party and became one of its first vice-presidents and its deputy leader in the Dáil. Although forced to resign from the party over his opposition to neutrality in 1942, he later rejoined Fine Gael and became its leader, 1959–1965.

William J. 'Wild Bill' Donovan (1883–1959) who was born of Irish ancestry in Buffalo, New York, won fame as the commander of the mostly Irish-American 'Fighting Sixty-ninth' during the First World War. An unsuccessful Republican Party candidate for state office in New York, he later became a trouble shooter for FDR, formed the OSS, and is generally regarded as the father of the CIA.

Denis Cardinal Dougherty (1865–1951), Archbishop of Philadelphia, was born in Pennsylvania of Irish parents. In 1921 he was created cardinal.

James A. Farley (1888–1976), born in New York of Irish ancestry, was a close associate of FDR, managed both the 1932 and 1936 presidential campaigns, was Chairman of the Democratic Party's National Committee, 1932–1940; and a member of FDR's cabinet from 1933 until 1940 when he resigned over the third-term issue. He was also state chairman of the New York Democratic Committee, 1932–1944.

John T. Flynn (1882–1964) was born in Maryland of Irish ancestry. He was an economist and writer, served as economic adviser to a number of US Congressional committees, and wrote a column for the *New Republic*, 1931–1940. A staunch isolationist, he was chairman of the New York chapter of America First.

Cordell Hull (1871–1955) served in the US House of Representatives, 1907–1921, 1923–1931, and the US Senate, 1931–1933. He resigned from the Senate in 1933 to become Secretary of State under FDR and served until 1944, when he resigned due to ill health, having served in that position longer than any other person in history.

John D. Kearney (b. 1893) was born in Montreal, Canada, of Irish parents. His father was from County Louth and his mother, Katherine O'Doherty, was from County Tyrone. He served as Canadian High Commissioner in Ireland from 1941 until 1945.

John H. Kelly (1879–1941) was born in Canada of Irish parents, both of whom had emigrated from Dublin. After a distinguished career in provincial politics in Quebec, he served as Canada's High Commissioner in Ireland from March 1940 until his death in Dublin following an operation in March 1941.

William Lyon Mackenzie King (1878–1950) was Canada's longest serving Prime Minister. He was a staunch advocate of Canadian independence within the Commonwealth of Nations.

Seán Lemass (1899–1966) first came to prominence as Minister for Supplies during the 1940s, but is best remembered as Taoiseach, 1959–1966, when he played a prominent part in attracting industry to Ireland.

Charles A. Lindbergh (1902–1974) first came to international prominence as an aviator by becoming the first man to make a non-stop solo flight from New York to Paris.

Seán MacBride (b. 1904), son of one of the executed leaders of the Easter Rising of 1916, was elected to the Dáil in 1947 and became Minister for External Affairs in the coalition government of 1948–1951. He is generally regarded as Ireland's foremost criminal lawyer. He won international prominence by being selected as a co-winner of the 1974 Nobel Peace Prize for his work as UN Commissioner for Namibia.

Joseph R. McCarthy (1909–1957) was born in Wisconsin of Irish ancestry. He was elected as a Republican to the US Senate in 1946 and became a prime mover of the Red Scare of the Korean War period. He accused the administrations of Roosevelt and Truman of '20 years of treason'. In 1954 he became only the second man in history to be censured by his colleagues in the US Senate.

John W. McCormack (b. 1891) was born in Massachusetts of Irish ancestry, served in the US House of Representatives, 1927–1970; was majority leader from 1940–1947, 1949–1953, 1955–1962; and Speaker of the House of Representatives, 1962–1970.

Frank MacDermot (1886–1975) served in the British army during the First World War, was elected to the Dáil in 1930, founder of the Irish Centre Party, later helped to found Fine Gael and became one of its first vice-presidents. He resigned from the party when it criticised de Valera for supporting the League of Nations' sanctions against Italy during the Ethiopian crisis. In 1938 he did not seek re-election to the Dáil but was nominated to the Irish Senate by de Valera.

General George C. Marshall (1880–1959) was Chief of Staff of the US army during the Second World War. He became Secretary of State, 1947–1949, during which time the Marshall Plan for the economic recovery of Europe was introduced. During the Korean War he served as Secretary of Defence and was awarded the Nobel Peace Prize in 1953.

Edward F. Mooney (1882–1958) was born in Maryland of Irish parents, named first Roman Catholic Archbishop of Detroit in 1933, and was created cardinal by Pope Pius XII in 1946.

Richard J. Mulcahy (1886–1971) took part in the Easter Rising of 1916, and was Chief of Staff of the IRA during the Black and Tan war. He served as leader of Fine Gael, 1944–1959.

William Cardinal O'Connell (1859–1944) was born in Lowell, Massachusetts, of Irish parents. In 1911 he was created cardinal. He was a strong supporter of self-determination for Ireland in the period following the First World War.

Paul O'Dwyer (b. 1908) was born in County Mayo but emigrated to the United States at the age of seventeen. He was a founding member and national chairman of the American Friends of Irish Neutrality, 1940–1941. Later he was a prominent critic of the Vietnam War and was the unsuccessful Democratic Party candidate for the US Senate in New York in 1968. His brother William served as Mayor of New York, 1947–1951.

Seán T. O'Kelly (1883–1966) was a founding member of Fianna Fáil and deputy leader to de Valera, 1932–1945. Later he served two terms as President of Ireland, 1945–1959.

Alfred E. Smith (1873–1944) was born in New York City of Irish and German ancestry. He served as Governor of New York, 1919–1921, and 1923–1929.

Francis J. Spellman (1889–1967) was born in Whitman, Massachusetts, of Irish parents, became the first American to serve in the Vatican secretariat, 1925–1932, where he formed a close friendship with Cardinal Pacelli who, as Pope Pius XII, appointed Spellman Archbishop of New York in 1939. During the Second World War the latter also acted as head of the Roman Catholic chaplains in the American forces. He was created cardinal in 1946.

Henry L. Stimson (1867–1950) served as Secretary of War, 1911–1913, in the administration of President William H. Taft, special representative to Nicaragua for President Calvin Coolidge in 1927, Secretary of State, 1929–1933, in the administration of President Herbert Hoover, and Secretary of War under Franklin Roosevelt, 1940–1945.

Samuel A. Stritch (1887–1958) was born in Nashville, Tennessee, of Irish parents, became Roman Catholic Archbishop of Milwaukee in 1930, was translated to the see of Chicago following the death of Cardinal Mundelein in 1939, and was created cardinal in 1946.

David I. Walsh (1872–1947), born of Irish ancestry, was Governor of Massachusetts, 1914–1918, and served in the US Senate, 1919–1946, during which time he voted against the Versailles Treaty.

INDEX

Abercorn, Duke of, 54–6
Acheson, Dean, 112, 130; biog., 231
Admiral Scheer, 91
Aiken, Frank, 21, 62, 71n., 76, 105, 108–21, 129, 133–4, 153, 195, 202, 207, 214–5; biog., 231
Allied Control Commission, 206–7
America First Committee, 40–1, 44, 117
American Friends of Irish Neutrality (AFIN), 90, 124, 134–5, 139
Andrews, Sir John, 53, 127–8, 165; biog., 231
Anglo-Irish Treaty (1921), xi, 2, 6–13, 50–1, 124, 172
Associated Press (AP), 103, 145, 195–6
Atlanta Constitution, 190
Atlantic Charter, 43, 164–5, 170
Attlee, Clement, x, 162–3
Azores, 177

Barnes, Harry E., 45
Barry, Kevin, 80
Beard, Charles A., 45
Belgium, 23, 28, 36, 40, 52, 68, 74, 102, 207
Berardis, Vincenso, 72–3, 120
Berehaven, 11, 51, 54
Bevan, Aneurin, 160
Bildersee, Barnett, 191
Boland, Frederick H., 72; biog., 231
Boland, Gerald, 71n., 210, 221
Boston *Traveller*, 40
Brennan, Robert, 81, 86, 89, 91, 93, 96, 112–13, 116, 129–30, 135, 138, 142, 155–6, 164, 189–90, 196–7, 203, 215
Brooke, Sir Basil, 53; biog., 231
Bruce, David K., 197–8; biog., 231
Burns, James McGregor, 35, 45

Byrnes, James F., 34, 39, 209; biog., 231–2

Cadogen, Sir Alexander, 127
Cahill, Joe, 152n.
Canada, 6–7, 16, 81, 92, 125–6, 186–8
Carson, William A., 211
Central Intelligence Agency (CIA), 105, 136, 197–8
Chamberlain, Sir Neville, 12–15, 17–18, 20–1, 52, 54, 61–5, 73–4, 86
Chicago Tribune, 30–1, 33, 37–9
Christian Science Monitor, 97
Churchill, Randolph, 158
Churchill, Winston S., ix–x, 12–13, 19–21, 30, 38, 41–3, 50–2, 68, 73–6, 85–92, 98–9, 101–2, 107–8, 123, 125–8, 139, 162, 165, 170–1, 177, 187, 193–4, 199, 203–4, 214, 220
Cohalan, Daniel, 4–6
Columbia Broadcasting System (CBS), 31, 99–100, 110
Commager, Henry A., 164
Committee for American Irish Defence (CAID), 135–6
Connolly, Charles, 89
Connolly, Joe, 121
Cooper, Duff, 50, 54, 122
Cork Corporation, 153
Corry, Martin, 147
Cosgrave, W. T., 7–9, 64, 87, 126–7, 131–2, 142, 160–1, 221; biog., 232
Costello, Major-General Michael J., 150
Coughlin, Fr Charles E., 27, 167, 169; biog., 232
Coyne, T. J., 121
Craigavon, Lord, 51–7, 60–4, 69, 74,

127, biog., 232
Cranborne, Lord, 102, 139, 141, 146, 162, 177
Cudahy, John, 14–15, 23, 28, 35–6, 40, 42, 44, 47, 117, 120, 167, 170; biog., 232
Curran, Fr Edward Lodge, 27, 167

Daily Express, 74–5, 124
Daily Mail, 137
Daily Telegraph, 124
Dallas Morning News, 190
Davin, William, 71n.
Davis, Norman, 116
Defence Conference, 71, 88, 103, 108, 189
De Gaulle, General Charles, x, 162
Denny, Harold, 76
De Valera, Éamon, addresses to USA, 15, 99–100, 110, 117–18; 120, 209, 213–14; American bases in N.I., 137–8, 143–4, 151, 162, 175; American opinion, ix, 3–4, 14–15, 18, 76–7, 87, 89–90, 101, 166–7, 209, 214; attitude towards Axis, 16–18, 52, 80, 98, 102–3, 128, 155, 159, 198, 201, 207–8, 211–12; benevolence towards Allies, 2, 16–20, 52, 71–2, 78, 83–4, 116, 134, 140, 157–9, 163, 166, 174, 198, 216–17, 221; censorship, 21, 82–3, 121, 128–9, 153, 207–8; critical of Gray, 96, 108, 120, 203; criticised by Maffey, 69, 92, 101–2, 104; expatriation of Axis personnel, 200, 205–6, 209–10; Hitler's death, 202–3, 208; interviews with American correspondents, 76, 93, 97; with Gray, 51–3, 57–8, 66–7, 94–5, 100, 103, 114–16, 126, 168, 183–5; with Kearney, 137, 144, 186–9; with MacDonald, 11, 61–3, 74; with Maffey, ix, 17–18, 20, 68–9, 77–8, 101–2, 109, 143, 172, 185–6; invasion scares, 70–7, 101–3, 145, 189; IRA, 10, 13–14, 16, 21–2, 67–8, 70–1, 74, 80–1; reasons for neutrality, 16–17, 64–5, 71–2, 93, 137, 140, 162–3, 211–13; refuses to expel Axis diplomats, 185–190; seeks American aid, 52, 57–8, 69, 99–100, 103, 108, 110, 149, 178;

speeches and statements, 15, 68, 71–2, 76, 87, 99–100, 110, 126–7, 134, 140, 143, 164, 176, 189, 209; treaty ports, ix, 11, 20, 51, 59, 61–5, 87, 89, 94–6, 98, 105, 129, 136–7, 162–3, 167–9, 172, 174–7, 214; Ulster question, 3, 11–15, 18, 51–3, 61–5, 68–9, 80, 122–3, 126–8, 139, 143–4, 152, 161, 164, 165–8, 173, 176, 180–3, 209, 211–13, 217–20; visits to USA, 4–6, 9, 15, 165; other references, *passim*
Devoy, John, 4–5
Dillon, James, 64, 71n., 88, 95–6, 111, 114–15, 123, 131–2, 142, 149, 189, 220–1; biog., 232
Donovan, William J., 105–6, 136; biog., 232–3
Dougherty, Denis Cardinal, 151; biog., 233
Dulanty, John, 50, 125

Economist, 92–3, 101
Eden, Sir Anthony, later Lord Avon, x, 21, 50, 163, 182, 222
External Association, 6–7, 11, 53

Farago, Ladislas, 198
Farley, James A., 33, 150–1, 167, 207–8, 223; biog., 233
Fegen, E. S. Fogarty, 91
Fianna Fáil, 2, 9, 10, 71, 80, 120, 131, 143, 160–1, 167–8, 176, 199, 206
Fine Gael, 1, 70–1, 88, 120–3, 130–2, 149, 160–1, 196, 221
Finland, 83
Fitzgerald, John F., 35
Flynn, John T., 33, 44, 117–8, 120; biog., 233
Forgan, J. Russell, 197, 223
Fort Worth Star-Telegram, 97, 190–2
Franco, General F., 2
Friends of Irish Freedom, 4

Gaelic-American, 4–5, 26–7, 37
Gallup poll, 27, 44, 101, 164, 192–3
Gleason, S. Everett, 45
Gneisenau, 155
Goebbels, Josef, 42
Goertz, Hermann, 70, 197, 210
Gray, David, background, 47–8;

American note (draft 1), 171–4, 181; (draft 2), 174–8, 181; (draft 3), 180–2, 182–5, 189; arms for Ireland, 53–4, 57–8, 82, 100, 103, 129, 130, 132, 145, 148; Axis representatives, 165, 167, 170, 172, 179–82, 185, 198, 216; censorship, 82–3, 109, 153, 207, 215; conscription, 122–3, 126, 128, 167; contingency proposals for securing Irish facilities, 54, 95, 130–3, 149–50; critical of Irish neutrality, 86, 94, 114–15, 128–9, 133, 152, 207, 211–13, 216–17; discrediting de Valera, x, 162–8, 173, 181, 193, 198, 206, 217–20; economic pressure, 141–3, 147–9, 168, 206; encouraged by FDR, 104, 134, 154; expatriation of Germans, 205–6, 209–10; Irish involvement in American politics, 100, 111, 114–15, 132–3, 207–8, 213–15; IRA, 67, 80–1, 100, 152; meetings with Churchill, 50–1, 162, 170–1; with FDR, 168–71; (for other meetings *see* Attlee, Cosgrave, Craigavon, de Valera, Kearney, Maffey, and Walshe); predicts U.S. involvement in war, 45, 82, 94, 131; supports interventionist policy, 32, 46, 49, 82, 103–4; Ulster question, 49–64, 152, 161–2, 164–70, 173, 176, 207–8, 217–18; U.S. troops in Northern Ireland, 137, 143–4, 151–3, 179–80, 182; other references, x, 32, 49–64, 66–7, 69, 76, 78–84, 86–7, 91, 93–6, 98, 100–1, 103–5, 108–9, 111, 114–16, 122–3, 126, 128–34, 136–7, 141–5, 147–54, 157–8, 161–83, 185–6, 189, 193–6, 198–203, 205–13, 215–20
Gray, Maud, 48
Green, Roger, 195–6
Green, Thomas, 80
Gunther, John, 202

Hanson, Richard, 92
Harriman, W. Averell, 170, 223
Harte, Francis, *see* Green, Thomas
Hartle, General E. P., 151
Hayes, Stephen, 140

Hearne, John J., 125
Head Line shipping company, 108
Held, Stephen K., 70–3
Hempel, Edouard, 16, 18, 70, 72–3, 79, 80, 83–6, 103, 111, 120, 155, 180–1, 185, 195, 202–3, 211–12
Hickerson, John D., 190, 208
Hitler, Adolf, 14, 20, 31–2, 42, 45, 52, 66, 75–6, 79, 90, 96, 105, 113, 133, 141, 190, 202–3, 207–8, 211–12, 216, 220
Hold, Rush D., 90
Holland, 28, 68, 75
Hoover, Herbert C., 36, 40, 99
Hull, Cordell, x, 57, 69, 77, 105–6, 111, 113, 129, 138, 148, 165, 169, 173–8, 180–1, 199; biog., 233
Hurley, Bishop Joseph, 169

Iceland, 43–4
International Truth Society, 27
Irish-Americans, ix–x, 2–6, 24–44, 49, 79, 87, 89–90, 96, 101, 112, 114, 117–20, 133, 134–6, 139, 154–5, 162, 165–7, 169–70, 173, 207–8, 213–14, 219
Irish Echo (New York), 89
Irish Oak, 117
Irish Pine, 117
Irish Press, 9, 83–4, 112, 191, 195
Irish Republican Army (IRA), 1–2, 7, 9–10, 13–14, 16, 21–2, 52, 67–8, 70–1, 74, 80–1, 100, 123–4, 140, 151–3, 212, 220–1
IRA *War News*, 21
Irish Times, 121, 124–5, 199, 207
Irish World (New York), 26, 119
Italy, 2, 29, 50, 55, 198

Japan, 45–6, 82, 141, 198
Jervis Bay, 91
Johnson, Denis, 76

Kearney, 44
Kearney, John D., 136–7, 141, 144, 151, 158, 162–3, 173–4, 179–80, 186–9, 193, 196, 202, 205, 215, 220, 223; biog., 233
Keating, Seán, 135
Kelly, John H., 92
Kennedy, John F., 35, 169
Kennedy, Joseph P., 12, 28, 34–5.

38, 57, 76, 82, 169, 207
Kerlogue, 159
King, Frank, 194
King, William Lyon MacKenzie, 61, 92n., 125, 127, 187–8; biog., 233
Knightly, Mike, 121
Knox, Frank, 29–30, 40, 58, 89, 111

Labour Party, 10, 70
Langer, William L., 45
Lausanne Treaty (1923), 14, 168
League of Nations, 2–4, 6–7, 14, 16, 22–3
Lehman, Herbert, 167
Lemass, Seán, 62, 120, 221; biog., 233
Letter from America, 150–1, 208
Life, 35, 40
Lincoln, Abraham, 199
Lindbergh, Charles, 41, 44, 117–20; biog., 233–4
Lloyd George, David, 7–8
Longford, Lord, 10, 104
Lough Foyle, 105–6, 137
Lough Swilly, 11, 105–6

Macauley, William B., 50
MacBride, Seán, 22, 81; biog., 234
McCarran, Patrick A., 27
McCarthy, Bishop Joseph, 169
McCarthy, Joseph R., 219; biog., 234
McCormack, John W., 39, 112, 207, 223; biog., 234
MacDermot, Frank, 134; biog., 234
MacDonald, Malcolm, 11, 13, 61–3, 72–5, 125
MacEntee, Seán, 78, 153
McGlynn, Michael, 135, 223
McGranery, James, 112
McGrath, Patrick, 22, 67, 80
McKenna, Lt. Gen. Daniel, 151
McNicholas, Archbishop John T., 40
MacRory, Joseph Cardinal, 123, 152–3, 164, 182–3
MacSwiney, Terence, 22
MacWhite, Michael, 50, 198
Maffey, Sir John, later Lord Rugby, ix, 17–18, 20, 54, 60, 62–3, 68–9, 77–8, 83, 92–3, 101–2, 109, 126–7, 136–7, 143, 147, 160–3, 172–4, 176, 180, 185–7, 189, 194, 202, 205, 214–16

Maguire, Conor, 161
Maloney, Cattie (née Barry), 80–1
Manchester Guardian, 166n.
Mansergh, Nicholas, 214
Margesson, David, 50
Marlin, Ervin R., 197–8, 223
Marshall, General George C., 174; biog., 234
Menzies, Robert, 127
Montini, Giovani, later Pope Paul VI, 198
Montreal Gazette, 92
Mooney, Archbishop Edward, 169, 208; biog., 234
Morrison, Herbert S., 162
Mulcahy, Richard, 64, 71n., 108, 120–1, 131, 189, 221; biog., 234
Murphy, Seán, 50
Murray, James A., 207

National Broadcasting Corporation (NBC), 76
National Clearing House Gazette, 19
National Union for Social Justice, 27
New York Daily Mirror, 112
New York *Daily News*, 37–8, 145
New York Enquirer, 36–7, 90
New York Herald-Tribune, 87, 97, 191–2
New York Times, 33, 76, 97, 99, 124, 164, 191-2, 194, 202
News Chronicle, 124
Nicolson, Harold, 50
Northern Ireland, 8, 11, 15, 49–65, 69–70, 75, 106, 118–19, 122–8, 137–8, 143, 151–2, 155–6, 161–2, 167–8, 171, 175, 179–80, 182–4, 212–13, 217–18
Norton, William, 71n., 127
Norway, 66, 74, 83, 102
Nye, Gerald, 25

Observer, 92
O'Connell, William Cardinal, 40, 117, 151; biog., 234
O'Connor, James F., 41
O'Dwyer, Paul, xi, 89–90, 124, 223; biog., 235
Office of Strategic Services (OSS), 197–8
Office of War Information (OWI), 150
O'Flanagan, Fr Michael, 80

O'Higgins, T. F., 71n., 88, 131, 195
O'Kelly, Seán T., 78, 111, 120, 153; biog., 235
O'Neill, Thomas, 10, 104

Paris Peace Conference (1919), 4, 7, 165
Pius XII, 49, 51, 176
Plunkett, Jack, 67
Plunkett, Joseph M., 67
PM, 97, 191
Pocket Guide to Northern Ireland, 155
Poland, 17, 40, 83, 150, 170
Portugal, 98, 177
Potocki, Count Jerzy, 36–7
Press Association (PA), 194

Queenstown (Cobh), 11, 19
Quisling, Vidkun, 66

Radio Éireann, 71, 204
Reilly, John J., 87
Reston, James, 192
Reynolds, Col. John, 148
Ribbentrop, Joachim von, 73
Robertson, Norman A., 187–8
Rome, 199n., 208
Roosevelt, Eleanor, 48, 104, 154, 201
Roosevelt, Franklin D., 24–45, 47–9, 51, 81, 84, 87, 89–90, 98–101, 104, 107, 110–14, 116, 120, 126–7, 129–30, 134, 137, 141, 145, 149, 154, 163, 167–9, 170–1, 174–5, 177–8, 194, 214, 220
Round Table, 128
Ruben James, 44

Salazar, Antonio, 177
San Francisco *Leader*, 26, 37, 89, 118, 144–5
Sayers, Michael, 191
Scharnhorst, 155
Sinn Féin, 3–4, 6, 9
Smith, Alfred E., 25, 27, 33, 150; biog., 235
Smith, J. Harris, 198
Smuts, Jan Christiaan, 73
Smyllie, Robert M., 121, 199, 207–8
Snell, Lord, 97
Social-democraten, 102
Spain, 2, 40, 146

Spellman, Archbishop Francis, 208; biog., 235
Starving Europe Campaign, 36, 40, 99, 117
Stephan, Enno, 197
Sterling, Frederick, 170
Stettinius, Edward R., 208
Stimson, Henry L., 29, 40–1, 57–8; biog., 235
Stokes, Richard, 160
Stritch, Archbishop Samuel, 169; biog., 235

Taylor, Myron C., 134
Thomsen, Hans, 33, 36–7
Time, 199
Times, The, 97, 124, 156
Tojo, Hideki, 190
Traynor, Oscar, 71n.
Tully, Grace, 32

Ulster Protestant, 176
Ulster question, *see* Northern Ireland
U.S.S.R. (Soviet Union), 2, 83, 141, 170, 206
United Irish Societies, New York, 27, 38; Philadelphia, 38; Chicago, 38; San Francisco, 38

Versailles Treaty (1919), 3–4, 26, 162, 218–19

Wailes, Edward T., 209
Wallace, Henry, 11, 129
Walsh, David I., 30–2, 38, 117, 120, 167; biog., 235
Walshe, Joseph P., 56, 72, 77–80, 85–7, 129, 136, 155, 158, 193, 198, 208
Warlimont, General Walter, 75
Washington Evening Star, 97
Washington Times-Herald, 37–9
Weber-Drohl, Ernst, 198
Welles, Sumner, 58, 89, 93–4, 96, 114, 129–30, 149, 155–6, 192
Westminster Gazette, 5, 155
Westminster, Statute of, 10
Wheeler, Burton K., 136
Willkie, Wendell, 33–4, 37, 104–5
Wilson, Woodrow, 4, 6–7, 24, 165
Winant, John G., 127, 134, 152, 177, 181–2
Wolfe, R., 157, 201